W9-DJH-019

The Catholic Voter in American Politics

The Catholic Voter in American Politics

The Passing of the Democratic Monolith

William B. Prendergast

GEORGETOWN UNIVERSITY PRESS / WASHINGTON, D.C.

Georgetown University Press, Washington, D.C. 20007

Printed in the United States of America.
10 9 8 7 6 5 4 3 2 1 1999
THIS VOLUME IS PRINTED ON ACID-FREE OFFSET BOOK PAPER.

Library of Congress Cataloging-in-Publication Data

Prendergast, William B.
The Catholic Voter in American Politics : The Passing of the Democratic Monolith / William B. Prendergast.
p. cm.
Includes bibliographical references and index.
1. Catholics—United States.—Political activity—History. 2. Republican Party (U.S. : 1854–)—History. 3. Elections—United States—History. 4. Voting—United States—History. I. Title.
E184.C3P74 1999
324.973—dc21
ISBN 0-87840-724-3 (hardcover)

98-44649

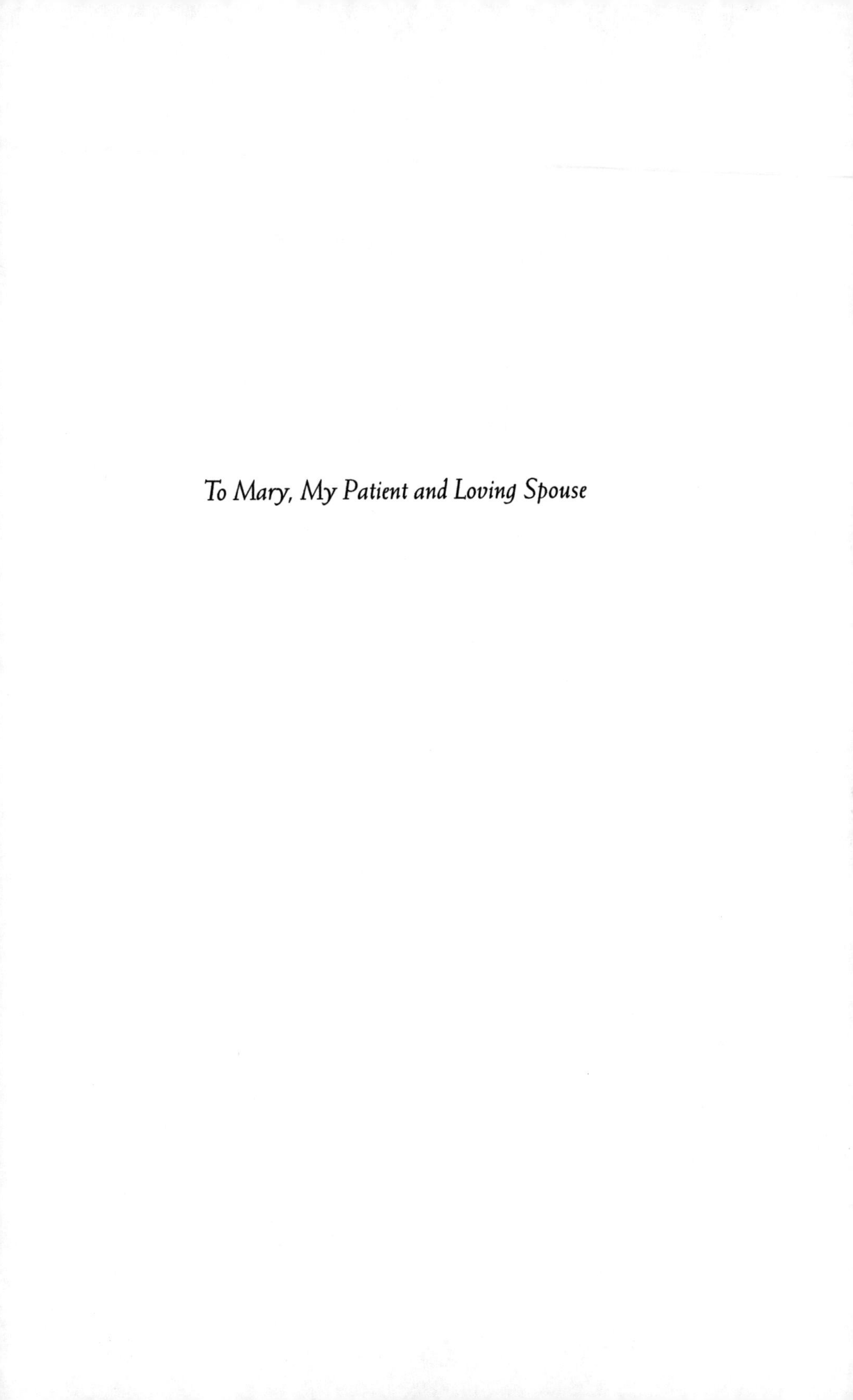

To Mary, My Patient and Loving Spouse

Contents

3

Republicans and the Catholic Electorate 1880–1908: From Hostility to Cautious Rapprochement 69

4

The 1928 Election and the Legacy of Al Smith 93

5

Catholics After World War II: They Liked Ike 116

6

Kennedy and the Return of the Prodigals 135

7

Catholics in the Turbulent Sixties and Seventies 149

Prologue

"Catholicism and Republicanism are as plainly incompatible as oil and water." So declared the staunchly Republican *Chicago Press and Tribune* of 17 July 1860 in the heat of a presidential campaign. And when the result of the fateful election of that year became known, a Cincinnati Catholic paper asserted that "no Catholic votes" contributed to Lincoln's victory (Foik 1969, 167).

In the second half of the twentieth century, Catholic votes made an important contribution to the election of Eisenhower, Nixon, Reagan, and Bush. And in 1994, a majority of Catholic ballots were cast for Republican candidates for the national House of Representatives.

Although in 1996 a majority of the Catholic electorate supported Bill Clinton, the pattern of Catholic voting behavior in that election should not blur a longer range perspective. Over a span of at least thirty years before that contest, a pronounced shift of Catholics away from the Democratic Party had occurred. There is historic irony in this shift which brought to the Republican Party, spawned in part from the Know-Nothing movement, substantial support from the descendants of those it once reviled. Tracing and explaining the changing partisan attachment and voting pattern of Catholics is the task of this book.

The influences that throw some light on the change in voting behavior we are exploring can be grouped under three headings: changes in the Catholic population, changes in the parties, and changes in the political environment.

Chapter 1 of the book, dealing with the first of these categories, attempts a profile of the Catholic population of the nation, highlighting politically salient changes that may help to explain shifts in voting behavior and party allegiance. Each of the succeeding chapters discusses the political behavior of the Catholic population in an era of change in the voting patterns of a large segment of the electorate.

Our interest lies in the political, not the ecclesiastical or theological. We are concerned with those in the pews, not those on the altar—except to the extent that the clergy may influence the political views and behavior of the laity.

Two constituencies, Catholics and white southerners, bulwarks of the New Deal coalition, defected from the Democratic Party in sufficient strength to enable Republicans to win the presidency in seven elections after the Second World War. Severe Republican losses among Catholics made possible the victories Bill Clinton achieved in 1992 and 1996.

A leading pollster has concluded that "no Democrat will ever be elected president without heavy Catholic support, and no candidate—Democrat or Republican—can take the Catholic vote for granted" (Gallup and Castelli 1987, 190–91). In recent elections the second clause of the statement has been more clearly demonstrated than the first. At the least it can be said that neither national party can safely ignore so large a group of floating voters.

Acknowledgments

It is impossible to list all who have in some way helped to bring this book into existence over the long gestational period preceding publication. It must suffice to say that I am grateful to many who must remain nameless.

Among those I can name, first place must be accorded to my spouse, Mary Comeford Prendergast, to whom the book is dedicated, for support, encouragement, and suggestions which improved the final product, as well as assistance in the drudge work that falls upon an author who lacks research and secretarial staff.

Several members of Congress submitted to interviews which yielded helpful insights and useful information. Among them were Representatives Henry Hyde of Illinois, Christopher Smith of New Jersey, Peter King of New York, Rick Santorum of Pennsylvania (who thereafter advanced to the Senate), and Vin Weber of Minnesota.

Chairman James Nicholson of the Republican National Committee shared his experiences in the service of the party with me as did some of his predecessors—particularly Bill Brock and Frank Farenkopf. In addition, there are things in this book reflecting my association at various times with former Representative Melvin R. Laird, Gerald R. Ford (as a member of Congress), and three chairmen of the Republican National Committee—Thruston Morton, William E. Miller, and Ray C. Bliss. Among the staff members of that Committee who were particularly generous in supplying information were Rev. Donald Shea and Kieran Harrington, Director of Coalitions.

I was fortunate in securing access to surveys conducted by Wirthlin Worldwide of McLean, Virginia, for President Reagan's campaigns in the 1980s.

Journalists Russell Shaw, George Weigle, and Linda Chavez shared with me invaluable insights about the Catholic community in general and its relationship with political parties, as did Professor Dean Hoge of the Catholic University of America.

My thanks go also to the following for permission to include in this book some material from earlier writings of mine which appeared in their pages:

America "Interpreting the Catholic Vote in 1992," 169, No. 11 (Oct. 16, 1993), 15–20.

Commonweal "Shifting Allegiance, 'Romans' and 'Rebels' Go Republican," 122, No. 1 (Jan. 13, 1995), 4–6.

Notre Dame Magazine "No Catholics Should Apply," 25, No. 4 (Winter 1996/97), 22–23.

Thanks also to the magazine *First Things* for permission to draw upon the article "Who Elected Clinton? A Collision of Values" by John C. Green, James L. Guth, Corwin E. Smidt, and Lyman A. Kellstedt (No. 75, Aug./ Sept. 1997, 35–40).

And to the Baton Rouge *Advocate* for permission to cite findings from a poll after the 1996 election commissioned by the newspaper and conducted by Professor Edward Renwick of Loyola University in New Orleans. The poll probed the effect of ecclesiastical exhortation on the behavior of Louisiana voters.

Finally, I am grateful to the able personnel who guide the Georgetown University Press, particularly Director John Samples, Patricia Rayner, Deborah Weiner, and Gail Grella. Such skilled professionals have made arduous tasks almost a pleasure.

The standard exoneration of others to the effect that any errors that crept into the text are solely the responsibility of the author goes without saying.

1

American Catholics: A Historical Profile

Abundant scholarship has been devoted to mining the history of the American Catholic community from its modest beginnings as a small sect huddled in parts of the mid-Atlantic states through its emergence as the nation's largest church. In attempting to draw a profile of the community, this chapter relies on the research of many scholars who have dug into the country's religious history, and particularly the story of America's Catholics. It focuses attention on events, experiences, and characteristics that are politically salient. It looks especially at influences bearing on political involvement, party preference, voting behavior, and attitudes on issues of public policy. Finally, it deals particularly with the relationship between the Catholic population and the Republican party.

The Growth of the Catholic Population

In 1785 Father John Carroll reported to authorities in Rome that there were about twenty-five thousand Catholics in the United States, residing principally in Maryland and Pennsylvania (Ellis 1967, 152). When, after having been designated the first American Catholic bishop, he assembled the clergy subject to his jurisdiction, twenty-two priests responded to his call.

In 1997 *The Official Catholic Directory* reported there were 48,097 Catholic clergymen ministering to 61,207,914 churchgoing members of their faith organized in 19,677 parishes spread throughout the nation.

A word of caution about the numbers: The more or less official count of the Catholic population, reported annually in *The Official Catholic Directory*, rests on nothing resembling a census or even on a uniform consistent methodology throughout the nation (Greeley 1990, 111–14; Celio 1993, 10–14). This count, based for the most part on estimates supplied by local clergy, is bound to be an underestimate, reflecting only the number of relatively active parishioners.

Several surveys have revealed a substantial gap between the number of self-identified Catholics and the Church's official count. In 1990, when *The*

TABLE 1–1. Growth of the Catholic Population

Year	*Number of Catholics*	*As Percentage of Population*	*Number of Parishes*	*Number of Clergy*
1790	35,000	1.0	—	22
1820	195,000	2.0	124	150
1840	663,000	3.9	454	499
1850	1,606,000	6.9	1,073	1,108
1860	3,103,000	9.8	2,385	2,235
1880	6,259,000	12.5	6,407	6,056
1890	8,909,000	14.1	7,523	8,419
1900	12,041,000	15.8	6,127	12,080
1910	16,363,000	17.7	9,017	16,651
1920	20,000,000	18.8	10,608	21,129
1930	20,204,000	16.4	12,403	27,043
1940	21,403,000	16.2	13,132	34,048
1950	27,766,000	18.3	15,292	43,189
1960	40,871,000	23.5	16,350	54,067
1970	47,872,000	23.7	18,224	59,528
1980	49,812,000	22.3	18,794	59,059
1990	57,019,948	23.0	19,860	53,112
1997	61,207,914	23.0	19,677	48,097

Sources: 1790–1920: Gerald Shaughnessy, *Has the Immigrant Kept the Faith? A Study of Immigration and Catholic Growth in the United States*, 189. 1930–1997: The Official Catholic Directory.

Official Catholic Directory reported that 52.5 million Church members resided in the fifty states and the District of Columbia, a Gallup poll suggested that there were 62 million self-identified Catholics in the nation. A contemporaneous study, the National Survey of Religious Identification (NSRI), conducted by scholars at the City University of New York, concluded that Catholics constituted 26.2 percent of the nation's adults, suggesting a total Catholic population of 65 million (Kosmin and Lachman 1993, 15). The sizable group of 10 million or more self-identified members of the Church who escaped the attention of those who compile the official count was called by one writer "the second largest religious denomination in the United States" (Castelli 1987, 33–34), an exaggeration but not very wide of the mark.

Roman Catholics, however and by whomever counted, are by far the nation's largest religious body. According to Gallup's estimates, Protestants collectively constituted 56 percent of the population in 1990, outnumbering the Catholic population by more than two to one. Of individual Protestant denominations, however, only the Baptists claim more than 10 million adherents, followed by the United Methodists, with a reported membership somewhat less than 9 million.

The growth of the Catholic population from less than 1 percent to one-quarter of the nation over two hundred years has not been even (see Table 1-1). Throughout the nineteenth century the rate of increase consistently exceeded the growth rate of the nation as a whole. It achieved its most impressive proportions between 1840 and 1860 (when it more than trebled, growing from 663,000 to over 3 million) and between 1880 and 1910 (when it swelled from 6 to 16 million). By the 1850s the Catholic Church had joined the ranks of the major religious groups in the United States in membership. In the thirty years bridging the current and the last century, it clearly became the largest denomination as its adherents increased from more than 12 to almost 18 percent of the country's population.

Because of immigration restrictions and the depression, the Catholic population increased more slowly in the two decades following the first World War, but the post–war years of the forties and fifties brought a resumption of an impressive growth rate. Since 1960, the Catholic population has been increasing at a rate no greater than the nation at large and may recently have lagged behind the national average.

If the expansion of Catholic ranks slowed during the final decades of the twentieth century, nevertheless they grew at a time when mainline Protestant denominations were experiencing a marked decline in membership. According to Gallup polls, between 1947 and 1990 the Catholic population increased from 20 to 25 percent of the American people as the percentage in Protestant churches dropped from 69 to 56. Of religious denominations with more than 1 million members, only Roman Catholics, the Assembly of God, the Mormons, and the Southern Baptists reported membership gains during these years (Princeton Religion Research Center 1991, 1).

The Immigrant Church

During much of the nineteenth century and the early years of the twentieth, the rapid growth of the Catholic population was due in major part to two waves of European immigration. In the 1840s and 1850s the immigrants were predominantly Irish and German. At the turn of the century the homelands of the immigrants were mainly countries of eastern and southern Europe. The Catholic immigrants of this later wave included such diverse

TABLE 1–2. Catholic Population Growth: The Immigrant Factor

Decade Ending	*Increase in Native Catholic Population*	*Increase in Immigrant Catholic Population*
1840	95,400	240,000
1850	198,900	726,100
1860	482,000	985,000
1870	620,000	741,000
1890	1,315,000	1,250,00
1900	1,782,000	1,225,000
1910	1,806,000	2,316,000

Source: Shaughnessy, *Has the Immigrant Kept the Faith?*, 134, 145, 172, 178, 182.

nationalities as Italians, Poles, Lithuanians, Slovaks, Bohemians, Croats, Ruthenians, Hungarians, Slovenes, and Ukrainians.

How important immigration was to the growth of the Catholic Church in these two eras is shown in estimates arrived at by Gerald Shaughnessy in his book *Has the Immigrant Kept the Faith?*, the most careful study made of the Catholic population down to 1920. This study concluded that additions to the Catholic population through immigration exceeded the increase in native-born Catholics in each decade between 1830 and 1870, with a particularly high excess of immigrants over natives between 1840 and 1860. Likewise, in the first decade of the current century, more than half of the increase in Catholic numbers was attributable to immigration (Shaughnessy 1925, 189) (see Table 1-2).

In the last third of the twentieth century, immigration once again helped to swell the ranks of Catholics in the United States. The new Catholic immigrants, predominantly Hispanic, came from Mexico, Central and South American countries, and Cuba. In the years between 1971 and 1992, more than 7 million people emigrated legally from the countries of Latin America to the United States, perhaps 70 percent of them Catholics. Like these immigrants, Puerto Ricans, who have settled principally in the urban centers of the Northeast, have also added substantially to the Hispanic flavor of the mainland Church.

In addition, the Asian immigrants of the last decades of the twentieth century—notably Filipinos and, to some degree, Vietnamese and Koreans—include an appreciable number who profess Catholicism. About 1 million arrived in this country from 1971 through 1992, from the Philippines, a nation in which 80 percent of the people are Catholics. Among the newly arrived Catholics from Asia perhaps 25 percent of 700,000 immigrants from Vietnam and 20 percent of an equal number from Korea were Catholics.

For millions of Catholics—particularly many of English, German, Irish, and mixed extraction—the immigrant experience is so remote that its power to color their thinking and influence their behavior has waned. Many Irish Americans whose great-great-grandparents came to this country to escape the Potato Famine may display a sentimental attachment to the land of their ancestors by a green necktie on St. Patrick's Day, but they no longer hate all things English and no longer subscribe to Irish American publications.

In many ways, the ethnics have undergone assimilation. They have lost their accents, left their ghettos, become Kiwanians, married outside their national group, and taken up golf and softball instead of bocce (Alba 1995, 3–18). Yet, for large numbers of American Catholics (including those of Irish and German descent), some consciousness of their immigrant roots is still very much alive. Even as late as 1964, before Hispanic immigration had reached major proportions, 60 percent of American Catholics either were immigrants or had at least one immigrant parent. Even among Catholics of Irish and German descent, 31 percent of the former group and 35 percent of the latter were of the first or second generation (Abramson 1973, 26). Andrew Greeley was not far off the mark when he wrote in 1971, "if we include the third generation, the overwhelming majority of the Catholic population still has one foot in the immigrant ghetto" (1971, 153). Writing more recently, Dolores Liptak observes, "Millions of turn-of-the-century immigrants still form the core of present Catholic membership. They account for the Church's ethnic base as 20 percent Italian, 16 percent Irish, 16 percent German, 16 percent Hispanic and 12 percent Slavic with the remaining 20 percent . . . current influxes of European, African and Asian minorities" (1989, 75).

The Ethnic Diversity of the Catholic People

No other religious group in the United States holds within its ranks so varied a mixture of ethnic strains as the Catholic Church. The first Catholics of English North America were the early settlers in Maryland—white masters and black slaves—and their descendants. Well before the arrival of the *Ark* and the *Dove* in St. Mary's City, however, French and Spanish missionaries had planted the Church in the New World in other places which were later to become part of the United States. The settlement of St. Augustine antedates the establishment of any colony in English North America, and as early as 1511, San Juan, Puerto Rico was designated the first Catholic episcopal see in the New World. The absorption of French and Spanish territory by the United States in the early nineteenth century brought into the Church a flock along the Gulf of Mexico and the Mississippi Valley somewhat different from the original Anglo-American Catholic people.

Among non-English groups it was the French who exercised the most important influence on the American Catholic Church in the early period after independence. The handful of priests then serving in the United States, like some leading Catholic laymen, had received their education in France. In the aftermath of revolution, many French clerics, driven from their native land and its possessions, found refuge in America. The refugees helped to satisfy the desperate need of the Church for clergy. Men of learning and culture, they also made important contributions to the educational mission of the Church, founding the first seminary to provide priests in the United States and constituting a significant part of the faculty of the first schools serving a lay student body. Prominent among the prelates of the Church in the United States in the first half of the nineteenth century were bishops with such French names as Blanc, DuBois, Flaget, Maréchal, Portier, and Cheverus (Ruskowski 1940). And when the bishops collectively first addressed their flock in 1829, they issued their pastoral letter in French as well as in English.

Although the first German Catholic congregation in America—Holy Trinity in Philadelphia—was formed in 1787, it was not until the nineteenth century that Irish and German immigrants began significantly to alter the ethnic composition of American Catholicism. The flow of immigrants of these nationalities became a flood in the 1840s and 1850s with the Potato Famine in Ireland and revolution and economic distress in the German states. With this influx of newcomers Catholicism became an immigrant Church, and, in ethnic terms, Catholic came to signify most commonly Irish or German.

Another flood of immigrants arrived in the years between the late nineteenth century and the First World War, mainly from southern and eastern European countries. Many who came in this wave of newcomers were Catholic, particularly among the Italians, Poles, French Canadians, Lithuanians, Slovaks, and Croatians.

As a result of immigration from all corners of Europe as well as from Canada, church services were conducted in a language other than English in 4,700 Catholic parishes in the United States at the time of the First World War. As late as 1940 at least thirty-five foreign languages were regularly in use in American Catholic churches. The most numerous national parishes of the period were Polish (449), Italian (308), and German (237). Even in the mid-1980s, 11 percent of the parishes in the United States were classified as "national parishes" (Castelli and Gremillion 1987, 54).

In recent years the two immigrant groups that have contributed most to swelling Catholic Church membership have been Hispanics and Asians.

Growing at a rate five times as fast as the non-Hispanic population, Hispanic Catholics now rank with the Irish, the Germans, and the Italians as the most numerous of the many ethnic groups in the American Church. The 1990 census reported a count of 22.3 million Hispanics, nine percent of the nation's population, with a birth rate higher than that of non-Hispanic America. The tenuous relationship of many Hispanics to the Church leads to a wide range of estimates of the Catholic Hispanic population—perhaps 14 to 17 million (Kosmin and Lachman 1993, 137–42; Gonzalez and LaVelle 1985). If the population trend of recent years continues (and a large majority of Latinos continue to embrace their historic faith), the time is not far distant when Catholics of Hispanic stock will outnumber any other ethnic group in the American Church.

The ethnic diversity of American Catholicism is not matched by racial diversity. Only 5 percent of the nation's Catholics are black. Nevertheless, more blacks are found in the Catholic Church than in any other religious denomination except the Baptist and the Methodist Churches (Davis 1990).

Geographic Distribution of the Catholic People

The tide of immigration from Ireland and Germany after 1840 not only increased the Catholic population of the United States substantially; it also altered drastically the pattern of settlement of Catholics within the country. Approximately two-thirds of the members of his small flock that John Carroll could account for in 1785 were located in Maryland and most of the remainder in Pennsylvania. Down through the first decades of the nineteenth century, the bulk of the Catholic population was located in certain southern and border states. Baltimore was the first episcopal see established in the United States, and among the other earliest dioceses were those of Bardstown, Kentucky; Charleston, South Carolina; and Richmond, Virginia (Miller and Wakelyn 1983).

With the arrival of the immigrants the centers of Catholic settlement shifted from southern and border states to the northeastern quadrant of the country. The Irish immigrants overwhelmingly settled in cities, notably New York and Boston. German immigrants, often landing in Baltimore, were more likely to settle there or in Pennsylvania or to move on to midwestern locations. Along the eastern seaboard, New York was the northernmost city that experienced a heavy influx of German immigrants during the first half of the nineteenth century. In the Midwest, although a significant number of Germans settled in rural areas, the bulk of the immigration was nevertheless directed to cities such as Cincinnati, Louisville, Milwaukee, St. Louis, and Cleveland.

Similarly, the Catholic immigrants of the late nineteenth and early twentieth centuries settled in cities while exhibiting some regional preferences—

French Canadians for New England, Italians for the mid-Atlantic states, Poles for the Midwest.

In 1990 60 percent of the nation's Catholics still lived in the area between the Atlantic and the Mississippi and north of the states of the Confederacy. Geographical concentration has been reduced, however, as Catholics have dispersed to areas in which they were sparsely represented until relatively recent years. In 1952 only 6 percent of the nation's Catholic population lived in the South; by 1990 about 15 percent of the Catholics were Southerners—a change attributable chiefly to migration from the North. Likewise, a dramatic increase has occurred in the Catholic population of the southwestern states owing to both Hispanic migration and the movement of non-Hispanics to the Sun Belt.

During the years 1960–1990, as the number of Catholics in the nation increased by 40 percent, in Texas the Catholic population grew by 95 percent, in Florida by 250 percent, and in Georgia by 320 percent. California, in which a growth rate of 125 percent in the Catholic population since 1960 had raised the total to almost 8 million, had by 1995 passed New York as the state with the largest number of Catholics.

Another major change of the years following World War II has been the movement of Catholics, along with other whites (and a growing number of blacks), out of central cities into suburban areas. Perhaps the most extreme example of the desertion of the cities is found in Detroit, where the Catholic population has declined from 1 million to 100,000 during this time (Murnion and Wenzel undated, 65–68). Similarly, as reported in *America*, 27 May 1995, Archbishop John R. Quinn, observing that "The San Francisco of the 40s and the 50s is gone," announced that attendance at Sunday mass in the city had dwindled from 120,000 in 1961 to 47,000 in 1994. Church officials in Baltimore estimated that the Catholic population of that city shrank from 150,000 immediately before World War II to 33,000 in the mid-1990s (*Washington Post* 19 September 1995).

In 1952, in the nation as a whole, almost half of the Catholics lived in central cities and one-third in suburbs. By 1980, one-quarter of the Catholic population resided in cities and one-half in the suburbs, with the rest in smaller communities and the countryside (Miller and Traugott 1989, 76).

The Catholics who fled the cities appear to have retained a taste for urban living, for they are still congregated in heavily populated areas. In only 30 percent of the nation's 3,105 counties and comparable jurisdictions were there, as of 1990, more Catholics than members of any other single religious group. But in 81 of the 97 counties with more than 500,000 residents, Catholics constituted the largest denomination. Catholics also outnumbered any other sect in 80 of the 102 counties with a population between 250,000 and 500,000.

As is true of estimates of the size of the Catholic population in the nation, there is considerable disparity among the estimates drawn from different sources for individual states. Table 1–3 provides two calculations of the number of Catholics in thirty-nine states and the District of Columbia, all with a Catholic population of appreciable size, along with the electoral vote of each jurisdiction.

The estimate in the column headed NSRI is that of the National Survey of Religious Identification conducted by the Graduate School of the City University of New York and based on a national sample of 113,000 Americans. It is probably a more accurate estimate of the number who call themselves Catholic than the percentages in the column captioned OCD, which gives the figures of the *Official Catholic Directory.*

A reader with an eye for the political implications of this table cannot fail to note that Catholics appeared to exceed 20 percent of the population in each of 31 states with an aggregate total of 382 electoral votes, with 62 seats in the United States Senate and 320 in the House of Representatives.

The Socioeconomic Status of the Catholic People

The vast majority of the Catholic immigrants of the nineteenth and early twentieth century arrived in the United States poor and uneducated. They came hoping to escape poverty, oppression, and discrimination and to find for themselves and above all for their children material comfort, dignity, and respect. By and large, the children, the grandchildren, and the great-grandchildren of these immigrants have found in America what their ancestors were seeking.

In the history of the upward climb of America's Catholics, the period of World War II serves as a dividing line. Although Irish Catholics may, as Andrew Greeley avers (1981, 112–15), have made "a dramatic quantum leap" in social status at the beginning of the twentieth century, the bulk of the Catholic population, mired at lower levels, appears to have made relatively sluggish progress through the depression years. The postwar period, however, brought a change due, among other factors, to the educational opportunities opened to veterans by the GI Bill of Rights. A scholarly study written in 1967 declared, "At the end of World War II, Protestants in the United States ranked well above Catholics in income, occupation, and education; since then Catholics have gained dramatically and have surpassed Protestants in most aspects of status." (Glenn and Hyland 1967, 79–85). The 1990 National Survey of Religious Identification arrived at a similar conclusion, reporting that "a social revolution has occurred since the 1950's" propelling Catholics (particularly white Catholics) into society's middle and upper classes (Kosmin and Lachman 1993, 256).

TABLE 1–3. Two Estimates of the Catholic Population and the Electoral Vote for 39 States with Highest Catholic Percentage, 1990 (As Percent of Total Population)

State	*Electoral Vote*	*Percent Catholic*		*State*	*Electoral Vote*	*Percent Catholic*		*State*	*Electoral Vote*	*Percent Catholic*	
		NSRI	*OCD*			*NSRI*	*OCD*			*NSRI*	*OCD*
Rhode Island	4	61.7	63.1	Nebraska	5	29.4	21.2	Iowa	7	21.5	18.7
Massachusetts	12	54.3	49.2	Minnesota	10	29.2	25.4	Hawaii	4	—	21.4
Connecticut	8	50.4	41.8	Michigan	18	29.2	25.2	Missouri	11	20.3	15.7
Louisiana	9	46.8	32.4	California	54	28.9	24.0	Indiana	12	19.5	12.6
New Jersey	15	45.9	41.3	Montana	3	27.6	15.7	Washington	11	19.0	10.8
New York	33	44.3	40.5	Delaware	3	26.4	17.5	Wyoming	3	18.0	13.1
New Hampshire	4	41.3	26.8	South Dakota	3	25.7	20.7	Kansas	6	17.3	14.9
Wisconsin	11	38.6	31.8	Colorado	8	25.1	14.7	District of Columbia	3	16.1	12.8
New Mexico	5	37.3	30.8	Maryland	10	24.9	17.4				
Vermont	3	36.7	25.6	Ohio	21	24.2	19.7	Oregon	7	15.3	9.8
Pennsylvania	23	33.2	30.9	Arizona	8	23.9	17.9	Kentucky	8	13.3	9.9
Illinois	22	33.1	31.6	Nevada	4	23.9	13.1	Virginia	13	12.2	6.2
Maine	4	31.2	21.5	Texas	32	23.2	21.0	Idaho	4	11.5	7.3
North Dakota	3	30.1	27.1	Florida	25	23.2	12.4				

Sources: National Survey of Religious Identification (NSRI); Official Catholic Directory (OCD).

Income Levels in the Catholic Community

In 1957, the last year in which the Census Bureau published any kind of survey classifying people by religion, its report suggested that Catholics had at least caught up with the nation's white Protestants. Indeed, it found that the median income of Catholic families was 10 percent higher than that of white Protestant families. However, when Catholic families residing in urban areas were compared with urban white Protestant families, no difference in median income was found between the two (U. S. Census Bureau 1957; Mueller and Lane 1972, 76–98).

More recent surveys seem to concur that, in a ranking of income, the median for Catholic households is close to that for the nation, above the collective Protestant median but lower than that of Jewish, Episcopalian, and Unitarian households. In upper income brackets, according to Gallup surveys (Gallup and Castelli 1989, 101), Catholics seem to be somewhat overrepresented and to be underrepresented in the lowest quartile.

TABLE 1–4. Income of Catholic Households, 1990
(Catholic Households as Percentage of All Households in Each Group)

Income Level	*Catholic Percentage*
All Households	25
$50,000 and above	28
$30,000–$49,999	27
$15,000–$29,999	25
Below $15,000	20

Source: Gallup Poll, Princeton Religion Center, *Emerging Trends* 13, no. 7 (Sept. 1991): 2.

Within the Catholic community sharp differences in economic status emerge when income figures are analyzed on the basis of race and ethnicity. The National Survey of Religious Identification, conducted in 1990, reported the median income of white Catholic households to be 17 percent higher than that of Hispanic Catholics and 27 percent higher than the median income of black Catholics. The figure for Hispanic Catholics, however, is 7 percent higher than the median income reported by the Census Bureau for Hispanic households as a whole in 1990. Even more impressive is the finding that the median income of black Catholic households exceeds that of the total black population by 16 percent (Kosmin and Lachman 1993, 256).

For most of the ethnic groups of the Catholic community a correlation seems to exist between time of arrival in the United States and position on the income scale. Father Andrew Greeley, in *The Irish Americans: The Rise to Money and Power*, asserted not only that the Irish had attained economic preeminence among the various divisions of ethnics in the Catholic community but also that they had achieved a higher economic and educational status than any other Gentile group. Furthermore, his research led him to conclude that the Irish of Chicago (his hometown) held a more exalted position on the socioeconomic scale than the Irish of New York, Boston, or Minneapolis.

Without belittling the extraordinary rise of Irish Americans, it is fair to note that other ethnic groups—later arrivals—have been following a similar course and often on a faster track. The important fact about Catholics is that the great majority of them have risen out of an economic underclass. Their ancestors wielded pick and shovel to build the nation's railroads and canals, mine its coal, construct its skyscrapers, pave its streets, and—in short—do all the dirty jobs that fall to those at the bottom of the economic ladder. Another important fact is that most Catholics who today enjoy the comforts of living the life of upper- or middle-class America are not so far removed from those ancestors that they have totally forgotten their modest origins.

Although the great majority of the Catholic people enjoy relative affluence, a substantial part of the community does not. Clustered at the lower end of the income scale are Hispanics and Asians—relatively recent immigrants. But also near the lower end are black Catholics whose economic status can be explained only by reasons other than late arrival in this country.

Making *Who's Who*

One measure of change in the status of Catholics has been provided by Purdue University Sociologist James D. Davidson and his colleagues (Davidson 1994, 419–40). They compared a count by religious denomination of the individuals listed in *Who's Who in America* in the early 1930s with a similar study of the listings in 1992–93. Over this period of sixty years the percentage of this elite group identified as Catholic rose from 4 in the earlier period to 23 in the nineties. In the more recent period the number of Catholics in this compilation of notables exceeded the number of members in any other single denomination. Episcopalians were in second place, constituting 18 percent of the individuals listed.

The greatest proportionate gain in terms of representation in *Who's Who* over the years selected for the research was achieved by members of the Jewish faith, who registered a tenfold increase. Next came the Catholics, with a fivefold increase. The percentage of individuals listed who identified themselves with any Protestant denomination fell from 82 in the 1930s to 56 as the nineties began.

Significant differences are found when the representation of individual religious denominations in *Who's Who* is measured against their membership in the general population. By this measurement, despite a spectacular advance since the 1930s, Catholics had still not quite arrived at the point at which their numbers in this compilation of notables reflected their numbers in the country at large. Catholics, along with Lutherans, Methodists, and Reformed Churches, were marginally underrepresented. By contrast, groups like the Baptists and Disciples of Christ were severely underrepresented, and Episcopalians, Unitarians, Quakers, and Jews were overrepresented.

Davidson's studies provide interesting clues about the path that has led to progress for Catholics listed in *Who's Who*. The field of activity in which Catholics had achieved their greatest level of prominence by 1930 was politics, and politics continued to serve as a major highway to success for Catholics. In the late seventies it was still the career field in which Catholics were most heavily represented. Catholic notables in business and in cultural fields, although increasing substantially, did not add to the bulk of *Who's Who* to the extent that Catholic politicians did.

Changing Intergenerational Occupational Status

Change in the occupational status of successive generations of Catholics affords another perspective for the measurement of progress. During the half century between 1910 and 1960, when the percentage of the national labor force classified as professional doubled, the percentage of Catholics practicing the professions quadrupled. And, as this was happening, the percentage of the Catholic workforce in blue-collar occupations fell by 15 percent even as the nation's blue-collar workforce was undergoing a strong expansion (Abramson 1973, 39).

A National Opinion Research Center survey conducted in 1964 comparing occupations of fathers and sons revealed interesting and sometimes surprising variations in the upward mobility of the major Catholic ethnic groups (Abramson 1973, 40–42). Irish Catholics registered the greatest intergenerational change (from 38 percent of fathers in white collar occupations to 66 percent of the sons), followed by Catholics of English ancestry, then Lithuanians, Germans, Italians, and Poles bunched closely together. On the other hand, the Catholic ethnic group showing the least mobility was the Spanish-speaking, with 16 percent in white-collar occupations in the fathers' generation and 18 percent in the sons'. Eastern Europeans and French Canadians, although experiencing greater upward mobility than Hispanics, lagged behind the other major ethnic groups in the Catholic community.

Rising Educational Levels

Another barometer of the upward mobility of the Catholic people is found in indexes of educational achievement. A 1952 survey indicated that 10 percent of adult Catholics were college graduates and 38 percent had ended their education with elementary school (Miller and Traugott 1989, 73). By 1986, 17 percent of the adult Catholic population held college degrees, 44 percent had spent some time in college, and 78 percent were high school graduates. During this time Catholics at least caught up with their white Protestant neighbors. In 1952 only 15 percent of the nation's college graduates were Catholic; by 1986 the figure had risen to 25 percent. As the percentage of adult white Protestants with college degrees trebled, the percentage of college graduates among adult Catholics quadrupled.

TABLE 1–5. Changes in Educational Levels of Successive Generations of Italian-Americans

Cohort	*Percentage Attending College*	*Percentage Receiving Bachelor's Degree*
Men born 1916–1925	25.8	12.1
Men born 1956–1965	61.9	30.2
Women born 1916–1925	16.5	4.9
Women born 1956–1965	61.2	27.8

Source: Richard D. Alba, "Assimilation's Quiet Tide," *The Public Interest* 119 (Spring 1995): 6–7.

Recent years have brought an intensification of the progress of Catholics in ethnic groups whose American roots were planted after 1890. For them, the younger the age cohort, the more impressive the educational attainment. Italian American men, a group largely Catholic, provide a typical illustration (see table 1-5). Of members of this group born in the decade from 1916 on, 12 percent graduated from college; of members born in the decade beginning in 1956, 30 percent were college graduates. Even more striking progress was made by women of Italian ethnic origin during this period of forty years. Their college graduation rate rose from nearly 5 percent in the earlier decade to almost 28 percent in the later period (Alba 1995, 5–7).

Catholics and Labor Unions

Catholic workers were closely identified with the labor union movement in the United States from the time it took form as the Knights of Labor in the last quarter of the nineteenth century. Union leadership has been disproportionately Catholic from Terence V. Powderly to Philip Murray, George Meany, and the two contestants for the presidency of the AFL-CIO in 1995, Thomas Donohue and John Sweeney. Under the leadership of Cardinal Gibbons, the most prominent and influential American bishops encouraged the development of unions and participation of Catholic workers in them. In 1886, after Canadian bishops had secured from the Vatican a condemnation of the Knights of Labor in their country as a secret society, Gibbons went to Rome in a successful mission to forestall similar action against the organization in the United States (Browne 1949; Ellis 1952, I:491–95, 511–21; Higgins 1993, 46–50).

As the structure of the country's economy has changed, union membership has declined from 33 percent of the labor force in 1955 to 16 percent in 1993. When government workers are eliminated from the comparison, the decline appears even more precipitous. Of the nonagricultural workers in private employment, only 11 percent were union members in 1993.

In line with this change in the nation's labor force, the percentage of Catholics belonging to unions has plummeted. In 1952, 41 percent of Catholic households included a union member; by the late 1980s the percentage had shrunk to 24 (Miller and Traugott 1989, 76). This drop in addition to reflecting shifts in occupational status in the labor force, has an implication in the field of political behavior. For many families it ended a relationship impelling them toward attitudes and actions supportive of the Democratic Party. It should be noted, however, that Catholics still constitute a disproportionately large share of union membership. And Catholics, whether union members or not, register a higher level of approval of unions than do Protestants or Jews or those with no religious affiliation (Gallup and Castelli 1989, 204, 215–26).

Black Catholics

A special note about the socioeconomic status and the educational achievement of black Catholics is in order. In terms of education, black Catholics are an elite group, as likely as white Catholics to be college graduates and 40 percent more likely than other blacks to hold college degrees. The median income of black Catholics is substantially above that of other blacks, but it is still substantially below that of white Catholics (Kosmin and Lachman 1993, 271–73).

Catholics and Anti-Catholicism

Part of the Catholic experience in the United States has been adaptation to a society in which many of their fellow citizens regarded them with suspicion, and even with contempt and hatred. Throughout the history of the nation there have been convulsions of mass bigotry directed against Catholics that rose and subsided, only to rise again (Billington 1938; Higham 1955; Kinzer 1964; Knobel 1996).

Between 1830 and 1860 anti-Catholicism took a violent turn in several communities. In the 1830s a mob in Boston destroyed an Ursuline convent and girls' school, terrorizing the nuns and the students. In the 1840s Catholic churches were pillaged and burned in Philadelphia with injuries and loss of life, and a similar episode may have been averted in New York when armed parishioners surrounded their churches ready to repel an attack. In the forties an anti-Catholic movement known as the American Protestant Association sprang up in several places, notably in New York and Pennsylvania. In New York City the movement succeeded in electing its candidate to the mayor's office and gaining control of municipal government in 1844 and 1845. The 1850s brought the flowering of a more widespread anti-Catholic movement in the Know-Nothing Party. It gained control of the legislatures of several states, and one of its members was elected speaker of the United States House of Representatives. For a time it seemed poised to succeed the Whigs as one of the two major parties vying for political power nationwide.

In the century after the Civil War, two organized large-scale anti-Catholic movements attained substantial influence in the political life of the nation. In the 1880s and 1890s it was the American Protective Association, which flourished in states of the Midwest. In the 1920s the Ku Klux Klan was for a time an important force in the South and the Midwest.

Such movements—overt, organized, aggressive, sometimes threatening violence, frankly preaching bigotry, and appealing principally to the ignorant and the disadvantaged—have almost entirely disappeared.

Less blatant forms of anti-Catholicism have also declined greatly since John F. Kennedy entered the White House and Pope John XXIII convened the Second Vatican Council. One indicator is found in the changed response the Gallup poll recorded over the course of two decades to the question, "If your party nominated a qualified Catholic for president, would you vote for him?" As late as 1959 this question drew a negative answer from 25 percent of the respondents. By 1978 the negative responses had fallen to 4 percent.

Apprehension that Catholic power threatened American freedom, a fear which made bestsellers of books authored by Paul Blanshard in the 1950s, abated rapidly during the sixties. One indication of this change is found in contrasting public reaction to proposals to appoint an ambassador to the Vatican in two presidential election years three decades apart. In 1952 a storm of protest forced Harry Truman to abandon his proposal to name General Mark Clark to such a post. By 1984 Ronald Reagan was able to establish diplomatic relations with the Holy See without serious political risk.

Yet, even in the late twentieth century many Catholics not particularly given to paranoia recall vividly encounters with anti-Catholic prejudice in their formative years. Michael Novak speaks of "two forms of bigotry arrayed against" Catholics, particularly against "the children of southern and eastern Europe." One he describes as "the bigotry of intellectuals . . . the animosity of the educated against those less educated" (1972, 141). The second he calls "Nordic racism," which permeated the schooling he received. The message of his schools, he writes, was,

> What is a Catholic but what everybody else is in reaction against? . . . To be modern is decidedly not to be medieval; to be reasonable is not to be dogmatic; to be free is clearly not to live under ecclesiastical authority; to be scientific is not to attend ancient rituals, cherish irrational symbols, indulge in mythic practices.

"It is hard," he concludes, "to grow up Catholic in America without becoming defensive, perhaps a little paranoid, feeling forced to divide the world between 'us' and 'them'" (1972, 55).

Andrew Greeley, priest-novelist-sociologist, cites the opinion of Pat Moynihan that "anti-Catholic nativism has even greater durability than racism and anti-Semitism in American life." He finds a strong strain of anti-Catholicism in a "certain kind of academic liberal," whose attitude toward Catholics he bluntly summarizes in the words "these folks hate our guts" (1981, 107–8).

John Kennedy's advisers, planning a campaign for the vice presidency in 1956, assumed that many liberals would oppose him because of his religion. Indeed, an authoritative biographer of Eleanor Roosevelt attributes "her strenuous opposition to John F. Kennedy's bid for the presidential nomination" in 1960 to her "distrust of the church as a temporal institution" (Lash 1973, 160).

Even in the 1990s, isolated events served as reminders that anti-Catholicism lives on. Violent actions disrupted Catholic services in New York, Washington, and Boston. An editor of the *Philadelphia Inquirer* described the Church as "an unAmerican institution" (Boldt 1990) and, like the *New York Times*, chided bishops for speaking their minds on abortion, reminding them that they are of a minority group to whom the majority has generously granted tolerance. Noting such occurrences, George Weigel observed, "new forms of an old bigotry, anti-Catholicism, are befouling American public life" (1992, 93).

Yet things have changed drastically. "No Irish Need Apply" signs have not appeared at the entrance to the job market within the memory of anyone now living, even though the expression is still recalled in Catholic households. The anti-Catholicism that still exists emanates more often from secular sources than from Protestant churches. And its impact on Catholics has waned, for American Catholics are no longer a mute, impotent, beleaguered minority. They no longer feel like outsiders possessing less than full membership in the society and the body politic.

Catholic Institutions

The religious experience of practicing Catholics is not limited to an hour spent in church on Sunday morning. They have multiple ties linking them to their Church through an elaborate network of institutions. These teach and inform, promote solidarity among the faithful, and unify them in a wide array of cultural, educational, charitable, and social activities. Diverse as their purposes are, they have one common objective—reinforcing the faith of their members.

The Catholic educational system, bringing parents, faculty, and administrators as well as students into a common enterprise, is the most conspicuous of these institutions. In 1996, more than 3.3 million students were enrolled in Catholic schools across the nation from kindergarten through university graduate schools. In addition, 4.2 million young Catholics attending public elementary and high schools received religious instruction in church-sponsored classes organized as the Confraternity of Christian Doctrine.

Since the 1960s the Catholic school system has undergone a sharp contraction. Student enrollment in the elementary schools has declined by almost 50 percent and by 40 percent in the high schools. The exodus of Catholics from big cities, the escalating costs of maintaining schools, and the loss of teaching nuns have taken this toll. In the nineties, however, a reversal of this free-fall drop in enrollment began to appear as modest gains were made in five successive years.

Catholic colleges and universities have not suffered the shrinkage that struck the Church's lower-level schools. In the thirty years since the mid-sixties, despite the disappearance of approximately sixty small institutions, the collective student bodies of Catholic colleges and universities have grown by about 60 percent.

Religious publications also serve an educational purpose, linking the Church to an adult audience. Not everything that is published with "Catholic" in its masthead is supportive of orthodox teaching and ecclesiastical authority, but most of the 25 million subscribers to Catholic newspapers, magazines, and newsletters published in the United States read a Catholic message. Magazines, with a circulation of almost 15 million, account for the bulk of the readership of these publications.

There are many diverse Church-related organizations with aggregate membership of several million that aim to strengthen the bonds among

Catholics, promote religious devotion, spread the teaching of the faith, and satisfy the need for socialization. Among the best known are the Knights of Columbus, the Holy Name Society, the Catholic Daughters of America, and the Catholic Youth Organization. Although many other churches have publications and auxiliary organizations, probably none spread out with as great a reach as those connected to the Catholic Church.

Other large-scale Catholic organizations are maintained for charitable and humanitarian purposes, serving as outlets for service and symbols of the beneficent social role of the Church. Six hundred and five Catholic hospitals are in operation in the United States. Another Church-sponsored organization spread throughout the nation is Catholic Charities USA, which in 1994 provided some form of social service to 11 million people.

Vatican II and the End of Catholic Separatism

Vatican II confirmed and expanded a movement already well advanced in the United States to remove barriers between the Catholic population and the rest of America—particularly Protestant America. It eliminated several obstacles to interfaith cooperation and in the process served to lessen some of the lingering suspicion with which Catholics were viewed by other Americans. Among the documents of the council which had this effect were the Decree on Ecumenism, the Declaration on the Relationship of the Church to Non-Christian Religions, and the statement in which the hand of American bishops was strongly involved—the Declaration on Religious Freedom (Abbott 1966).

In the nineteenth century and even into the twentieth, there was a considerable degree of segregation—in great part voluntary—among immigrant Catholics. In ethnic enclaves they found a reproduction of the European village from which they came—neighbors who spoke their language and offered help and a church with sights and sounds to which they had been accustomed since childhood. Outside lay a world as unfriendly as it was unfamiliar.

Churchmen often encouraged Catholic separatism, fearing that contact with non-Catholics in an environment hostile to the Church would lead to loss of faith. In the nineteenth century this fear led Archbishop Hughes of New York to engage in a bitter quarrel with brother priests who proposed to induce Catholics to quit urban slums in the East and resettle on open lands in the West.

The complex organizational web spun by American Catholicism came about in part as a means of segregating Catholics from other Americans and from cultural influences feared likely to lead them away from the Church. Catholic elementary schools were established initially to guard children against the Protestant atmosphere of public schools. Similarly, the Knights of Columbus was meant to provide for Catholic men an alternative to fraternal organizations considered hazardous to their faith.

A defensive separatism had been largely discarded by American Catholics long before Vatican II. As early as 1893, Cardinal Gibbons of Baltimore and other Catholic prelates participated in a significant ecumenical event held in connection with the Chicago Columbian Exposition. Despite criticism from some members of the hierarchy, they joined with representatives of other faiths in a Parliament of Religions. What was then a bold undertaking would encounter little protest today. Catholic churchmen from pope to parish priest have moved far along a path toward closer ties with those of other faiths in an ecumenical tide that has washed away the separatism of an earlier age.

A Declining Church?

Several trends can be cited that seem to show that since the 1950s the commitment of American Catholics to their Church has weakened substantially (Greeley 1990, especially ch. 5–7; Steinfels 1994). Whereas more than 70 percent of the Catholic people were in the habit of attending mass weekly in the earlier period, fewer than 50 percent did so in the mid-nineties. Catholics appear to be considerably less generous than Protestants in the percentage of income contributed to their churches (Harris 1993, 8–9; 1994, 14–16). The contraction of the Catholic school system (table 1-6) has resulted in a growing number of young Catholics who are religiously illiterate, lacking a strong tie to their Church. An aging and dwindling corps of priests and nuns foreshadows serious shortages in the religious ministry. Abandonment of their calling by large numbers of priests not only has left a void in clerical ranks but has also shaken the faith of many Catholics. Some doctrines of the Church, notably relating to the indissolubility of marriage and artificial contraception, are widely ignored and rejected by the laity. Several prominent Catholics holding political office are out of step with ecclesiastical authority on the subject of abortion. Dissenting groups calling themselves Catholic who are dissatisfied with a hierarchy they deem "unprogressive," particularly on sexual and feminist issues, though constituting a small minority of Church membership, enjoy the favor of the media and probably confuse the public.

In *The Churching of America* sociologists Roger Finke and Rodney Stark point to "declines in the vigor of American Catholicism" of the sort we have noted as evidence that the Church will begin to "wilt" (1992, 261). It is true that the unity and the uncritical acceptance of authority that were once hallmarks of American Catholicism have suffered erosion. Certainly the Church's problems of preserving the faith of its people and ministering to

TABLE 1–6. Trends in Religious Vocations and Catholic Schools, 1968 and 1997

	1968	*1997*	*Percentage Change*
Priests	59,640	48,097	-19
Nuns	181,421	87,644	-51
Elementary schools	10,406	7,164	-31
Pupils	3,917,919	2,053,819	-48
High schools	2,181	1,357	-37
Students	1,115,351	652,687	-42
Colleges/Universities	297	241	-18
Students	435,716	690,826	+58

Source: The Official Catholic Directory.

them are extremely serious. Yet the figures on church membership cited by these authors show that Catholicism has not gone the way of mainstream Protestantism. Despite fissures, divisions, and dissent that trouble many churches in the late twentieth century, American Catholicism has far more adherents than any other denomination, and its share of the nation's church-affiliated population has been steadily increasing. Part of the explanation of this relative success of the Church in America may lie in the character, the personality, and the accomplishments of its leader, John Paul II, who commands extraordinary respect from the majority of American Catholics and has had an influence in world affairs unmatched by any other religious leader in modern times.

Political Activism of Catholics

Despite their relatively small numbers and the disabilities imposed on them, Catholics were active participants in political life in several places even in the nation's infancy. Nowhere were they more active than in the District of Columbia after its establishment as the nation's capital. Robert Brent, the first mayor of the city, was a member of the most distinguished Catholic family of Virginia. In addition, during the first two years of Washington's municipal government, the positions of chief judge, president of the board of aldermen, and president of the common council, as well as five of twelve seats on that body, marshal of the district, clerk of the court, and city administrator were all held by Catholics (Warner 1994, 152–59).

Irish Catholic immigrants plunged into local politics soon after arrival in the United States. They were quick to seize the opportunity to find employment and exercise influence by mobilizing urban voting blocs. In communities distant from the eastern seaboard, Irish immigrants, often among the early settlers, rose speedily to positions of civic leadership. St. Louis, for example, elected a Catholic as its mayor in the 1840s, when nativists dominated local government in New York and exercised considerable power in Philadelphia. The mayor chosen by the voters of St. Louis was Bryan Mullanphy, whose immigrant father arrived in Missouri when the ink was hardly dry on the Louisiana Purchase to become a wealthy businessman and philanthropist.

In time the Democratic Irish political boss (or bosses) became a common feature of big northern cities, and in a few exceptional places like Philadelphia there were even Republican Irish bosses. So pervasive did the phenomenon seem by the mid-1890s that one observer of the political scene titled an article "The Irish Conquest of Our Cities" (Bobcock 1894, 186–95).

With demographic changes and Good Government movements in urban America this era passed. The old machine vanished almost everywhere along with the boss, particularly the Irish boss. Irish mayors still govern in Chicago and Los Angeles in the 1990s, but the chief executive of a major American city in this decade is more often African-American or Italian.

A comprehensive study measuring public participation in a broad range of political activity was undertaken by Verba and Nie in 1972. In the ranks of voters and of workers in political campaigns, it found a substantially higher representation of Catholics than would be expected on the basis of the size of the Catholic population. As voters, Catholics exceeded by 16 percent the figure reflecting the Catholic share of the population. The number of Catholics participating in political campaigns was 21 percent above the number expected on this basis (Verba and Nie 1972, 98–101).

A later study conducted by Paul Kleppner reported on voting turnout of nonsouthern whites by religious group in both presidential and off-year elections during the years 1952–1980 (table 1-7). Kleppner reported a Catholic turnout in the neighborhood of 78 percent during this period, four to five percentage points higher than for Protestants but seven to ten points below the Jewish turnout in these elections. In off-year elections a similar relationship in turnout among the three groups was found.

Kleppner also adjusted the turnout figures for the three religious groups to take into account differences among them in age, education, income, and sex. With these adjustments he discovered a higher turnout rate among Catholics than among Jews or Protestants in off-year elections and rough equality between Catholic and Jewish turnout in presidential elections between 1964 and 1980 (Kleppner 1982, 124).

TABLE 1–7. Voting Turnout of Non-Southern Whites by Religious Groups in National Elections, 1952–1980

	Unadjusted		*Adjusted*	
	1952–60	*1964–80*	*1952–60*	*1964–80*
Presidential Elections				
Protestant	72.9	66.7	72.8	67.0
Catholic	78.0	70.4	78.9	70.8
Jew	85.1	81.1	81.7	71.3
Off-Year Elections				
Protestant	54.9	50.5	54.9	50.6
Catholic	65.9	55.1	67.1	56.2
Jew	72.2	65.8	66.6	55.4

Source: Paul Kleppner, *Who Voted? The Dynamics of Electoral Turnout, 1870–1980* (New York: Praeger, 1982), 124.

The Hispanic community has been a glaring exception to the high turnout rate among Catholics. Even when allowance is made for the large number of noncitizens as well as for the youthfulness of the Latino population, the turnout of Hispanics in elections appears to be the lowest among the nation's ethnic and racial elements. In the presidential elections of 1988 and 1992, 29 percent of the Latino population of voting age reported going to the polls, a figure approximately half that for the total population.

Poverty, lack of education, a linguistic barrier, unfamiliarity with the culture and the political system—conditions which restrict the turnout of Hispanics—are passing. The Latino population of the United States, which increased five times as fast as the rest of the nation in the 1980s, will become an important political force (O'Hare 1989, sec. 4–4). The sleeping giant may have started to stir in 1996 when the turnout of Hispanics rose in absolute numbers while that of almost all other groups declined from the level of 1992.

Catholics and Political Parties

For many years to be a Catholic in religion was to be a Democrat in politics. The vast majority of Catholics voted the Democratic ticket from alderman to president. In national contests Catholics supplied a considerable share of the vote cast for Democratic candidates outside the South. In the big cities of the North they supplied as well a great part of the leadership of the party at the local level from the late nineteenth century through the Second World War. Their rise to positions of power at the state and national level through the Democratic Party was slower. Not until the second decade of the twentieth century was a Catholic elected to the office of governor in New York or Massachusetts. The era in which Catholics secured substantial representation in appointive and elective office in the national government opened only with the inauguration of Franklin D. Roosevelt as president.

The identification of Catholics with the Democratic Party began with the arrival in force of immigrants, particularly the Irish, and their settlement in major eastern cities. Before that time the Catholics who gained political prominence were mainly Federalists and Whigs. During the early period after independence, men like Charles and Daniel Carroll of Maryland, Thomas Fitzsimons of Pennsylvania, and Richard Brent of Virginia served in the United States Congress as Federalists. William Brent was a founder of the Whig Party of Louisiana, and, during the period between the 1820s and the 1840s, Louisiana elected to the governorship and the national House of Representatives the Catholic Whig Edward Douglass White. Baltimore merchant Luke Tiernan, also a Catholic, was called by Henry Clay "the patriarch of the Whig party in Maryland." Even Roger Brooke Taney, another Marylander, began his political career as a Federalist before becoming a leader of the Jacksonian Democratic Party in 1825.

On into the 1850s the voting behavior of recent Catholic immigrants diverged from that of the older Catholics. Justice Taney noted the split in Maryland. And, responding to the complaint of Know-Nothings in Kentucky that Catholics were all voting Democratic, Bishop Martin J. Spalding of Louisville conceded the charge was true of immigrants but asserted that native Catholics divided their votes evenly between Whigs and Democrats (1855, 151).

The most eminent historian of Catholic America, John Tracy Ellis, traces the party attachment of Catholics in the first half of the nineteenth century in these words:

> The great majority of Catholics in the early national period consulted their own interests and found them best served by the Federalist Party.... After the breakup of the Federalists their choice lay between the Democrats and the Whigs. Ultimately it did not prove a difficult decision for most Catholics to make, for if at first some of them leaned toward the Whigs, they were quickly disillusioned when they discovered the flirtations of that party with the nativists. . . . The Democrats were by far the stronger proponents of religious freedom, and it was that party—not the

Whigs—which extended a welcoming hand to the foreign-born. (1956, 75)

The dictum that Catholic equals Democrat became true with the large-scale immigration of Catholics from Ireland and Germany and largely held true until the 1890s. In the presidential elections from 1896 on, cracks appeared in the heretofore solid Catholic Democratic vote and spread after the First World War. The erosion of Catholic loyalty to the Democratic Party was reversed, however, in 1928 when a united Catholic electorate was galvanized to support Governor Alfred E. Smith for president.

Though never again as monolithic as in 1928 (even in 1960), the Catholic vote remained overwhelmingly Democratic from the depression of the thirties through the post–World War II years. In 1956 Eisenhower broke through the barrier by gaining 50 percent or more of the vote cast by Catholics in a presidential election, a feat later duplicated by Nixon, Reagan, and Bush.

No Democratic nominee for the presidency secured a majority of the vote cast by Catholics in the four presidential elections between 1980 and 1992—a record broken by Bill Clinton in 1996. Since the late 1960s, and particularly during the 1980s, the percentage of Catholics self-identified as Democrats has declined sharply. On the other hand, the Republican gain in adherents among Catholics during this period was far from commensurate with the Democrats' loss.

The Clergy and Politics

A myth widely propagated in anti-Catholic publications of the last century and still not quite defunct is that faithful Catholics receive directions on how to vote from their priests, perhaps following orders that originate in Rome. In fact, with relatively few exceptions, American Catholic clergymen have heeded the admonition addressed to them in the late eighteenth century by their first bishop, John Carroll, to remain aloof from politics (Ellis 1956, 73). Even when representatives of other faiths carried on campaigns questioning the fitness of any Catholic to serve as the nation's president in 1928 and in 1960, the Catholic clergy avoided overt partisan involvement. In 1980, Pope John Paul II reaffirmed Carroll's rule by bringing about the termination of the political careers of two priests, Robert Drinan of Massachusetts and Robert Cornell of Wisconsin, both of whom had served as Democratic members of the United States House of Representatives. As they were setting in motion campaigns for re-election, the two were notified by their religious superiors of a Papal decision requiring them to abandon their plans. In explanation of his decision, John Paul II said, according to the *New York Times* of

13 May 1980, "politics is the responsibility of laymen, and a priest should be a priest."

There have been clerics, however, who have ignored Carroll's advice. One of the most conspicuous was Archbishop John Ireland of St. Paul, who made clear his affiliation with the Republican Party, notably in the McKinley campaign in 1896. In the present century Franklin D. Roosevelt received vigorous support in his campaigns from Monsignor John A. Ryan of Catholic University and in 1932 from Charles E. Coughlin, "the radio priest," who told his largely Catholic audience that their choice at the polls was between "Roosevelt or Ruin." By 1936 Father Coughlin had come to believe that FDR was a "great liar and betrayer" and involved himself in launching a third party which nominated William E. Lemke for president. In the campaign of 1972 George McGovern drew support from Auxiliary Bishop Thomas Gumbleton of Detroit, who has consistently positioned himself well to the left of his colleagues.

The emergence of abortion as a national issue has prompted a somewhat more conspicuous level of involvement by bishops in campaigns than had been customary in earlier times. In 1976 remarks by the president of the National Council of Catholic Bishops on the positions of the two major presidential candidates on abortion were widely construed as approval of Ford and disapproval of Carter, although several steps were taken by spokesmen for the bishops to counteract this impression. In 1984 Cardinal O'Connor of New York issued well-publicized statements critical of Geraldine Ferraro's view that there was more than one Catholic position on the subject. Four years later, Archbishop John Whealon of Hartford and Auxiliary Bishop Austin Vaughan of New York announced their withdrawal from the Democratic Party, Whealon by the dramatic gesture of burning his party membership card (*New York Times*, 26 August 1988).

When in 1996 President Clinton vetoed a bill banning a form of abortion called partial birth abortion, his action was denounced by numerous bishops. The American cardinals assembled in Washington in an unsuccessful effort to persuade Congress to override the president's action. But even when a moral issue which the bishops regarded of major magnitude was before the nation, few members of the hierarchy ventured any clear signal of their preference in the presidential contest.

Fragmentary evidence suggests a spread of bipartisanship in the ranks of Catholic bishops since the election of John Paul II to the papacy. A 1989 survey comparing members of the hierarchy appointed by Pope Paul VI between 1963 and 1978 with those selected by his successor in the following years pointed to this conclusion. Of the earlier group of bishops, 59 percent were Democrats and 17 percent Republicans. Those appointed by John Paul were nicely balanced, 38 percent Democrats and 38 percent Republicans (Gelm 1990, 38).

Although Catholic Church leaders and organizations have been loath to intervene in political campaigns to support or oppose specific candidates, they have been active participants in many campaigns to promote or defeat public policy measures affecting their moral principles or their interests. Whenever abortion or euthanasia is on a ballot, the Church's spokesmen, press, and auxiliary organizations will be leaders in the fight, seeking to mobilize the Catholic community to cast pro-life votes. Similarly, the Church as an organization will vigorously campaign when legislators or voters are making decisions affecting its school system or its social service agencies.

Since the end of World War I, a Catholic lobby, the U. S. Catholic Conference, has been maintained in Washington by the bishops. Parallel organizations exist in the capitals of many states. With a legislative program of broad scope more attuned to the agenda of Democrats than Republicans except on matters relating to abortion and education and with a minimum of direction from the bishops, the staff of the United States Catholic Conference works with great skill to influence legislative and executive action (Hertzke 1988, 81; Byrnes 1991, 25–29; Reese 1992, 218–19).

The Influence of Religious Belief on Voting Behavior

Several political movements in our history have been rooted in religious belief, including such causes as abolitionism, civil rights, and Prohibition. Several religious bodies have entered the political arena to advance causes related to their faith and put in office candidates sympathetic to them.

No organization of Catholics similar to the Moral Majority or the Christian Coalition has sprung up to mobilize Catholics into a political force. With financial and organizational support from the Christian Coalition in its initial stages, a political association named the Catholic Alliance came into being after the 1992 election. In the 1996 campaign the Alliance claimed to speak for 30,000 Catholics, but, struggling with organizational problems and regarded with distrust by some Church personages, it failed to develop into even a pale imitation of Reverend Pat Robertson's political legions. (Gerner 1995, 15–20).

Without pressure or direction, committed Catholics, like strong believers of other faiths, are likely to consult their religious convictions when they are in the polling booth. Yet religious belief does not appear to be a dominant influence on the voting behavior of most Catholics in the closing decades of the twentieth century. A survey published in 1987 (Castelli and Gremillion, 189), which sampled the nationwide population of white, non-Hispanic "core

Catholics" (registered parish members), asked, "Are your voting decisions determined by your religious beliefs and values?" The responses fell into the following four categories, with the percentage of respondents in each indicated below:

Completely determined	9
To a large degree	34
To a small degree	35
Not at all	21

Those whose faith had an important bearing on their votes constitute a substantial number of voters. Yet even among this committed group, only a minority said their religious belief had much to do with how they voted.

The Catholic Conservatives

Writing of *The Conservative Intellectual Movement in America Since 1945*, George Nash concluded that much of this movement "seemed Catholic in composition"; he called it "the cutting edge of the postwar 'coming of age' of America's Catholic minority" (quoted in Allitt 1993, 3). Among the Catholics who became prominent spokesmen for postwar conservatism were William F. Buckley, Michael Novak, Garry Wills, Russell Kirk, Thomas Molnar, John Lukacs, James Hitchcock, Francis Wilson, Ross Hoffman, and L. Brent Bozell. *National Review*, the publication Buckley founded, became the more or less official organ of this movement.

The conservative message which such writers expounded found a receptive audience among many Catholics, particularly the most orthodox and traditionalist. In the political order it had a part in generating the formation of the Conservative Party in New York, which was largely Catholic in its leadership. The party's most noteworthy accomplishment occurred in 1970, when its candidate for the United States Senate, James Buckley, defeated the nominees of the two major parties for the office. In this victory the vote of Catholics played a decisive role. In later years New York's Conservative Party, although not losing its separate identity, has tended to become an adjunct of the Republicans, adding its endorsement to most candidates nominated by the GOP.

The conservatism that attracted a significant following in the Catholic population after World War II was not the thorough-going doctrinaire brand held by many conservatives. Nor did it hew to the line preached in the *Wall Street Journal*. Catholic conservatism had strong foreign policy content, with heavy emphasis on anticommunism. In the field of domestic policy, it was not inclined to criticism of government programs promoting social welfare.

Nor did it oppose government action to strengthen civil rights and to expand economic and educational opportunity.

This brand of conservatism was primarily concerned with what Scammon and Wattenberg called "the social issue" in a seminal work (1970) written at the end of the tumultuous decade of the 1960s to call attention to the emergence of new influences on the voting behavior of many Americans. The authors (both loyal Democrats) argued that new concerns, largely cultural, were threatening to displace economic issues as the major determinant of election outcomes, thereby jeopardizing the dominant position which the Democratic Party had held in American politics for the better part of four decades.

The so-called social issue gnawed with particular intensity at the consciences of deeply religious Christians. The complex of conditions to which this label was applied seemed to them to exemplify the moral decline into which the nation had fallen. Riots in the streets and on the campus, the escalating crime rate, the breakdown of the family, deteriorating schools, sexual permissiveness, the spread of abortion, the epidemic of drug use, urban decay, the decline of the work ethic, disrespect for the uniform and the flag, the whole Vietnam protest movement—these were the principal symptoms of a moral rot infecting society.

In response to a shift of voter attention from economic to cultural concerns, code words playing on values of prime importance to many believers assumed greater importance in the political vocabulary—words like "religion," "prayer," "patriotism," "law and order," "discipline," "home and family," "neighborhood," and "work." Politicians attuned to this conservatism learned to end their speeches with "God bless America." New issues appeared in platforms and entered political debate.

Catholics were particularly responsive to many of the new issues. Not long after World War II the bishops began to deplore the spread of secularism and to criticize judicial decisions which they interpreted as closing much of public life to religion. Later, in 1973, in *Roe v. Wade* came the Supreme Court ruling that shocked many Catholics into heightened political activism. The constitutional protection which a majority of the justices established for abortion was to generate continuing debate and to bring long-term involvement of the hierarchy in the political arena in support of the Right to Life movement.

Another shock was the resistance to the war in Vietnam, which brought to the fore the question of patriotic duty. Catholics grew up in a Church that gave particular emphasis to the virtue of patriotism—so strong an emphasis that many critics within and outside the Church used the derisive expression "superpatriotism" to describe the attitude it encouraged (Dolan 1985, 450; Byrnes 1991, 42).

The tactics of the Vietnam protesters—desecration of the flag, disruptive demonstrations in support of the nation's enemies, lawlessness and violence—were deeply offensive to most Catholics, even when a protester appeared in the garb of priest or nun. In this troubled time, as in earlier conflicts, Catholics were overrepresented in the armed forces and the service academies. And, as in earlier wars, they were grossly underrepresented in the ranks of conscientious objectors. Catholic college campuses were relatively tranquil when other institutions erupted in protest. As ROTC units were attacked and driven off other campuses, with only one exception, they stayed at Catholic schools.

A third shock was provided by the turmoil that accompanied changing relations between whites and blacks. The reaction was particularly strong when urban neighborhoods and schools populated by white ethnics began to change their complexion under government mandate.

Christians of many persuasions in many parts of the world have failed to demonstrate respect for Christ's second command to those who would be His followers: Love thy neighbor. At some times and places Catholics have been the offenders. The antipathy of Catholic immigrants toward blacks was noted in a report to Rome by a papal representative in the middle of the nineteenth century. The representative, Archbishop Gaetano Bedini, wrote of the deep hostility of Irish immigrants at the bottom of the economic ladder toward "Negroes, whom they despised and feared as their competitors" (Connelly 1960, 199).

Somewhat more than a decade later this hostility erupted in the Draft Riots in New York City, bringing death and injury to blacks at the hands of an infuriated mob. The intervention of Archbishop Hughes helped to bring this ugly episode to an end. In the twentieth century clashes have occurred pitting residents of Irish, Polish, and Italian enclaves against blacks in some major cities as their racial patterns changed.

As America's blacks flocked to join the ranks of voters, nine out of ten became Democrats. In many places, particularly in the South, this influx combined with whites' desertion of the Democratic Party tended to separate the two major parties on the basis of race. A similar, but far weaker, effect can be discerned in changing voting behavior among some white ethnic Catholics who collided with blacks entering what they regarded as their neighborhoods and schools (McGreevy 1996).

Racism was unquestionably one factor in the civil strife that engulfed several communities particularly in the decade after the mid-sixties, exacerbating fears and tensions about the changes urban America was undergoing. But to attribute the reaction of whites to phenomena like mounting crime, deteriorating housing, unsafe streets, and undisciplined schools to racial prejudice is to oversimplify and misinterpret their motivation.

Summing Up

The preceding discussion has suggested several characteristics and experiences of the American Catholic people that have, in varying degrees, had some influence on their political attitudes, party attachment, and voting behavior. Much of the discussion has dealt with the climb of the bulk of the Catholic population out of the immigrant underclass, which brought a change profoundly affecting their political decisions.

The great Catholic migration from cities to suburbs and from the Northeast to the Sunbelt also has had its effects on political outlook and behavior. The move itself was often a rejection of conditions in the city, as well as its dominant political party. A new environment brought with it new friends and associates, home ownership, and often either a competitive political order or one dominated by the forces opposing the party in control of the city which the migrants fled.

The immigrant origins of Catholics have relevance to political attitudes in many ways. Some vestige of attachment to the Old Country survives well beyond the immigrant generation. As a result there is probably a livelier interest in foreign policy, or, at least in selected foreign policy issues, among the Catholic people than among those of older American stock. This interest led candidates for many years to compete for Catholic votes by outdoing each other in reviling England as Ireland's oppressor. In campaigns following World War II, the theme of anticommunism brought a strong response from those whose ancestral lands had become "captive nations." Yet another example is found in the case of Cuban émigrés, who, alone among the Hispanic population, have frequently given decisive majorities to Republicans because of dissatisfaction with the policy of Democratic administrations toward Castro.

Aspiring politicians in the past were not hesitant to appeal to the tribal loyalty and the prejudices of their ethnic group. Tim Campbell, Tammany Congressman, was blunt in his standard speech to Irish audiences in his campaign against Samuel Rinaldo in 1890. The issue before the voters he defined as "the Dago Rinaldo. . . . He is from Italy; I am from Ireland. Are you in favor of Italy or Ireland?" (Allswang 1986, 74). James Michael Curley in his many campaigns employed a somewhat similar, if less primitive, message to rally the Irish of Boston to repel the Brahmins of Beacon Hill and the Ku Klux Klan.

"Vote for one of our own" has not lost its potency as a campaign slogan. Ethnic and racial solidarity visible in the voting patterns of several groups remains a fact of political life. In recent times it has operated most conspicuously to advance the careers of politicians of the black race and those of Italian and Hispanic ethnicity.

Religious ties, too, have been helpful in winning votes. The tendency of Catholics to vote for a coreligionist, at its strongest in the presidential contests of 1928 and 1960, has also been found in milder form in many races for various offices in several states (Fenton 1960). A 1960 study of voting behavior concluded that a Catholic candidate could expect from coreligionists a vote 10 percent higher than that given to a non-Catholic of the same party (Campbell et al. 1960, 319–21). In that same year when it became clear that no office—not even the White House—lay beyond the reach of a Catholic, any such bonus a Catholic might receive in the normal election thereafter was sharply reduced. For Catholics, as for others, as the immigrant experience becomes a fading memory, the impulse or pressure to vote for a candidate of one's faith or ethnic stock loses its force.

Catholics have changed, and so has their Church, in ways that have dispelled much suspicion and hostility. The emergence of Catholics from vestiges of self-segregation has helped. So has the modification of teachings, some of which seemed to demean other faiths and to assert for the Catholic Church a privileged position in the political order.

The social issue which Scammon and Wattenberg saw emerging in 1970 has, if anything, gained importance since then. It has helped to spawn a gradual development of alliances among members of religious groups that were noted in the past for an adversarial relationship. Most noteworthy is a convergence of the political agenda of many traditional Catholics and Evangelicals and a tentative collaboration between the two in quest of common political goals.

At the threshold of the twenty-first century, the Catholic community in the United States looks back on a history impossible to summarize in a word. But if any word captures the most universal aspect of the community's experience, it may be "homogenization." Catholics went through the melting pot and came out very much like other Americans.

2

Immigrant Catholics and Elections of 1844–1860

Between 1840 and 1860 the United States underwent a number of fundamental transformations—economic, political, social, and demographic. The pattern of life and the composition of the population changed drastically as the impending storm that was to fracture the Union gathered force.

Major Currents of the Mid-Nineteenth Century

Demographic change contributed to unsettling established ways of life. Fed by heavy immigration that began in the late 1840s as well as by high birthrates among both the immigrant and the native population, the national headcount soared, increasing by 35 percent in the decade before the Civil War.

The nation's villages were becoming towns and cities. Between 1840 and 1860 the urban population increased from less than 2 to more than 6 million. Though urban areas were mainly small towns, New York City by 1850 had become a metropolis of 700,000 people, followed by Baltimore, Boston, Philadelphia, New Orleans, and Cincinnati—each with more than 100,000 inhabitants.

Immigrants from Ireland and Germany accounted significantly for the growth of the urban population. The communities in which the newcomers settled lost their homogeneity, absorbing in the span of a few years a large alien community—for the most part, impoverished and uneducated, living in squalid overcrowded tenements, exhibiting strange customs and traditions, speaking a foreign tongue or a type of English smothered by a brogue or other strange accent, and most practicing a religion known to native Protestant America for Inquisitions and Gunpowder Plots.

Steadily, particularly in the northern states, a rudimentary industrial economy took shape as factories and mills dotted the towns of New England and the mid-Atlantic states. The system of canals was completed, and railroads spread out to connect the population centers of the East and the Midwest. The new immigrants turned to the tasks of digging the earth and tending machines that went with these changes in the structure of the economy.

Horace Greeley advised young men lured by cheap and fertile farmland in the heartland and by California's gold, to go west, and a substantial number—not all young—followed his advice in a great migration facilitated by the spread of the railroad system to the middle region of the country.

Slavery came to dominate the nation's political agenda amid deepening sectional strife. Beneath quarrels about the war with Mexico and the acquisition of Texas in the 1840s lay a conflict over disturbing the balance between slave and free states. To many Northerners, enlargement of the nation's boundaries appeared to be a Southern plot. Texas, ominously, was brought into the Union by legislation that made possible its division into five slave states. The expansion of national territory whetted an appetite for still more. The doctrine of Manifest Destiny was proclaimed, and, as though to give it effect, American-directed filibustering expeditions were carried out in Nicaragua and Cuba.

The Compromise of 1850 enacted by Congress in the hope of dampening the sectional conflict failed to achieve its purpose. By its terms, the Missouri Compromise, which had fixed a boundary to slave territory and helped to stifle discord for more than three decades, was abandoned. The elimination of that boundary set the stage for the battle over the admission of Kansas and Nebraska to statehood. With the *Dred Scott* decision, hope of confining slavery to areas in which it was already established glimmered.

The political system suffered shocks that the parties that had been dominant for two decades could not withstand. A major realignment of the electorate occurred, largely along sectional lines. The Whig Party, deprived of two great leaders by the death of both Henry Clay and Daniel Webster in 1852, did not survive to contest another presidential election with a candidate of its own. In the struggle to succeed the Whigs as the major opponent of the Democrats, the Republicans prevailed in 1856 and by the end of the decade absorbed their two rivals, the Free Soil Party opposed to the slave power, and the American Party opposed to foreigners and Catholics.

Slavery was not the only question that divided Americans in the 1850s. Perhaps of greater significance in generating antagonism between Catholics and Protestants were two issues fought out at state and local levels rather than in the national forum. One was the result of the movement for a common school system to provide universal elementary education. In the early 1850s this movement attained a major objective with the passage of compulsory attendance legislation in New York State and Massachusetts. The most bitter controversy attending the common school movement revolved around whether religion was to have a place in the curriculum and, if so, whose religion would be favored. Among several causes of friction between Catholics and Protestants in the nineteenth century none was longer lasting than disputes about the subject of education (McCadden 1964; Ravitch 1974; Glenn 1988, 215–35).

A second divisive issue that spread across the nation in the 1850s was introduced by the temperance movement. The passage of the Maine law in 1851 outlawing alcoholic beverages in that state encouraged campaigns for similar legislation elsewhere. Although the division of public opinion on this issue did not clearly follow religious lines, the strongest supporters of temperance laws were native Protestants of puritanical outlook, and among the staunchest foes were Irish and German immigrants.

Catholics at Mid-Century

The American and Foreign Christian Union, a leading Protestant publication surveying the signs of an increasing Catholic presence, asked in its issue of July 1850 the rhetorical question, "In 1830 who would have dreamed that in just two decades America would harbor 29 bishops, 30 dioceses, 1,081 priests, 1,073 churches, 17 colleges, 29 ecclesiastical seminaries, and 91 female academies in addition to numerous orphan schools and asylums?"

The two decades had indeed been years of impressive growth for the Catholic Church. Membership rose from 300,000 adherents to 1.6 million and from 2.5 to 7 percent of the nation's population. By the end of the fifties their numbers were to double to more than 3 million—10 percent of the nation—making Catholicism one of the country's largest religious bodies.

By 1850 the Catholic population had spread throughout the Northern states although still concentrated near the eastern seaboard. The growth and the dispersion of the ranks of the Church's followers are reflected in the creation of new dioceses—Hartford, Pittsburgh, Chicago, Milwaukee, and Little Rock in 1843; Walla Walla in 1846; Albany, Buffalo, Cleveland, and Galveston in 1847; Wheeling, Savannah, St. Paul, Santa Fe, and Monterey in 1850. Whereas in 1840 Dubuque was the westernmost residence of a Catholic bishop, ten years later the hierarchical organization stretched from border to border and coast to coast.

The first National Council of the American Catholic Church convened in Baltimore in 1852. Of the six archbishops and twenty-six bishops whom it brought together, only eight were Americans by birth. The gathering was symbolic of three developments—the emergence of the Catholic Church on the national scene, its growth, and its strongly immigrant character. Most of the work of the council dealt with internal Church matters of religious practice and discipline and the role of bishops vis-à-vis the laity. It avoided mention of matters of public policy, including slavery. The bishops, however, spoke of the need to educate children in the faith and decreed that "schools be established in connection with all the churches" throughout the nation, thus founding the system of parochial schools.

Since 1840 education had been a battleground in communities in which a substantial number of Catholics had settled. Why the bishops were critical of the public school system is understandable in the light of the following description of the common school of the era:

> The groups which captured the schools did so by making them militantly middle-class, militantly Protestant, and militantly nativist. . . . Concerted effort was made to ridicule and defame the culture and the folkways of the lower-class children. Their religion (predominantly Catholic), their languages, and their foreign habits and values were continually denounced. Whatever pride in their homeland they were able to keep alive after the migration experience was ridiculed and even cursed as evidence of subversive intentions. (Church and Sadlak 1976, 156)

Anti-Catholic feeling, which had flared up notably in New York and Philadelphia midway through the 1840s, reached its apogee in the years between 1853 and 1856. The American Party, popularly called the Know-Nothings, claiming a membership of more than 1.5 million in its lodges, seemed to spring up overnight throughout the nation to win control of many state and local governments and to elect a substantial number of its members to the United States Congress. The sobriquet Know-Nothing, applied to the American Party by its critics, was based upon the practice of members of the semisecret party to respond "I don't know" to any questions asked about the movement.

The strength of the Know-Nothing movement was concentrated in the East. In places like California where Catholics were among the original settlers, Know-Nothingism was a rather feeble and ephemeral phenomenon. As one writer observed, "the ratio of religious and social prejudice diminished in proportion to the distance from the older and settled communities of the East, so that on the West Coast it hardly existed" (Potter 1960, 540).

The watchword of the Know-Nothings, "Americans must rule America," suggests equal hostility to all foreigners, but their special concern was "the aggressive policy and corrupting tendencies of the Roman Catholic Church." And within the Catholic Church the group that was the major object of Know-Nothing wrath was the Irish. The common indictment of Irish Catholics was well summarized in New York's *Irish American* just before the elections of 1854, in which the Know-Nothing movement registered spectacular gains in Congress and in several states. Addressing "fellow countrymen and friends," the paper observed,

> You have at present opposed to you a bitter, inimical, and powerful secret society called the Know Nothings; opposed to you, to us Irishmen particularly, on the grounds that we are impudent and voracious cormorants of petty places under government; that we are ignorant, turbulent, and brutal; that we are controlled by our clergy; that we are willing subjects of a foreign prince, the Pope; that we are only lip-Republicans; that we are not worthy of the franchise; that by the largeness of our vote and the clannishness of our habits we rule or aspire to rule in America; that we are drunkards and criminals; that we fill the workhouses and prisons; that we heap up taxes on industrious and sober and thrifty citizens. (Quoted in Knobel 1986, 132–33)

Not unrelated to the outpouring of anti-Catholicism in the 1850s was a growing visibility of Catholics in urban politics. In New York and some other northeastern cities a Catholic vote large enough to have a bearing on the outcome of elections had come into existence. This vote prompted the Democratic Party to which it was solidly attached to nominate an increasing number of Catholics for local office and the state legislature and to share with them the spoils that came with electoral success.

Even at the national level, the political importance of the Catholic population gained recognition. In 1852, the Whig Party for the first time in a national campaign actively sought the votes of Catholics. The victorious Democratic candidate for president in that contest, Franklin Pierce, chose James Campbell as his postmaster general. Rewarded for delivering votes in Pennsylvania, Campbell was the second Catholic to occupy a cabinet post in the 64 years since Washington's first inauguration. Also in 1852, for the first time New York City elected an Irish American to the United States House of Representatives to hold a place which for many years thereafter remained an "Irish seat." Significantly, in their pastoral letter of 1852, the bishops took the opportunity to lecture their flock on the obligations attached to suffrage with a thinly veiled admonition against selling one's vote.

The Campaign of 1844

The first presidential campaign in which the nation's Catholics received significant attention was the contest of 1844 pitting the dark horse candidate of the Democratic Party, James Polk, against the Whigs' Henry Clay. Also in the race was James G. Birney, nominated by the Liberty Party to express dissatisfaction with the failure of the major parties to oppose slavery.

Opposition to slavery had earlier brought Birney together with Daniel O'Connell, leader of the fight for Catholic emancipation in Ireland. Noting the importance of Irish immigrants "especially in New York" (Fladeland

1955, 204–5), Birney overtly appealed for their votes, lavishing praise on O'Connell and voicing his party's "sympathy" for Ireland.

Birney also vigorously denounced the anti-immigrant movement in a year in which nativists were active in the streets and at the polls, a year in which Catholic churches were burned in riots in Philadelphia and a nativist administration was elected to office in New York City. He sought to enlist the immigrant in the fight against slavery by arguing that the same spirit that sustained human bondage produced discrimination and violence against immigrants.

As a result of his antinativist campaign, Birney became the target of a charge that in later elections was to become a standard device for exploiting prejudice. Birney was accused of being a Catholic. The evidence cited was the fact that one of his sons had for a time attended St. Xavier's School in Cincinnati. The unfounded allegation was considered threatening enough by the candidate to require refutation by publication of a series of letters from the son involved as well as from other relatives attesting to the Protestantism of the entire Birney family.

The election returns contain no evidence that Birney's campaign for Irish immigrant votes was productive. The Irish did not rally to the antislavery cause even when their hero O'Connell, along with others of his compatriots, in 1842 addressed a strong appeal to Irish Americans to unite for the abolition of slavery.

Birney's candidacy, however, may well have had a decisive influence on the 1844 election, which Henry Clay lost by the narrowest of margins. Had Clay captured New York State, in which he ran 5,100 votes behind Polk, his lifelong dream of becoming president would have been realized. Birney received 15,800 votes from New Yorkers.

According to the commonly accepted interpretation of the election, this vote for Birney came mostly from Whigs dissatisfied with Clay's stand on the issues of slavery and the annexation of Texas. In an election as close as that of 1844, however, in which a switch of 2,600 votes in New York would have changed the result, it is hard to assign credit or blame for the outcome to any single issue or group of voters.

Clay himself took this view in analyzing the reasons for his narrow loss. "If there had been no native party," he wrote, "or if all of its members had been truer to their principles; or if the recent foreigners had not all been united against us; or if the foreign Catholics had not been arrayed on the other side; or if the Abolitionists had been true to their avowed principles; or if there had been no frauds, we should have triumphed" (Sellers 1971, 1: 798).

Millard Fillmore, defeated in his race for governor of New York, narrowed the list of those responsible for the rebuff suffered by the Whigs to two groups, writing to Clay, "The Abolitionists and the foreign Catholics have defeated us in this State. May God save the country from the effects of foreign influence" (O'Driscoll 1937, 284–85).

As time went by, the belief that Clay was denied the presidency by the votes of immigrant Catholics became an article of faith among Whig politicians while other reasons for his defeat tended to fade from their recollection. Ten years after the election of 1844, Congressman Lewis D. Campbell of Ohio, then a Know-Nothing on the way to becoming a Republican, was still deploring the Catholic influence that affected the outcome:

> Because Theodore Frelinghuysen was nominated on the ticket with Henry Clay . . . the influence of the Catholic Church—I mean especially that of the foreign Catholic Church, I do not include the American Catholic Church—was brought to bear against him; and wherever you find a foreign Catholic vote in . . . the election of 1844, you will find, particularly in your large cities where the power was wielded, that the power was exercised for the prostration of Harry of the West, for the reason, as admitted to me by a priest . . . that Theodore Frelinghuysen was a leading Presbyterian and President of the American Protestant Bible Society. (McLaughlin 1885, 85–86)

Bishop John Hughes of New York in private correspondence labeled Frelinghuysen "a sincere, honest, and honorable bigot." (Letter of Hughes to Pintle and Prentice, 29 July 1844, Archives, Archdiocese of New York). But Catholics could find more compelling reasons for voting against Clay than his choice of a running mate. In some major cities, notably New York and riot-wracked Philadelphia, Whigs and nativist groups formed an alliance in 1844 to divide elective offices with each other. One result of the alliance was the election of six avowed nativists to the United States House of Representatives, four from New York and two from Pennsylvania.

James Harper, publisher of the magazine bearing his name and of the most widely read anti-Catholic book of the time (a spurious"confession" of life in a Canadian convent), was elected mayor of New York in the spring of 1844 as the candidate of the nativist American Republicans with the active support of the local Whig Party. In helping to place the city under nativist control, local Whigs believed they had struck a deal, with the municipal election as its first phase. The second phase of the bargain, they understood, would come with the fall elections, in which nativists were expected to support the Whig candidates for president and governor in return for Whig votes for nativist nominees for Congress and the state legislature.

Bishop John Hughes predicted after the success of the Whig-nativist coalition in the spring municipal election that thereby "Henry Clay had been destroyed" and warned his friend Thurlow Weed against the danger to the Whig Party of alliances with the forces that would proscribe immigrants (Weed 1884, 2: 134).

Horace Greeley was among those who voted for the nativist ticket in New York's spring municipal election in the belief that the coalition formed in that campaign would reunite in the fall to give the Whig presidential ticket a plurality of two to five thousand votes in the city. In November these hopes were dashed. Nativist candidates captured three of the four congressional districts within New York City, but Clay lost the city to Polk. In the *New York Tribune*, 12 November 1844, Greeley ruefully confessed to feeling "like some silly countryman who has been decoyed into some disreputable haunt, had his clothes and money stolen, and then been kicked into the street. . . . The Natives take all and we get nothing."

Greeley belatedly came to the opinion Bishop Hughes had expressed. After surveying the 1844 returns across the nation, the *Tribune* found in them a warning against Whig alliances with Nativism. "In Ohio," Greeley reported in the November 14 issue of the paper, "Whigs expressly, in Maryland and New Jersey tacitly repudiated Native Americanism. In Connecticut they did not encourage it. In New York and Pennsylvania they followed a different course. Look at the results."

Thurlow Weed's *Albany Evening Journal* concurred with Greeley in its election postmortem: "We have lost the state by a course which has driven adopted Whig citizens against us. . . . While favoring and uniting with the Native American Party, was it reasonable to ask or expect those whom that party proscribes to vote our ticket?" (*New York Tribune*, 13 November 1844).

In the Whig campaign of 1844, an anti-Catholic theme appeared in places which immigrant Catholics had not penetrated as well as in areas to which immigrants were beginning to swarm. A substantial piece of Whig campaign literature was produced by William G. "Parson" Brownlow, Methodist minister and journalist of Jonesboro, Tennessee, later a Know-Nothing and finally a Republican governor and United States senator. His tract was titled *A Political Register Setting Forth the Principles of the Whig and Loco-Foco Parties in the United States*. The praise for Clay in this work is almost overshadowed by forty pages of anti-Catholic diatribe.

American freedom was threatened, Brownlow wrote, by growing Catholic power in "an unholy alliance" with the Church's chosen instrument, the Democratic (or LocoFoco) Party. The most acute danger at the time, he thought, as did Lyman Beecher, was the Catholic "conspiracy" to control western areas of the country then being settled.

The operation of the unholy alliance was described by the *Western Christian Advocate* in its July 1850 issue:

> It is well known that the Romanists as a body, with few exceptions, take one side in politics; and there is little doubt but their political preference is decided at Rome, and comes from the eternal city through the bishops, priests, and other officers of the Papal See, to the members of their Church in this country. During the past twelve or fourteen years, as a body, the Romanists have gone to the side of the Democrats.

The remedy was clear. To thwart this dangerous conspiracy, Protestants should vote for Whigs as solidly as Catholics were voting for LocoFocos.

Doubtless Polk received a large majority of the votes cast by immigrant Catholics clustered in a few large cities. But not all Catholics were immigrants or Democrats. The islands of Catholicism populated by descendants of the early English settlers in rural Maryland and Kentucky remained staunchly Whig in 1844, giving Clay more than 60 percent of their vote.

The Campaign of 1852

In 1852 the Whig Party, for the first time in a national campaign, actively sought to attract immigrant voters. Faced with defections from both its northern and southern wings because of its ambiguous stand on the Compromise of 1850, the Whig high command moved to offset its anticipated losses with votes from the burgeoning ranks of the Catholics. Truman Smith of Connecticut, a manager of the campaign, wrote to Thurlow Weed in New York, "you must devote your whole time to bringing the Catholic element into full play. No one can do this as well as you can & in short you can do it and must . . . we want you . . . to devote yourself exclusively to this work" (Gienapp 1987, 24).

The Whig appeal to Catholic voters in 1852 rested on an attempt to link the Democratic candidate Franklin Pierce to a provision of the New Hampshire Constitution barring Catholics from holding public office. In 1850 Pierce had presided over a convention to revise the Constitution and had failed, Whigs alleged, to make a zealous effort to eliminate the discriminatory provision. In fact, repeal of the provision was supported by Pierce and recommended by the convention but was not accomplished because the voters failed in a ratifying referendum to provide the two-thirds majority needed for adoption of the revision.

Despite the flimsy basis for the charge, Pierce was accused of hostility toward Catholics in vigorous attacks in the press and on the stump waged chiefly by William E. Robinson, an Irish immigrant and journalist for Horace Greeley's *Tribune*, Robinson, engaged to speak and write on behalf of the Whig candidate, General Winfield Scott, produced pamphlets with titles such as *Franklin Pierce and Catholic Persecution in New Hampshire*.

Scott, "Old Fuss and Feathers," credited with the victory achieved in the Mexican War, served as general in chief of the United States Army from 1841 to 1861, retaining the title even as he campaigned for the presidency. Into a tour ostensibly conducted to inspect military installations in several states, he incorporated several campaign events, including attendance at the dedication of the new Catholic cathedral in Louisville.

Scott peppered his speeches with awkward tributes to Irish and German immigrants. In Columbus, Ohio, for example, he responded to a questioner in his audience with this fulsome flattery:

> I think I hear again that rich brogue that betokens a son of Old Ireland. I love to hear it! I heard it on the Niagara in '14 and again in the Valley of Mexico. It will always remind me of the gallant men of Erin who in such great numbers have followed me to victory. (Gibson 1951, 56–57)

Scott's main campaign promise aimed at immigrant voters was a pledge to reduce the naturalization period for aliens serving in the armed forces. Neither this pledge nor the attack on Pierce seems to have pried Catholics away from the Democratic ticket. On the contrary, according to the New York *Herald*, the Whig strategy lost two Protestant votes for each Catholic vote it gained. (Gienapp 1987, 30–31)

Greeley, who during the campaign had expressed confidence that Catholics would back Scott, concluded after the election that the "cry about Gen. Scott's former Nativism, the citations from Whig papers of former years against Foreigners, Popery, &c . . . proved too powerful" (Nichols and Nichols 1971, 2: 999). To Catholics, the Whigs and their candidate lacked credibility. In his quest for the presidential nomination going back to 1840, Scott had cultivated the support of nativists. His record in this regard was amply documented in a pamphlet composed by Francis Preston Blair in his last campaign as a Democrat, *Memoir of General Scott from Records Contemporaneous with the Events*. And, in the two previous presidential campaigns Whigs had joined in alliances with the foes of Catholicism. In 1848, in fact, the Native American party had been the first to endorse Zachary Taylor for president (Bauer 1985, 223).

The *Irish American* expressed its doubts about the sincerity of the Whig concern for Catholics in 1852, noting that Whigs never nominated a Catholic for office. It responded to Scott's praise of the Irish brogue by calling him "a great deludherer" (Gibson 1951, 57).

Whatever effort was made to elicit support for Scott from members of the Catholic hierarchy was completely unproductive. Thomas J. Semmes, a prominent Catholic Democrat from Louisiana, wrote Archbishop Hughes inquiring about the "rumor" that he and other members of the hierarchy "entertain and express the opinion" that Catholics should vote against Pierce because of New Hampshire's "religious test clause." Hughes responded by opining that the country would be adequately served by either of the contestants for the presidency. He denied "any ecclesiastical influence" over Catholics, who, Hughes predicted would divide their votes between the two candidates.

The Archbishop's letter declaring neutrality in the presidential contest was published in the *Pittsburgh Catholic* of 2 October 1852 and carried in several other diocesan organs including the *Boston Pilot* and the *New York Freeman's Journal and Catholic Register.* Although commenting on aspects of the campaign, these papers expressed no preference for either Pierce or Scott. The Catholic press, however, did reject the charge that Pierce was responsible for the religious test clause of his state's constitution. In its issue of 4 September 1852, the *Pilot* pointed out that he had opposed it in the New Hampshire constitutional convention of 1850.

On the other hand, the campaign tactics of the Whigs were roundly criticized. The Catholic papers of Boston and New York directed scornful fire at William E. Robinson, who acted as the Whig spokesman to Irish Catholics. Robinson, though an Irish immigrant, was not a Catholic. His association with the *Tribune* and Greeley was an added handicap. "There is not in all America, we believe, a man more hostile to Catholicity than Horace Greeley," declared the *Pilot* in the 4 September issue. The *Freeman's Journal* of 2 October 1852, called Robinson "a tool of the New York *Tribune*" and added, "Unless Gen. Scott's friends could stop the mouth of the Irish Protestant hireling . . . and repudiate the contemptible effort he has made to persuade his employers that he has influence with the Catholic Irish, the result will be a largely increased vote for Gen. Pierce."

The *Pilot* of 28 August 1852, expressed exasperation with the Whig appeal to Catholics:

> For the last month the Whig canvass against Pierce has almost entirely consisted in an effort to hoodwink us Catholics. . . . Let them speak to us as they do to all other citizens, let them canvass the merits of Frank Pierce, of his policy—let them try to show that Scott would make a better President. The Whig leaders made a special appeal to the Catholic vote—a thing we do not like . . . when they singled us out thus . . . they must think us all, Catholic voters, to be knaves, sheep, or asses.

At times the *Pilot* treated both parties with scorn. It asserted that the old party system was disintegrating and that a realignment was about to occur. "Both parties are dying—let them die," it editorialized on 18 September 1852." They have lived long enough. Stand by the coffins, follow them to the tomb and bury them decently."

On the eve of the election, 6 November, the *Pilot* expressed evenhanded skepticism toward both parties, warning its readers "the zeal of politicians for Catholic interests will cool after this weekend," The campaigners would cease praising "warm hearted Irishmen" and soon revert to such expressions as "superstitious Papists and priest-ridden Paddies."

The church-related press of New York and Boston gave no endorsement to either of the presidential candidates. Neutrality, however, would be too strong a word for the campaign coverage provided by the papers of these two major dioceses. The *Pilot*, although asserting "We have not written a line in favor of Pierce or Scott," manifested some tilt toward the Democratic side. Its articles on the campaign, the paper said, sought only to "thwart the demagogues and prick the windbags" (9 October; 6 November 1852).

The *Pilot* vigorously defended Pierce against the charge of bigotry, declaring that "the stories told to Catholics about Pierce are *false*. They are made out of whole cloth" (28 August 1852). Ridiculing the effort to connect the Democratic nominee with a provision of the New Hampshire constitution adopted before his birth, the paper published the following heavy-handed satire in its issue of 4 September 1852:

LIFE OF FRANKLIN PIERCE
4004 B.C. Is born in Concord, N.H.
4002 B.C. Is expelled from Eden
4001 B.C. Kills his brother Abel
2674 B.C. Burns the Temple of Diana and pockets the fire insurance
2107 B.C. Orders Daniel to be devoured by lions
74 A.C. Puts his mother Agrippina to death
5 A.C. Plays his fiddle while Brooklyn is burning
58 A.C. Murders the two young Princes in the Tower
1780 A.C. Plots with André to betray the American cause
1815 A.C. Endeavors to ruin the teeth of a poor child with Wild's candy
1853 A.C. Is inaugurated as President
1854 A.C. Swears allegiance to Queen Victoria and Louis Napoleon and governs the United States in their names
1855 A.C. Makes himself perpetual dictator
1856 A.C. Puts all Whigs to a horrible death.

Even more insistently than in 1844, the losers in 1852 blamed their defeat on the foreign Catholic vote. Pierce's appointment of the Catholic James Campbell of Pennsylvania to the position of postmaster general was taken as confirmation of the administration's debt to foreigners. Some critics expressed alarm at the prospect that the Pope would henceforth have access to everybody's mail.

An extreme interpretation of the election was offered by Anna Ella Carroll, who took great pride in everything about her ancestors, the leading Catholic family of colonial times, except their religion. Speaking of the 1852 contest, she wrote:

> Has not the outcome of the last Presidential election been the result of the foreign vote? Did not the Romish Church contract, bargain, to sell its influence at the ballot box to cause that result? Was not the consideration any member of the Cabinet that Church might demand? Did it not call for the Postmaster General because that officer could best facilitate their movements? Did not the Pope name him and have assurance of his appointment before the American people heard it? (Carroll 1856, 108–9).

An unknown statistician provided to the Know-Nothing party a measurement of the foreign vote in 1852. Although he did not reveal the methodology behind his results, he calculated that, in fourteen states casting a majority of the electoral college votes, 258,548 "foreign votes" were cast. Pierce carried these states with a collective plurality of 120,004, and in each of them his margin was smaller than the size of the foreign vote. Leading the list was New York, captured by Pierce with a plurality of 27,901, thanks to 93,317 "foreign" voters.

This suspect analysis was presented to the Congress by Nathaniel Banks, then a Know-Nothing, as evidence that the power of "the foreign vote and the Catholic influence" had tipped the balance in 1852. In the *Congressional Globe* of 14 December 1854, he deplored the bidding for this vote on the part of both parties, for the Democrats, he said, had matched "the flattery of foreign voters by General Scott." He analyzed the election as a demonstration that "American citizens and Protestants, dividing upon minor questions of policy," can easily give a balance of power to a party of diminutive numbers that eschews division." In 1856, he asked, may not both parties "go down on their knees to those who may hold the balance of power in that contest?"

And so, for Banks, who was to exercise an influence matched by few other individuals in bringing the Republican Party into existence on the national level, the election of 1852 was a call to replace the old parties with a new political organization uniting "Americans and Protestants" to defend the Republic and its institutions against "foreigners and Catholics." In short, these specifications for a party that would save the nation pointed toward the emerging American Party. They did not describe a party in which Catholics would feel welcome.

The Formation of a National Republican Party

Between 1854 and 1856 as the Whig Party disintegrated, anti-Democratic political coalitions took shape in northern states. Without direction from the national level guiding this development, the pace, the composition, and the orientation of the shifting coalitions differed from state to state. Whigs, Free Soilers, nativists, and Democrats in varying combinations and under different names, galvanized by the struggle over Kansas, joined together to offer slates of candidates opposed to the slave power.

The off-year election of 1854 in the North brought bad news to both of the old parties. The sole consolation for Democrats was salvaging a close victory in Illinois. For the Whigs it was winning the governorship of New York by a hair, although even here the party's control of state government depended on satisfying a strong nativist bloc of legislators. In 1847 the Whigs held a majority of the seats in the national House of Representatives; eight years later they held none.

In Michigan and Wisconsin a new party carrying the name Republican prevailed in both state and congressional races. In the following year Republicans were able to derive some added satisfaction from the election of two governors, albeit on fusion tickets—Salmon Chase in Ohio and James Grimes in Iowa.

All in all, however, if there was a winner in the contests of these two years in northern states, it seemed to be the Know-Nothing Party, which emerged from nowhere to capture on its own four New England states (all except Maine and Vermont), Kentucky, Maryland, Pennsylvania, and Texas and to dominate or act as a leading partner in fusion movements that swept Indiana, Ohio, and Maine. In Virginia and in Tennessee, on the other hand, the Know-Nothing Party was rebuffed in gubernatorial elections. Democrat Henry A. Wise defeated the Party's candidate in Virginia (Simpson 1985, 109–14) as did Andrew Johnson, future Republican president but then still a Democrat, in Tennessee (Trefousse 1989, 95–98).

For those seeking to establish a viable anti-Democratic party outside the South, the elections of 1854 and 1855 seemed to indicate that such a party could be put together only through a fusion of forces of widely differing views on matters other than disapproval of Democrats. The major elements of a new party would be Whigs and Know-Nothings, for the experience gained in 1854–55 argued that fusion seemed to succeed "wherever the Whigs encouraged it and the Know Nothings also lent their support" (Gienapp 1987, 165).

No sooner had the Know-Nothing movement achieved startling success in state after state than its disintegration as a national political party began, its ranks divided by the Kansas-Nebraska Act. The southern wing of the party withered as its opponents tarred it as a Trojan horse for abolitionists and other extremists threatening the region. This was an important reason for its loss in the 1855 gubernatorial race in Virginia. In the North, paradoxically, the movement began to lose followers who found it unwilling to take a strong stand against slavery.

Certainly other factors contributed to the decline of the Know-Nothings. Alarm about Catholics and other foreigners, however widespread, was an insubstantial foundation for a viable national political party. Not only did the party lack other ideas, but it could not make credible the danger it claimed was threatening the nation, nor could its limited program of restrictions on Catholics and other immigrants be presented convincingly as an adequate prescription for the problems of the times. The conduct of Know-Nothings in office in states in which they came to power, notably such actions as the junkets of Massachusetts lawmakers to investigate nunneries and religious schools, also helped to discredit the party.

Finally, the Know-Nothing Party dissolved because many of its leaders were not true believers but cynical politicians using it as a vehicle to win office and attain power. Horace Greeley recognized this aspect of the movement in a letter to Schuyler Colfax in June 1856. Writing on the eve of a convention held by dissident Party members known as North Americans, Greeley expressed the hope that Colfax and others whom he called "bogus Know Nothings" would coalesce with the Republican Convention scheduled to meet in Philadelphia shortly thereafter (Iseley 1947, 165). Many ambitious politicians were bogus Know-Nothings, including Henry Wilson and Nathaniel Banks, who, after using the party to advance their careers, shattered it and joined the Republicans (McKay 1964, 32).

The Know-Nothing movement began to crumble in June 1855 in an American Party convention which split over the issue of slavery. Led by Henry Wilson of Massachusetts, a substantial number of northern delegates, known thereafter as North Americans, defected after losing a vote on section 12 of the party's platform. The position adopted by the majority of the delegates in section 12, which provoked the rebellion of the North Americans, was an acceptance of the Kansas-Nebraska Act opening the newly created territory to slavery.

The year 1856 saw the emergence of a national Republican Party. Although nonexistent in the South and feeble in border states, a Republican National Committee representing eighteen states and the District of Columbia was appointed at an organizing meeting held at Pittsburgh on Washington's birthday. It issued a call for the convention which was to select the party's candidates for president and vice president in Philadelphia the following June.

Those who guided the developments that produced the Republican Party recognized the need for winning the votes of nativists if a new anti-Democratic party was to succeed on a national scale. Even William H. Seward and

Thurlow Weed, despite their distaste for Know-Nothingism, as political realists conceded this. Horace Greeley, also contemptuous of nativist principles, observed that circumstances had flung "many thousands of good and true anti-Nebraska men" into the American Party. "I want these to act with us in the great struggle for which we are now preparing," he wrote, "and I would be careful to do or say nothing which would render such action difficult or embarrassing" (Iseley 1947, 153). Therein may lie the explanation of a change in policy of editor Greeley's *Tribune*, which somewhat abruptly softened its editorial attacks on the American Party.

Political Events of 1856

The Conventions of 1856

The election of 1856 was preceded by a bewildering succession of political conventions. In February the American Party assembled in Philadelphia to nominate Millard Fillmore as its presidential candidate in a convention which the *New York Times* characterized with the headline "Pro-Slavery Men Have It All Their Own Way." The party's minority faction, the North Americans, now having received a second rebuff after losing its platform battle in 1855, disavowed the convention's actions and resolved to meet separately in New York City in June.

As the American Party was meeting in Philadelphia in February, another somewhat inchoate group assembled in Pittsburgh to issue a call for the nominating convention of what was to become the Republican Party. It was hardly a coincidence that the timing of the North Americans' gathering set for June coincided with the Republicans' plan to assemble during that month in Philadelphia.

In May the Democrats met in Cincinnati to select James Buchanan as their nominee after a struggle that went on for seventeen ballots. They left no doubt about their stand on the issues raised by the Know-Nothings. The Democratic platform condemned in general all "secret political societies" and specifically denounced Know-Nothingism for conducting "a political crusade . . . against Catholics and foreign born" inconsistent with the American spirit of toleration and freedom.

Finally, in September the shreds of the Whig Party, brought together in convention in Baltimore, chose Fillmore as their candidate, disavowing, however, the "peculiar principles of the party" which had already selected him as its nominee for president.

The two rival conventions held in June—the Republicans in Philadelphia and the North Americans in New York—had a common aim in seeking fusion. However, a mixture of personal ambition and attachment to different, if not inconsistent, causes made fusion difficult to achieve. Agreement on candidates was the major problem to be resolved, but there were difficulties, too, in reaching accord on such matters as platform and status of the leaders of both camps in campaign organization and, in the event of victory, in participation in the spoils.

The North American convention was scheduled to open five days before the Republican gathering, thus raising a potential obstacle to fusion. If the North Americans selected their nominees before the Republicans convened, the Republicans might face a choice of meekly seconding the judgment of the Know-Nothings or splitting further an already divided anti-Democratic vote by offering their own ticket. The best solution to the problem, and the one successfully engineered, was to secure from the North American convention a nominee who would later withdraw, leaving a clear field for the Republican candidate.

As the delegates to the North American convention assembled, it became clear that the probable nominee of the Republican gathering, John Charles Frémont, was not their favorite candidate. On the first ballot taken in the New York convention, Frémont ran behind the Speaker of the House of Representatives Nathaniel Banks. Stephen M. Allen, the manager of Banks's campaign for the nomination, reported as the convention opened, "Some of our friends called on Frémont yesterday for his positions and his answers were quite unsatisfactory to some of them. All he could say on Americanism was that 'he sympathized with them and should not appoint foreigners to office.'" (Allen to Banks, 12 June 1856, *Banks Papers*) When the first ballot was taken, only 34 of the 117 votes cast went to Frémont.

Nathaniel Banks, the front-runner for nomination by the North Americans, had resolved privately that, if selected, he would withdraw in favor of Frémont. He led the pack of candidates on the first ballot, receiving, however, an unimpressive total of 43 votes—an indication of the uneasiness of the delegates toward the man to whom they were to offer the nomination. That Banks planned to yield to the nominee of the Republican convention was strongly suspected. In fact, Murat Halstead reported in the Cincinnati *Gazette* that New England delegates were working for Banks on the assumption that he would withdraw in favor of Frémont. It appears, however, that Stephen M. Allen, managing Banks's campaign, was not privy to his principal's plan. Allen sought to quiet the talk that Halstead was reporting. "One of the scarecrows that have come out to the conservative American portion of the convention," he told Banks, "is that *you would not accept* but would decline in favor of another candidate, thereby sinking the American party or forcing them to go back to Fillmore. I have pledged them that you would accept and are as good an American as ever took the stand" (Allen to Banks, 13 June 1856, *Banks Papers*).

Within the ranks of the North Americans, considerable opposition to fusion with the Republicans was expressed unless nativists exercised control of the merged organization. Samuel Hammond, editor of the Albany *Argus*, stated this view bluntly in February to those who walked out of the convention that nominated Fillmore and planned the New York convention. If any one expected New Yorkers at the North American convention "to unite with the Republicans, they were mistaken," he declared in the *New York Times* of 26 February 1856, "New York had no objection to letting Republicans go up with their kite, but it must be in the tail."

At the opening of the North American convention, a carefully worded letter from Edward D. Morgan, chairman of the Republican National Executive Committee, was read to the delegates. Inviting their attention to the call for a people's nominating convention in Philadelphia, the letter cautiously expressed a hope that it would be attended by representatives of all parties believing the extension of slavery to be the dominant issue. It dismissed as of secondary importance the name to be given to "the great movement which we desire to see successfully inaugurated," but it noted diffidently that "one of the parties which will be represented at Philadelphia has taken the name Republican," the name Thomas Jefferson gave to his party, in order to "embrace all who love the Republic."

This guarded notification, which did not quite rise to the standard of a specific invitation, was greeted at the New York gathering, the *Times* reported, "with general applause and a few hisses." Lieutenant Governor Thomas Ford of Ohio, one of the staunchest of nativists, eagerly seized on Morgan's letter as "an olive branch of peace" and "the first step towards hitching" the two horses of Americanism and Republicanism "to the same load." A committee to meet with the Republicans was named, headed by George Law of New York, a dark horse candidate for the presidential nomination.

The North Americans responded favorably to the quasi invitation, but they met an initial rebuff from the Republican convention. A motion offered by Joshua Giddings that the Americans' acceptance be laid on the table carried by an overwhelming majority. This action was later reversed and negotiations undertaken with the North Americans. No agreement could be reached with the New York convention, however. Murat Halstead acclaimed this impasse, writing, "Then and there the Republican Party parted company with the KN's forever. . . . The spectre of Sam [the code name which Know Nothings gave their organization], which has hitherto frightened tens of thousands of honest foreigners from the Republican camp, is at last exorcised" (Hesseltine and Fisher 1961, 103).

On June 16, 1856 the North American convention nominated Nathaniel P. Banks for the presidency. On June 18 the Republican convention nominated John C. Frémont. On June 19, knowing that Banks would decline to be their candidate, the North American gathering reassembled to reverse its action.

At the end of the North American convention, as it accepted the presidential nominee of the Republican convention—John Charles Frémont—but chose its own vice presidential candidate, William F. Johnston of Pennsylvania, Thomas Ford and others no longer spoke in metaphors suggesting that they and the Republicans were equal partners. Smarting from the treatment received from the Philadelphia convention, Ford declared, "our advances have been spurned, and instead of being treated like gentlemen, we have been treated like dogs." Nevertheless, he argued for union with the Republicans to bring about "the overthrow of Popery and Slavery." Although the Republican convention had not suggested overthrowing popery, Ford thought this inseparable from opposition to slavery, for the "power of the Pope and Domestic Slavery are linked together and they have upon earth but one mission—the extinction of human liberty" (*New York Times*, 21 June 1856).

The final round in the contest for power or status in the major anti-Democratic movement of 1856 was precipitated by the disagreement between Republicans and North Americans about the vice presidential nominee. Although the North American convention had accepted Frémont as its candidate for president, it had done so, its leaders insisted, because of assurances from "numerous and prominent leaders of the Republican Party" that William Dayton, the Republican nominee for vice president, would be "induced to withdraw" in favor of a candidate preferred by the North Americans. For two months Chairman Morgan and others sought without success to persuade Dayton to withdraw. In late August the nominee of the North American convention, William F. Johnston, reluctantly yielded after a conference in which, according to Morgan, Frémont pledged to give "fair play" to all his friends in the event of victory (Nichols 1923, 495–96).

The split in the ranks of the American Party at the national level was replicated throughout the northern states with a majority adhering to the North Americans and endorsing Frémont in one state convention after another. The North Americans insisted that they were the one true orthodox party of Americanism. When they bolted from the convention of the American Party in February, going their separate way, they had denounced the stand of the dominant faction not only on slavery but also on what Thomas Ford called "the Catholic test." The declaration justifying their action proposed by Ford and adopted by the seceders read, "The admission into the National Council and nominating convention of the delegates from Louisiana, representing a Roman Catholic constituency, absolved every true American from all obligation to sustain the action" (*New York Times*, 26 February 1856).

At the end of August two rival American factions of New York state convened in Syracuse. The North American group proclaimed itself to be "the true American organization of the State of New York," endorsed Frémont, and repudiated its rival, which had just endorsed Fillmore. The true American Order, based on the principles of "Freedom, Protestantism, and Americanism," admitted all Protestant American citizens but excluded Roman Catholics. The *New York Times* of 28 August 1856 explained, "The North Americans are, then, the Anti-Roman Catholic party, as contradistinguished from the Fillmoreites and Democrats—the former fraternizing with the Roman Catholics by embracing them in their organization, and the latter relying upon them as a considerable portion of their political power."

An assessment of the fusion achieved between Republicans and North Americans for the 1856 campaign must conclude that the nativists were outmaneuvered, deceived, and defeated in their attempt to control the new political movement. Both the organizing meeting in Pittsburgh and the Philadelphia nominating convention were controlled by nonnativists. The call for the Pittsburgh meeting made clear the single issue on which a new political movement was to be based, and it contained no echo of the Americanist creed. As Foner observed (1970, 249), if nativists were present at Pittsburgh, they were silent.

It was at the nominating convention, however, that Republicanism clearly distinguished itself from nativism and established its independence. Neither the rhetoric which the convention heard nor the platform it adopted nor the candidates it nominated had any apparent association with Know-Nothingism. The platform endorsed equality of rights for all citizens in a plank that repudiated at least a part of nativist doctrine. From speakers like Giddings and George Julian and the German leader from Cincinnati, Charles Remelin, the delegates heard denunciations of Know-Nothingism "as a scheme of bigotry and intolerance and a mischievous side issue." Such utterances were "enthusiastically applauded." (Julian 1899, 318–19). The disdainful treatment of the North Americans' bid for partnership at the time of the convention and the later rejection of the attempt to secure second place on the ticket for a nativist added to the perception that the Republican Party was not a branch of the nativist movement, much less the tail on its kite.

For many practical politicians an important motive for avoiding identification with the Americanist cause was the hope of winning a substantial share of the German—or at least the German Protestant—vote. The Germans had become a crucial part of the electorate in several midwestern states, some of which permitted the newcomers to vote before admission to citizenship. Unlike Irish immigrants, the Germans were not judged to be indissolubly wedded to the Democratic Party. Many responded to an antislavery appeal. And dynamic figures like Carl Schurz and Charles Remelin emerged to bring many of their countrymen into the Republican fold. In order to avoid alienating this promising source of strength, Republican leaders in midwestern states particularly avoided nativist doctrine.

The character of the party that would become the dominant anti-Democratic force in the massive realignment of the electorate in the 1850s was set in 1856. The Republican Party was to be antislavery, not nativist. And yet within that party, as junior but essential partners, were many who, representing the most uncompromising brand of Know-Nothingism, were to give the party the mark of anti-Catholicism for many years to come.

The Presidential Campaign of 1856

The campaign of 1856 developed into two contests. In the slaveholding states the contestants were the Democrats and the Americans; the candidates, Buchanan and Fillmore. In ten southern states and Missouri, Frémont received not a single vote. In each of four other states—Delaware, Kentucky, Maryland, and Virginia—fewer than four hundred votes were cast for the Republican presidential candidate. In northern states the contest was mainly one between Buchanan and Frémont, although Fillmore ran a respectable race in some states in the region, even finishing second to Buchanan in California. Maryland, the cradle of American Catholicism, was the only state carried by Fillmore.

Buchanan was elected with 45 percent of the popular vote and 174 votes in the electoral college. Frémont won 33 percent of the popular vote and 114 electoral votes, carrying eleven northern states but losing California, Illinois, Indiana, New Jersey, and Pennsylvania to Buchanan.

The principal theme of the Republican campaign was opposition to the slave power. The major issue as framed by leading Republican spokesmen was preventing the expansion of slavery, which required that Kansas be admitted as a free state. Republicans indignantly denied Fillmore's charge that abolition was their aim and that the election of Frémont would shatter the Union. Rejecting interference with slavery in states in which it existed, they nevertheless held out to abolitionists the hope that confinement of slavery to the South would lead ultimately to its extinction.

Republican leaders knew the potency of anti-Catholicism. Despite the rebuffs directed toward nativist leaders during the nominating process, Republicans recognized that they needed votes from rank-and-file nativist voters, particularly in the Northeast. Greeley's advice to avoid doing or saying anything that might discourage nativists from joining Republican ranks guided party leaders in a decision they made as the North Americans convened to select a presidential candidate. Frémont was prepared at that time to send to the North American delegates a letter all but rejecting nomination at their hands. He was dissuaded from doing so by "advisers." The letter, composed but never sent, read:

> I am hostile to slavery upon principle and feeling. While I feel myself inflexible in the belief that it ought not to be interfered with where it exists under the shield of state sovereignty, I am inflexibly opposed to its extension . . . beyond its present limits. Animated with these views . . . and having but little active sympathy with secondary questions, which are not involved in the great issue, I am naturally identified with the cause represented by the great Republican Convention about to assemble in Philadelphia. I could not therefore accept unconditionally the candidateship of the American party, inasmuch as I would feel bound by the decisions of that party with which I am identified. (Smith 1933, 354–55)

Frémont did accept the "candidateship" of the North American Party when it was offered and received the endorsement of its state organizations throughout the North. In New York, as already noted, Frémont's nativist supporters claimed to be the "true Americans." As the campaign unfolded, the North Americans seemed to assume responsibility for the negative campaign against Fillmore, questioning his credentials as a member of the American Order and his party's consistency in opposition to Catholicism.

In an unexpected way a "Catholic issue" was introduced into the campaign, putting the Republicans on the defensive. The allegation was raised (probably by Fillmore supporters with the *New York Express* in the vanguard and with some help from Democrats) that Frémont was a Catholic. Although the allegation was false, his French name plus the fact that a Catholic priest had officiated at the wedding of Frémont and Jessie Benton gave it some tinge of credibility.

Widely circulated and apparently believed by many, the report of Frémont's Catholicism caused considerable concern in Republican ranks. William Gienapp (1987, 368–69) believes that the "issue" that hurt Frémont most in the 1856 campaign was "the misconception that he was a Catholic." In any event, the Republicans labored to rebut the misconception, producing testimony from a number of sources that Frémont was in fact an Episcopalian, that his children had been baptized and reared in that faith, and that a Catholic clergyman officiated at his wedding only because it was impossible at the time to find any other cleric in Washington willing to brave the wrath of Senator Benton, the unhappy father of the bride.

Religious leaders of several churches, journalists, politicians, friends, and acquaintances filled the Republican press with statements declaring the Pathfinder innocent of the charge of Catholicism, but, strangely, Frémont himself uttered no word on the subject. A letter was prepared for his signature affirming his Protestantism, but, once again, advisers dissuaded him from transmitting it.

Horace Greeley, spreading the Republican message through a semi-weekly campaign edition of the *Tribune* widely circulated in the North, undertook to set the record straight. After believing initially that the charge about Frémont's religion should go unanswered to avoid the appearance of sanctioning a religious test for office, Greeley became convinced by mid-October that the falsehood was damaging the Republican cause. He ended up compounding confusion and aiding the attack on his candidate.

In response to letters "by the thousands" asking for proof of Frémont's Protestantism, Greeley published a pamphlet to dispose "completely" of the charge that Frémont was a Catholic. Greeley wrote, "there are two Frémonts, both of whom have belonged to the army; both resided in Washington; . . . they resemble each other . . . the Frémont who is the candidate for President is not the Frémont who was in the habit of attending the Catholic Church." When the second Frémont subsequently denied that he had ever entered any Catholic church, the props were effectively knocked out from under this imaginative explanation (*New York Tribune*, 16 October 1856; Iseley 1947, 192).

The decentralized character of the American political system and the usual chaos of American campaigns make it difficult to generalize on the subject of the place of nativists and nativism in the 1856 Republican campaign. Marked differences are discernible from state to state. In New York, but only in New York, did a state Republican platform condemn the Know-Nothing movement. The fledgling Republican Party in Connecticut under the leadership of Gideon Welles rejected fusion with the Know-Nothings. At the other extreme, in Pennsylvania Know-Nothings dominated the Republican Party apparatus. One of the state's leaders confessed that "the American party . . . constituted the great bulk of the Republican party" (Republican National Convention 1893, 57). Fusion was achieved for the election by an agreement between Republicans and Americans of the Keystone State on a joint slate of electors ready to vote for either Frémont or Fillmore in order to defeat Buchanan. And Thomas Ford was sent from Ohio to carry on his campaign against slavery and popery, his pockets bulging with $10,000 to secure the support of the press in Pennsylvania for Frémont. Know-Nothing influence was also strong in the Republican Parties of Massachusetts, Maine, Ohio, and Indiana (Nichols 1923, 494–96; Anbinder 1992, 52–74).

The press associated with the American Party, whether supporting Frémont or Fillmore, sounded themes of anti-Catholicism, and, particularly where Know-Nothingism had been strong since 1854, Republican orators and newspapers joined the chorus. On the other hand, Republican spokesmen of national stature seem to have avoided exploitation of anti-Catholic feeling, although the press and many politicians of local and statewide significance did not observe the same restraint. The preparation of official campaign publications was in the antinativist hands of the Republican Association of Washington, and the campaign textbook, featuring past speeches of Senator Seward, was completely devoid of any appeal to animosity toward foreigners or Catholics. One campaign publication, *The Pope's Bull and the Words of Daniel O'Connell*, was clearly a bid for Catholic support, citing papal condemnation of the slave trade and O'Connell's appeal to Irish Americans to support the abolition of slavery. And some Republican spokesmen, especially in midwestern states, lauded the immigrant and pointed to their platform's ringing endorsement of "equality of rights among citizens" as evidence that their party did not subscribe to nativist principles.

The Catholic Press and the 1856 Election

At several intervals from June until the election the *Pilot* warned its readers that the Republicans were conducting a campaign of "treachery" and "deception, "presenting "two faces" on Catholicity and naturalized citizens. Some Republican papers were "attempting to make it appear that the party has cut adrift from Know Nothingism," it declared, noting that in the West Republicans "boldly appealed to immigrants and Catholics." That such appeals were hypocritical was clear to the editor of the *Pilot*, published in Massachusetts, where nativism had scored its greatest triumphs and the Frémont campaign was run by people like Speaker Banks, Senator Wilson, and Governor Goodrich, all leaders of the Know-Nothing movement a few years earlier. In July, when the Massachusetts Know-Nothing convention endorsed Frémont in preference to Fillmore, the *Pilot* needed no further evidence of the hostility of the Republican candidate toward Catholics.

Further evidence was not lacking, however. Following the action of the state convention of the American Party, the *Boston Bee*, the party's organ in Massachusetts, endorsed Frémont. The *Bee* minced no words in expressing its opinion of the Catholic Irish and their political activity: "Guided by these bonded murderers, the priests of Rome, who would butcher every Protestant in the United States if they had the power . . ., [Irish Catholics] are forced . . . to vote with the Democracy" (*Pilot* 1 November 1856).

The strong involvement of the Know-Nothing movement in the 1856 campaign through both the American and the Republican Parties led some Catholic papers to jettison their customary policy of neutrality in presidential contests. Notable among the papers hitherto neutral that became active partisans in 1856 was New York's *Freeman's Journal*. Like the *Pilot*, it gave strong support to Buchanan.

Other papers, like the *Pittsburgh Catholic*, maintained the customary position of the Catholic press, limiting coverage to a few bare factual accounts of the results of nominating conventions and other major events without expressing a preference among the presidential candidates. Only after the election did the *Catholic*, on 29 November 1856, reveal an opinion on the Republican Party and then through publication of a letter signed "A Democratic Voter." The Republican Party, the writer asserted, is "hostile to Catholics as a class." This hostility, although "not always in their platforms," has been manifested "in those papers claiming to be its organs . . . in those men claiming to be its leaders" and in the alliance it sought with a secret oath-bound organization sworn to deprive Catholics of their constitutional rights and to "make them a proscribed, persecuted, and enslaved class."

Unlike the Pittsburgh paper, the *Pilot* contained frequent political commentary from June through November, attacking the Republican more frequently than the American Party and leaving no doubt of its support of Buchanan. As noted, the paper was concerned lest its readers be deceived into thinking the Republican Party was not hostile to Catholics and repeatedly called attention to the well-known ex-Know-Nothings now working to elect Frémont. The difference between the two parties opposing the Democrats, according to the *Pilot* on 5 July and 1 November 1856, was that whereas "Fillmoreites are frank and flat-footed" in their anti-Catholicism, "Frémonters" holding the same sentiments conceal them in some parts of the nation.

The charge that Frémont was a Catholic, greeted at first with some uncertainty by the *Pilot*, was later used by that paper as an additional argument for rejecting the Republican nominee. By October 1856 the *Pilot* was accusing the Republican nominee of abandoning "the faith of his father and of his youth and early manhood" because of political ambition. Similarly, the editor of the organ of the Archdiocese of New York, James McMaster, alleged that at one time Frémont had professed to be a Catholic. This charge drew Archbishop Hughes into the controversy. Dissociating himself from his editor, Hughes said in the *Pilot*'s 18 October 1856 issue that he knew "nothing reflecting on the private and personal character" of Frémont.

The campaign commentary in the Catholic press emphasized the contrast between Republican connections with the Know-Nothing movement and the Democratic repudiation of nativism. Beyond this, other considerations were cited to justify support of the Democrats. Both the *Freeman's Journal* and the *Pilot* argued that Buchanan was less threatening to the South and to national unity than Frémont. Republicans with abolitionists in their ranks could be expected to interfere with slavery, precipitate sectional conflict, and disrupt the Union. Whatever the evils of slavery, the papers agreed, forcing its termination on the South would produce a greater evil and would violate the Constitution as well.

Another argument for preferring Buchanan was based on the background of the two candidates. According to the *Pilot*, 18 October 1856, Frémont's limited résumé of military and political service was tarnished by a court-martial and questionable financial transactions, whereas Buchanan boasted an unblemished record of experience in high government posts as congressman, cabinet member, and ambassador.

Election Postmortems

Few, if any, of those who organized the Republican campaign of 1856 held hopes of victory. This pessimism led Thurlow Weed to persuade a restless Seward, certainly the party's best known aspirant for the presidency, to stay out of the race and wait for 1860. After Democratic victories in state elections in Indiana and Pennsylvania in October, realists conceded the likelihood that Buchanan would be the next occupant of the White House and began planning for the next election.

When the returns were in, Republicans could find reason for encouragement in the remarkable vote received by their ticket. Nowhere had the party existed for more than two years. With little time to organize and communicate a message to the electorate, it had in its first national campaign emerged as the dominant party in the North, winning eleven of sixteen free states. It was clearly a sectional party, but its strength lay in the growing section of the nation from which most future states would be carved.

Despite the impressive showing, Republicans were conscious that the American political system awards no prize for running second, and postelection analysis centered on the "mistakes" that had probably cost Frémont votes that could have been won. The fact that the combined Frémont-Fillmore vote in California, Illinois, and New Jersey exceeded the vote for Buchanan and almost equaled the Democratic vote in Pennsylvania and Indiana led some to conclude that Republicans had not done enough to conciliate North Americans. Even as staunch an opponent of the Know-Nothings as Thurlow Weed expressed this view, writing to Simon Cameron after the election, "The first, and I still think, fatal error was in not taking a Vice President in whose nomination the North Americans would have concurred cordially" (Crippen 1942, 152).

In flat disagreement with this conclusion, the strongly antislavery Republican Association of Washington argued that Republicans had in too many places allied themselves too closely to the Know-Nothing cause. In a declaration addressed to "the Republicans of the United States" on 29

November 1856, they denounced "the timid policies of the Republicans in New Jersey, Pennsylvania, and Indiana, in postponing their independent action, and temporizing with a Party got up for purposes not in harmony with their own." For the future, they declared, "The true course of the Republicans is to organize promptly, boldly, and honestly upon their own principles, so clearly set forth in the Philadelphia platform, and, avoiding coalitions with other parties, appeal directly to the masses of all parties that would divert the public mind from the one danger . . . Slavery Propagandism allied with Disunionism" (Cooper and Fenton 1888, 70–71).

Yet others believed that slavery had been overemphasized by party spokesmen and that the Republican program should be broadened to attract voters who did not regard this issue as "the one danger" threatening the nation. Greeley, never one for consistency, stated this point of view in a letter written in 1860 at a time when he considered ex-Democrat, ex-Know-Nothing Edward Bates to be the most desirable of the potential candidates seeking the Republican presidential nomination. "I know," he wrote, "the country is not Anti-Slavery. It will only swallow a little Anti-Slavery in a great deal of sweetening. An Anti-Slavery man *per se* cannot be elected; but a Tariff, River-and-Harbor, Pacific Railroad, Free-Homestead man, *may* succeed *although* he is Anti-Slavery" (Iseley 1947, 215).

Leading Republicans of the time seem to have had little interest in the vote of the burgeoning ranks of immigrant Catholics. Although "the German vote," thanks to Schurz and others, was looked on as worth cultivating as part of a Republican coalition, it was non-Catholic Germans—Protestants and the less extreme representatives of the Forty-Eighters—whose support was sought.

Cassius Clay, who had been educated in Catholic schools, was one, however, who sought to pry Catholics away from attachment to the Democrats. In 1857–58 he corresponded with Archbishop Hughes, offering somewhat novel arguments to convince the prelate that Catholics should be Republicans. Clay mentioned none of the causes that Greeley was urging the party to espouse. Rather, he based his argument to Hughes on the promotion of the interests of the Church.

Opening the correspondence on 28 December 1857, Clay noted that "almost all the Catholic vote went against us in the last election." "This," he wrote, "is not to the interest of the Republican party . . . not to the interest of Catholics." The free states, growing mightily in population, he declared, "cannot much longer be kept down by the sparse and feeble slave power" of a South that was clearly in decline. He concluded that Catholics for their "future security" should move to the winning side in the contest then gripping the nation.

The doctrine of Manifest Destiny, Clay charged, was a serious threat to the interests of the Church. This doctrine should alert Catholics to the intention of the Democrats to acquire "Catholic Mexico, Catholic Central America, Catholic South America, Catholic Cuba . . . to be plundered, revolutionized and religionized anew." In another flight of hyperbole Clay linked the Democratic Party in the United States with "that Democracy which carried on a bloody war in Europe against Catholicism" and denounced it as "the enemy of Catholicism—of Religion—of Justice—of Humanity." The Republicans, he wrote, "are the fast friends of Religion and Freedom. We offer you safety and peace . . . tolerance . . . equality. I pray you to change your alliances."

Archbishop Hughes answered with an unresponsive letter assuring Clay that Catholics vote "without any direction from their clergy" and that he himself had voted only once nearly thirty years earlier and then for Henry Clay, to the discomfiture of the majority of his congregation. Clay professed to be pleased with the reply of the archbishop, which he construed to say that Catholics "are not firmly wedded to any one party" and declared himself now "all the more emboldened to ask their favourable consideration of the principles" of the Republican Party (correspondence between Clay and Hughes, 28 December 1857; 6 February and 11 February 1858, Archives, Archdiocese of New York).

Agreement that immigrant Catholics voted solidly for Buchanan in the first national election contested by the Republican Party appears to have been universal. The pattern of the vote in 1856 made it difficult to construct a plausible argument that Catholics had a decisive influence on the outcome, for Frémont carried almost all the states with a large Catholic population.

Nevertheless, disgruntled Know-Nothings like Henry Winter Davis of Maryland judged that foreigners "have decided the government of this country." Davis pointed an accusing finger at "the Irish Brigade" which "saved the Democrats from annihilation. . . . They have elected, by these foreigners, by a minority of the American people, a President to represent their divisions."

The election of 1856, Davis asserted, manifested

> Every evil against which the American Party protested . . . men have forgotten the ban which the Republic puts on the intrusion of religious influence on the political scene. These influences have brought vast multitudes of foreign-born citizens to the polls, ignorant of American interests, without American feelings, influenced by foreign sympathies, to vote on American affairs. (McLaughlin 1885, 72–73).

The *New York Times* in its postelection interpretation of the presidential race, although not contending that the vote of those it classified as foreigners was decisive, began its editorial by remarking that, "the whole foreign vote—Irish and German—has been cast for Buchanan." The *Times* castigated the Germans for the error of their ways (not 10 percent of the Germans nationally voted Republican, the article complained) but reserved its choicest prose for the Irish, who had "gone in a drove—as they always do—for the regular Democratic ticket." In the most Irish precinct in the city in the area known as Five Points, the presidential vote, the paper reported, was Buchanan, 576; Frémont, 17; Fillmore, 13.

The Irish, the *Times* explained to its readers in its issue of 6 November 1856, will vote Democratic "as long as they remain Irish, and it takes at least two generations to convert them into Americans." Lacking the "faculty of independent action" they are

> Managed like herds by . . . skillful and experienced drivers. . . . Their ignorance and credulity make them ready dupes. . . . They care no more for the principles of Freedom . . . than they do for anything else of which they have no conception. . . . They never look ahead. . . . They look out only for themselves . . . there is nothing an Irishman loves like the opportunity to tyrannize over somebody.

Unnoticed in the massive realignment of the electorate that took place in 1856 was the shift in the voting behavior of the relatively small islands of Catholics of English extraction, descendants of the original Catholic colonists. Located in such rural counties as St. Mary's and Charles in Maryland and Marion and Nelson in Kentucky, they had steadfastly supported the Whig Party down through the years. But in 1856 they joined their coreligionists of recent immigrant stock by voting the Democratic ticket. Presumably they found the Republican Party both too anti-Catholic and too antislavery.

Republican Victory in 1860

The election of 1856 established the Republican Party as the major challenger to the Democrats and clearly pointed out one path by which it could achieve dominance in future national elections. The combined vote for Frémont and Fillmore amounted to 55 percent of the vote cast nationwide, and, by putting the two groups together, Republicans saw the promise of victory even without carrying a single southern or border state.

There were many auspicious signs that such a coalition could evolve. A substantial segment of the American movement had joined the Republicans in supporting Frémont. And after the 1856 contest the party that had offered Fillmore to the nation rapidly disintegrated. The last gathering of the American party as a national entity held in 1857 resulted in its dissolution. The Thirty-fifth Congress elected in 1856 included many members who had been listed as Americans in the previous Congress, but most of them were now Republicans. In the Thirty-fourth Congress fifty-one members openly bore the American designation; two years later, fourteen; after the election of 1858, only five.

In states in which Americanism had displayed great electoral strength in 1854–55, it was reduced to insignificance. In New York, for example, a leading Republican could say in 1859, "Nothing remains of the Know-Nothings except the smell and the *Express*" [the party newspaper] (Rawley 1955, 95). In state after state the party lost its most effective leaders. Only in a few border states did the nativist party maintain an independent existence, holding control of the government of Maryland until 1860.

David M. Potter offers this appraisal of the results of the absorption of northern Know-Nothings by the Republicans:

> No event in the history of the Republican party was more crucial or more fortunate. . . . By it the Republican party received a permanent endowment of nativist support which probably elected Lincoln in 1860 and which strengthened the party in every election for more than a century to come. But this support was gained without any formal concessions that would have forfeited the immigrant support also vital to political success. The Republicans were able to eat the cake of nativist support and to have too the cake of religious and ethnic tolerance. (Potter 1976, 259)

This analysis somewhat overstates the result. The disappearance of the American Party did not eliminate the voters it had attracted or change the opinions that had led these voters to rally to its cause. It is true that the Republican Party to which they flocked had to concede little to win their support and could safely repudiate some of their doctrines and virtually all of their legislative proposals (Silbey 1977, 155–65). Potter fails, however, to distinguish nativism from anti-Catholicism and to recognize that Republican religious tolerance did not exclude exploitation of anti-Catholic sentiment in the conduct of campaigns to elect Republican candidates to office.

Death came suddenly to the American Party because its cause was eclipsed in the late 1850s by other, graver issues involving life or death for the nation. Slavery and the preservation of the Union became overriding concerns. Beside these, other political causes receded in importance.

When the Republicans met in convention in the newly built Wigwam in Chicago on 16 May 1860, the leading candidate for nomination for the presidency appeared to be William H. Seward. He led the field on the first ballot, but his strength subsequently eroded, and a switch on the part of delegates from Ohio and Pennsylvania started the groundswell that won the nomination for Lincoln.

The convention rejected Seward because of doubts about his electability, doubts sedulously spread by an embittered Horace Greeley, who thought he had been spurned by his former friend. Several New Englanders, including Connecticut's Gideon Welles, joined Greeley in the campaign to undermine the Seward candidacy, as did the Republican candidates for governor in Pennsylvania and Indiana, who sowed fears that their states would be lost if Seward headed the ticket.

Seward's rhetoric in the past about an "irrepressible conflict" and "a higher law than the Constitution" tended, in the minds of more cautious delegates, to place him with extremists and hotheads on the issue of slavery. Lincoln, although holding a position indistinguishable from Seward's, benefited from a perception that he was more moderate and less likely, if elected, to precipitate conflict with the South.

But, certainly, Seward's record of sympathetic attention to the concerns of Catholic immigrants, particularly in the field of education, as well as his close friendship with Archbishop Hughes, also turned delegates against him. According to Alexander McClure, writing from the perspective of an insider in Republican politics in Pennsylvania, this was the decisive consideration for two leaders of the anti-Seward campaign at the convention, Republican gubernatorial candidates William Curtin of Pennsylvania and Henry K. Lane of Indiana. McClure wrote,

> The single reason that compelled Curtin and Lane to make aggressive resistance to the nomination of Seward was his attitude on the school question that was very offensive to many thousands of voters . . . who either adhered to the American organization or cherished its strong prejudices. . . . It was Seward's record on that single question that made him an impossible candidate for President in 1860. (Curry 1973, 185)

Twenty years earlier, as governor of New York, Seward had proposed state funding of schools in which the children of immigrant families would be instructed in their own language by teachers of their own choosing. The proposal, which would have included aid to church-related schools, was eagerly supported by John Hughes. It precipitated a long, bitter struggle and probably almost cost Seward reelection as governor. Out of the struggle came the Maclay Act, substantially altering the public educational system by ending its Protestant orientation but also barring any type of support for church-related schools (McCadden 1964, 205–7). The unsuccessful fight which Seward waged on the subject of education dogged his later political career.

Repeatedly throughout his years in Albany and Washington, Seward publicly denounced religious and ethnic prejudice. "This right hand," he once declared, "drops off before I do one act with the Whig or any other party in opposition to any portion of my fellow citizens on the ground of difference of their nativity or their religion" (Van Dusen 1967, 76). So strong was his distaste for the American Party that, when invited to meet at the Blair estate in late 1855 to lay plans which were to lead to the establishment of the Republican Party, he declined to attend because he wished to avoid any entanglement with Know-Nothings.

Lincoln likewise was contemptuous of movements that exploited hostility based on religion or birthplace. As early as 1844, when an outburst of anti-Catholicism erupted in arson, mayhem, and other violent forms in several places, Lincoln offered a resolution at a Whig meeting in Springfield, Illinois, affirming that the "sacred and inviolable" rights of conscience belong to Catholics and Protestants alike and denouncing "all attempts to abridge or interfere with these rights, either of Catholic or Protestant, directly or indirectly" (Ellis 1956, 63–64).

When the American Party was attracting widespread support in the 1850s, Lincoln wrote to Joshua Speed,

> Our progress in degeneracy appears to me to be pretty rapid. As a nation, we began by declaring that "all men are created equal." We now practically read it "all men are created equal, *except negroes*." When the Know-Nothings get control, it will read "all men are created equal, except negroes, *and foreigners and Catholics*." When it comes to this, I should prefer emigrating to some country where they make no pretense of loving liberty—to Russia, for instance, where despotism can be taken pure, and without the base alloy of hypocracy [sic!]. (Basler 1953, 2: 323)

Lincoln does not appear to have uttered these sentiments publicly, however, as he sought the presidential nomination. The *Chicago Tribune*, enumerating eight reasons why the party should choose Lincoln as its nominee, differentiated its candidate from Seward. Illinois's favorite son, the paper affirmed in May 1860, "is without a strain of Know Nothingism" but nevertheless "is acceptable to the great mass of American voters who will be compelled to choose between the candidate of Chicago and the Democratic nominee." Thus editor Joseph Medill sought to point out that Lincoln, unlike Seward, would be an attractive candidate to the voters whom Fillmore had captured in 1856. At the same time he wished to give reassurance to Carl Schurz and other German leaders that a man not yet well known to them held no prejudice against immigrants.

The Republican platform of 1860, in conformity with Greeley's prescription, offered a broader program than had the 1856 platform. Among its promises were tariff protection (with an eye on Pennsylvania), a Homestead Act, and a transcontinental railroad. The platform rejected nativism with a denunciation of legislation, state or federal, impairing the "rights of citizenship hitherto accorded to immigrants from foreign lands." And, in connection with its proposed Homestead Act, the platform made it clear that noncitizen immigrants would share in eligibility for its benefits.

To some, like Giddings, the more expansive platform seemed to mute the party's opposition to slavery. To satisfy him and other like-minded delegates, the convention added to the draft presented to it the words of the Declaration of Independence affirming the equality and divinely endowed inalienable rights of all men.

The Catholic Issue in the Campaign

Throughout his career Stephen A. Douglas had defended Catholics against the parties from nativist American to Know-Nothing that exploited the successive waves of prejudice sweeping the nation. Among the immigrant peoples, particularly the Irish, he enjoyed an extraordinary level of support.

Yet in the confused four-party contest of 1860, politics made the strangest of bedfellows. In New York the major anti-Lincoln coalition offered a slate of electors made up of Democrats and, in addition, some former Americans led by Erastus Brooks who were now adrift and ready to bargain with all comers (Editorial *New York Times*, 17 August 1860). This unexpected source of support appears to have done little to add to the vote for Douglas (Editorial *New York Times*, 12 November 1860).

In New York, as in other northern states Lincoln was the beneficiary of the bulk of the vote that had gone to Fillmore in 1856, and without it he might well have been defeated. In southern and border states many of the former Americans supported the newly formed Constitutional Union party whose candidate, John Bell of Tennessee, formerly a Whig, had also been at one time a member of the Know-Nothing Order.

The *Chicago Tribune* assumed a leading role in exploiting anti-Catholic feeling to turn voters away from Douglas. Resorting to the familiar tactic used against Birney in 1844 and Frémont in 1856, the paper orchestrated a series of articles which concluded that Douglas was secretly a Catholic. The discrediting information was introduced gradually in the *Tribune*'s columns, initially in July as a question: Is Douglas a Catholic? After printing rumor, gossip, speculation and facts of doubtful relevance repeatedly throughout the summer, the paper on 4 September asserted that the pieces of circumstantial evidence it had accumulated "seem to establish Judge Douglas' Catholicism beyond successful contradiction" (Keefe 1957, 244). The incriminating evidence—none of it secret—was that Mrs. Douglas was a Catholic, that she had enrolled the two Douglas sons in a school maintained by her church, and that Douglas had made financial contributions to various Catholic organizations. Having established to its satisfaction that Douglas was a Catholic and that he had concealed his religious affiliation, the *Tribune* warned its readers against voting for a vassal of the pope. Although Douglas had every right to choose whatever church he wished, the paper editorialized in its 17 July issue "as Catholicism and Republicanism are as plainly incompatible as oil and water, it is the right of the American people to refuse to entrust him with power whereby Protestantism and Freedom may be beaten down, and Popery and slavery built up."

Identification of Douglas with Catholicism became an important, if secondary, theme in the campaign waged in the Republican press. The *Tribune*'s allegation that Douglas had surreptitiously converted to the Catholic faith was echoed in party publications elsewhere, such as the *Cleveland Leader* and the *Pittsburgh Gazette*. Some publications warned that Democratic victory would give excessive power to a dangerous Catholic triumvirate to be formed by Chief Justice Taney, Archbishop Hughes, and President Douglas.

Catholic Voters in the 1860 Election

Studies of the 1860 presidential race point to the salience of religious affiliation and of Protestant-Catholic antagonism to voting decisions. A scholarly study of the election in Cleveland, for example, concludes that "the virulent animosity between Catholics and non-Catholics was the driving force behind the Republican victory in November 1860" (Kremm 1977, 69). A similar conclusion was drawn in another study dealing with voting behavior in Pittsburgh in 1860 (Kleppner 1966, 176–95).

When the election returns were in, the *Catholic Telegraph and Advocate* of Cincinnati fumed, "No Catholic hands have done this deed of treason. . . . No Catholic votes pursued the Southern citizen to injury and oppression" (Foik 1969, 167). That Catholics supported Douglas overwhelmingly is clear. They stuck with the party to which they had become closely attached and to a man who had been their outspoken champion against their attackers. The virulent anti-Catholic campaign conducted by many Republican organs reinforced the appeal of Douglas and his party to Catholic voters.

The question of slavery also turned Catholic voters away from the Republican Party. The Catholic press, unanimous in its support of Douglas, argued that the preservation of the Union and the maintenance of the constitutional right of the states to order their domestic institutions were at stake. These publications emphasized the danger of secession if the Republican Party were to control the national government. Admitting slavery to be an evil, they still tended to argue that the status quo was preferable to the evils that would attend its precipitous abolition (Rice 1944, 131–47). But foremost in their argument was concern about the danger of conferring power on a party so anti-Catholic in its orientation and so heavily populated by leaders of the movement that had harassed their Church in several states which it had recently controlled. To them this was the great issue of the campaign and the rationale for opposing the party of Lincoln.

The Civil War: A Changing Catholic Role in Society

During wartime, especially a war for national survival, divisions on issues irrelevant to the outcome of the conflict become submerged. So it was with Catholic-Protestant divisions during the Civil War. In fact, the war appears in some ways to have softened antagonism, dispelled some prejudice, and removed some barriers which confronted Catholics in the prewar era.

Northern Catholics outside the border states rallied to the cause of maintaining the Union. They were well represented in the ranks of the Union forces, including generals like Sheridan and Rosecrans. Massachusetts and Connecticut hastened to repeal laws prohibiting Irish and other ethnic military units, which they had forced to disband in the 1850s. Catholics in the armed forces gave the lie to charges that they were less than loyal to their country. Priests were enrolled as chaplains, and heroic nuns nursed the wounded. Military service forced hundreds of thousands of Catholics and Protestants into intimate association facing hardship and danger together, dependent upon each other, in a common cause.

In the slave states which stayed within the Union, some Church leaders were lukewarm toward the Union cause. Archbishop Peter Kenrick of St. Louis, who refused to join his fellow bishops in the practice of flying the Union flag from the cathedral, so alienated Seward that the secretary of state sought the removal of the archbishop. Southern bishops, with the exception of James Whelan of Nashville, who was forced into monastic retirement because of his sympathy for the North (Rice 1944, 148), loyally supported the Confederacy.

Two Catholic prelates undertook diplomatic missions. Archbishop Hughes, at the behest of Secretary of State Seward, visited the Papal States and France to persuade Catholic rulers to withhold recognition of the Confederacy. With the opposite objective Jefferson Davis commissioned Bishop Patrick N. Lynch of Charleston to undertake a futile journey to seek support from the South from Pope Pius IX.

One symbol of a changing climate appeared in Massachusetts. There, where a few years earlier the Know-Nothing party had all but monopolized public life, the legislature offered Bishop John Bernard Fitzpatrick of Boston a place on the board of overseers of Harvard University. The bishop declined this honor, but he accepted from Harvard the honorary degree of doctor of divinity granted in recognition of his credentials as "a scholar, gentleman, and divine." An additional credential, noted privately by a member of the Harvard Corporation, was "the loyalty shown by him and by the Irish who have offered themselves freely for the army" (O'Connor 1984, 197–99).

3

Republicans and the Catholic Electorate 1880–1908: From Hostility to Cautious Rapprochement

For two decades after the Civil War the Republican Party maintained control over the national government. Once Reconstruction ended and the restraints imposed on the South were loosened, its control became shaky, surviving close election contests until Grover Cleveland won the White House in 1884. Neither party could muster so strong a vote in the eighties as to justify a claim of dominance in the nation.

The balance between the parties changed in 1894. The election of that year, held at a time of severe depression, ushered in an era of Republican dominance in national politics which ran until terminated in another depression in the 1930s. Although Republican occupancy of the White House was interrupted in 1912, this hiatus occurred because of the factional strife that split the party. Woodrow Wilson, the beneficiary of the split, failed to secure a majority of the popular vote in either of his electoral triumphs.

The presidential election of 1896 signalled a major realignment of the electorate. American Catholics participated in this movement in the direction of the Republican Party as the nineteenth century came to its close, although a large majority remained loyal to the Democratic Party. Nevertheless, the defection of Catholics from the Democratic Party in presidential elections from 1896 on was substantial enough to end the appearance of monolithic adherence to that party. In the movement toward party realignment that took place around the turn of the century, Catholics were laggards, however, joining the drift toward the Republicans in force in the elections of 1904 and 1908.

Social and Political Change

The years around the turn of the century brought another spurt in population. There were 30 million more Americans in 1910 than in 1890—a 50 percent increase. Contributing greatly to this growth was a new massive wave of immigrants—new in more than one sense, for they came in great force from the countries of eastern and southern Europe. These new immigrants were Italians, Poles, Russians, Scandinavians, Bohemians, Slovaks, Serbs, Croats, Ukranians, and Greeks (along with Canadians, both English and French).

Three consequences of the new immigration are especially noteworthy. First, as the nation's economy was in the process of transformation, these immigrants provided the bulk of the labor force for factories and mines, succeeding older immigrant stock in the least desirable jobs. Second, from the ranks of the immigrants came recruits for political movements proposing radical, sometimes violent, change in the economic system. As the 1900s began, the Socialist and Socialist-Labor Parties succeeded the Populists as the principal third party. Third, fear that the new immigrants were a threat to the country's civilization and its economy brought a backlash. Exclusion of Asian immigrants for cultural and economic reasons became national policy in the late nineteenth century. On essentially similar grounds a movement to restrict the influx of immigrants from southern and eastern Europe was launched, fed in part by pseudoscientific publications asserting the superiority of Anglo-Saxon stock and predicting that immigration would lead to the suicide of the superior race.

The urban metropolis came into being. In 1900 New York, Chicago, and Philadelphia each had more than 1 million people, and thirty-two other cities had grown to more than 100,000. Into them poured the new immigrants. The census of that year revealed that 77 percent of Chicago's inhabitants were immigrants or children of immigrants. With the influx of newcomers to the cities came new slums, more poverty, more crime, and strengthened political machines. Lincoln Steffens wrote of pervasive corruption in municipal government in *The Shame of the Cities*, and countervailing reform movements came to life in many communities.

A restless people had spread throughout the vast empty spaces that made up the United States. In 1890 the superintendent of the census announced that the nation had been "so broken by isolated bodies of settlement that there can hardly be said to be a frontier line." This finding inspired historian Frederick Jackson Turner to undertake a landmark study of the significance of the frontier in the nation's history and conclude that, with its passing, a cause of American egalitarianism, individualism, confidence, and social harmony was slipping away.

Whether for this or other reasons more closely related to the major changes in the form of the economy, strife among economic groups in conflict boiled over into strikes and violent confrontations. Although the economy expanded manyfold, the expansion was not without painful periodic panics (as they were then called), impoverishing the most vulnerable and driving desperate men to violence in the railroad yards of Illinois and the coal mines and steel mills of Pennsylvania.

Factories replaced the small shop. Giant corporations, the "trusts," came to possess economic and political power so great that to many they appeared capable of crushing worker, farmer, and consumer. Devising methods of restraining this power became an important part of the nation's political agenda as, by fits and starts, the Progressive movement, the Square Deal, and the New Freedom strengthened the economic role of government.

The Populist Party, born of agrarian protest, received more than 1 million votes for the presidency in 1892 and, for a time, threatened to replace one of the major parties as the Republicans had once replaced the Whigs. Populism vanished, however, largely absorbed by the Democratic Party in 1896, but it left so strong a mark on the Democrats that a hostile press labeled the followers of William Jennings Bryan "Popocrats."

At the very end of the nineteenth century the United States acquired an empire through a brief and one-sided war with Spain. It became a world power, strengthening its claim to hegemony in the Western Hemisphere. A new century began with the Stars and Stripes flying all across the Pacific, even to the shores of the Asiatic mainland, and the parties debating the issue of imperialism.

Catholicism at the Turn of the Century

As the population of the United States grew by 50 percent between 1890 and 1910, the Catholic population increased by almost 85 percent—from 9 to more than 16 million. At some point in the 1890s the Catholic Church became the nation's largest religious denomination. In every major city outside the South, Catholics constituted at least a sizable minority of the population, and, in a few urban centers like Boston, a majority.

The flood of new immigrants, of course, accounted in part for this phenomenal growth, but, unlike the situation in the 1850s, most Catholics now were natives, not immigrants, the children and grandchildren of the Irish and Germans who had arrived here in the earlier period. At the turn of the century the children of the immigrants of the 1840s and 1850s were in middle age, and their children were marrying and forming families. Many of both generations—although far from a majority—had been educated in the parochial school system of the Church, which spread rapidly, particularly after the Third Plenary Council decreed in 1884 that each parish must establish a school.

Americanization of the Catholic population proceeded apace. The Catholic school system taught patriotism along with the four R's (Reading, 'Riting 'Rithmetic, and Religion), and the hierarchy constantly emphasized the Catholic's duty to be loyal to America. Ties to the old country weakened.

Symbolic of the change was the announcement in the Catholic *Telegraph* of Cincinnati upon the appointment of a new editor in 1890 that henceforth its columns would be devoted principally to "the New World, not the Old"—to the United States rather than Ireland and Germany, which had until then been the focus of a great part of its news coverage. (Connaughton 1943, xix–xxi).

The descendants of the earlier immigrants moved upward markedly. The sons of hod carriers entered white-collar and even professional ranks as lawyers and doctors. The daughters of cooks and maids became teachers and office workers (Greeley 1981, 115; Diner 1983, 94–99). From the ranks of the children and grandchildren of Irish immigrants came the leadership of the American Catholic Church and, in many northern cities, of the local Democratic organization.

By the 1880s the emergence of Irish officeholders and political bosses in urban politics became manifest. Tammany Hall under "Honest John" Kelly (husband of the niece of New York's Cardinal Archbishop John McCloskey) supported the successful candidacy of William R. Grace, who in 1880 became the city's first Catholic mayor. In the same year Massachusetts elected the first Catholic to serve in its congressional delegation, Harvard-educated Patrick A. Collins, and in 1884 Boston chose Hugh O'Brien to be its first Catholic mayor.

Democratic victories in 1890 and 1892 brought approximately twenty Catholics into the United States Congress, most from northeastern states but some also from Wisconsin, Missouri, and even Texas. During this time at least four Catholic Republicans served in Congress representing California, Maryland, Montana, and New York. One, Representative (later Senator) Thomas H. Carter of Montana, was elected chairman of the Republican National Committee in 1892, the first of his faith to hold this position.

The emergence of Catholics in public offices hitherto held only by others generated some uneasiness in an establishment that felt itself being displaced. The prospect of electing a Catholic mayor in New York City in 1880 was viewed by Elihu Root as turning the city over "to one sect to the exclusion of all others" and by the *New York Times*, on 30 October 1880, as leading to the "Romanization of the schools."

The increasing prominence of Catholics in political life also helped to stir up a new anti-Catholic tide with a wave that struck mainly in certain midwestern states. In Iowa in 1887 the APA, the American Protective Association, was formed with purposes essentially the same as those of the Know-Nothing Movement thirty years earlier—keeping political power out of the hands of Catholics. Although not the only organization with this purpose in the last two decades of the nineteenth century, the APA was the most prominent, most widespread, and most active (Desmond 1912; Kinzer 1964).

The activities of the APA were largely campaign-oriented, organizing support for candidates who favored its objectives and opposition to candidates who were Catholic or deemed friendly to Catholic interests. Its legislative program was thin. Its most serious cause was opposition to any form of public support of sectarian schools. Although its claim of 2.5 million members in 1896 appears to have been a wild exaggeration, it did have some influence, peaking in 1894, riding the Republican tide in Iowa, Michigan, and the states in between. After the midterm election of that year it asserted that twenty members of Congress, including five from Michigan, were APA members.

The congressional allies of the association were almost exclusively Republicans. In the 1890s an APA honor roll was published paying tribute to members of Congress who had opposed the proposal of Wisconsin to place a statue of Father Marquette in Statuary Hall in the Capitol. All but one of those on the honor roll were Republicans.

Such credibility as the American Protective Association commanded was damaged by publication of an absurd document in its paper *The Patriotic American* purporting to be a directive from Pope Leo XIII to his American subjects to massacre "heretics" on the Feast Day of Ignatius Loyola in 1893. Despite loss of credibility and influence, the APA continued a shadowy existence on into the twentieth century, and some of its leaders caught the new wave of bigotry by appearing as Ku Klux Klansmen in the 1920s.

The Spanish-American War and the acquisition of the Philippines brought an unprecedented involvement of leading Catholic churchmen, notably John Ireland, with officials of the United States government. Their activity was directed initially toward averting the conflict and later toward safeguarding the Church's interests in the newly acquired American territory in the Far East. The settlements arranged helped, through the sensitivity shown by Roosevelt and Taft, to display to Catholics a more benign image than the Republican Party had shown in earlier times. On the other hand, the postwar arrangements for governing the former Spanish possessions—condemned as American imperialism by many, including Bryan in his 1900 campaign—were strongly criticized in the Catholic press (Doyle 1976, 262–303; 332–39).

Republican Campaigns 1868–1880

Catholicism, an eminent political historian has observed, was "dragged into practically every presidential election in the post-Civil War generation" (DeSantis 1960, 67). In every national campaign to the end of the nineteenth century, "a Catholic issue" was raised, in most cases peripheral and minor.

The attention it received did, however, rise to a kind of crescendo in New York in two elections in which Catholic candidates sought high profile offices as nominees of the Democratic Party—in 1872, when Francis Kernan ran unsuccessfully for governor, and in 1880, when William R. Grace was elected mayor of New York City.

From the Civil War until 1884 the Republican Party did not shrink from playing upon anti-Catholicism in campaigns for national office. The hapless Horace Greeley, having quit the party of Grant to become the presidential candidate of the Liberal Republicans and of the Democrats in 1872, was a victim of this kind of attack. Ironically, having been denounced twenty years earlier by one Catholic editor as a bitter foe of Catholicism, Greeley in his 1872 race was branded by *Harper's* magazine as the candidate of the Jesuits and "Romish priests and bishops" (DeSantis 1960, 67).

Rutherford B. Hayes, campaigning for governor of Ohio in 1875 and for president in 1876, was particularly worried that inadequate emphasis was being given to what he called "the Catholic question." "We must not let the Catholic question drop out of sight," he wrote in 1875. And in 1876 he complained that "Catholic interference with political affairs, and especially with the schools . . . has not . . . been sufficiently used in the canvass." As for Democratic charges that his campaign smacked of Know-Nothingism, Hayes wrote that such charges were "more than met, not by denial or explanation, but by charging the Democrats with their Catholic alliance" (DeSantis 1960, 72; King 1899, 269–71).

The Republican National Committee met its candidate's demands by the issuance of Campaign Document No. 2 entitled *Vaticanism in Germany and in the United States*. Charging that an alarming "alliance of church and party" was taking shape in the United States, the document called on citizens to block

> the design of the Papal hierarchy to use the Democratic party as the political lever to . . . change . . . our form of government. . . . The Romish Church, inspired by Jesuitical teachings, is to make common cause with the Democracy, in its endeavor to overthrow the Republican party, and with it the free-school system which it sustains.

The Republican campaign four years later took up this theme again in a pamphlet entitled *Garfield or the Pope*.

Catholicism also entered the national political debate in the post-Civil War period as the result of a proposal for a constitutional amendment made by President Grant as his tenure in the White House approached its end. In September 1875, in an address to veterans of the Civil War delivered in Des Moines that was widely interpreted as a bid for a third term, Grant warned against the use of government funds for the support of sectarian institutions. His January message to Congress followed up this theme by calling for taxation of most of the property owned by religious bodies and proposing a constitutional amendment barring the states from using public funds for church-related schools.

The proposal became known as the Blaine Amendment after its sponsor, the "plumed knight" from Maine. It passed the House of Representatives but fell short of the required two-thirds vote in the Senate. The movement for the amendment bore an unmistakable Republican stamp. Of twenty-eight votes in its favor in the Senate, twenty-seven were cast by Republicans. And it was given a hearty endorsement in the Republican platform in 1876 and again in 1880.

Senator Justin Morrill of Vermont, commenting on opposition to the amendment, wrote, "The Catholics will rave but I suppose there is not one who ever voted for free men, free schools or the Republican Party in war or peace" (Klinkhamer 1956, 26). One Catholic Democrat, Representative Edwin R. Meade of New York, charged that Grant's Des Moines speech was "deliberately and wilfully prepared to incite rancor and hatred in the breasts of our fellow-citizens; . . . having for its immediate object to influence the Ohio election . . . then impending" (Klinkhamer 1956, 41).

The 1884 Campaign: Republicans Jettison Anti-Catholicism

In 1884, a significant change occurred in Republican campaign strategy. Avoiding any overt display of anti-Catholicism, the party made a serious effort to attract "the Irish vote." Although its presidential candidate was James G. Blaine, gone from its platform was any endorsement of the Blaine Amendment. For the first time in the party's thirty-year history, the national nominating convention heard an invocation pronounced by a Catholic priest. The priest selected, Dr. Charles O'Reilly of Detroit, was an official of the Irish National League of America, an organization through which Irish Americans were abetting the efforts of Parnell to secure land reform and home rule in Ireland.

Among American Irish, enthusiasm for the struggle led by Parnell in the mother country had been rekindled in the 1880s. It was manifested in the warm reception given Parnell (including an invitation to address Congress) when the Irish leader toured the United States in 1881, in the formation of an organization on this side of the Atlantic to aid his campaign in Ireland, and in the financial support which Americans provided for the cause of Irish freedom and land reform. Such developments encouraged some Republican leaders in the hope that Irish nationalism could be used to make inroads into a loyal Democratic constituency.

James Gillespie Blaine had certain credentials which were thought to appeal to voters of Irish ancestry. Perhaps most important was his public record of hostility toward England during his tenures as both secretary of state and member of Congress. In addition, his middle name was a reminder that his mother was an Irish Catholic (Russell 1931, 7). Blaine often expressed admiration for her Church; indeed, he did so in his official campaign biography. A major obstacle to a pursuit of the Irish Catholic vote was his sponsorship of the Blaine Amendment, but he managed to go through the presidential campaign without ever mentioning the constitutional amendment to which his name had been attached eight years earlier.

Finally, Grover Cleveland, Blaine's opponent, was somewhat flawed in the eyes of many of New York's Irish Catholics. As governor of New York he had vetoed an appropriation bill providing funds for the Catholic Protectory, a home for orphans—an action which drew a barrage of criticism from Catholic clergy and laity. At the Democratic Convention in Chicago, Tammany Hall vigorously opposed his nomination. Bourke Cockran called him a "pigmy," and Tammany agents spread the word that their governor was anti-Catholic. After the convention Tammany sulked for several weeks before voting to endorse Cleveland. Even after this action there were enough dissenters to fuel uncertainty about what Tammany would do on Election Day.

With the editorial support of Patrick Ford and his *Irish World* and of various Irish personages in Pennsylvania and New York whose speaking tours and other activities were financed by Republican sources, the Blaine campaign had serious hopes of making inroads in the Irish vote, partly by attracting a large part to Blaine and partly by benefiting from such fragments of that vote as were drawn to a maverick third-party candidate, Benjamin Franklin Butler, former Democratic governor of Massachusetts.

These hopes dimmed in the closing days of the campaign when the Reverend Samuel Burchard, spokesman for a delegation of ministers who met with Blaine, denounced the Democrats as the party of "Rum, Romanism, and Rebellion." In the few days remaining before the election, Democrats exploited this gaffe among the Catholics of New York and elsewhere.

Until Burchard made his impolitic remark, there were some reasons for the hope many Republicans held that a breakthrough in winning Irish voters was at hand, although the hope was based on a generous amount of wishful thinking (Gibson 1951, 388–89; Brown 1966, 136–42). Burchard's indiscretion was probably enough by itself to reverse any gains among Catholic voters. Its impact was magnified by Blaine's tardy repudiation of the minister's sentiments (Farrelly 1955, 38–39).

After the election those engaged in the effort to woo the Irish made self-serving claims of success, but the results cast doubt on the claims. Some erosion of support for the Democratic presidential ticket can be detected in

Irish areas of New York City, but even there a sampling of such areas shows Cleveland polling two-thirds of the vote. In five Irish wards in Brooklyn Cleveland received 70 percent of the vote cast. In Boston, with strong support from Congressman Patrick Collins and *Pilot* editor John Boyle O'Reilly, Cleveland amassed 71 percent of the vote in Irish wards (Brown 1966, 187).

Like Clay's loss in 1844, Blaine's defeat in 1884 can be attributed to a number of factors, any one of which could have influenced enough votes to provide Cleveland's narrow plurality of 1,100 votes in New York and with it a majority in the electoral college. Blaine's immediate reaction to the outcome was, "I should have carried New York by 10,000 if the weather had been clear on election day and Mr. Burchard had been doing missionary work in Asia Minor or Cochin China" (letter from Frank B. Loomis, 17 November 1884, Clarkson Papers).

In addition to whatever effect the Burchard remarks may have had on voting behavior, an analysis of the vote in New York State cannot ignore the twenty-five thousand votes cast for the Prohibition Party candidate, John P. St. John (probably mostly from Republican voters) or the seventeen thousand votes cast for the Greenback standard bearer, Butler. Further complicating the analysis, Blaine's bitter foe, Roscoe Conkling, was suspected of using his considerable influence to cut his party's candidate. Conkling's home county of Oneida, which gave Garfield a plurality of almost two thousand in 1880, was carried by Cleveland in 1884. And when a challenge to the vote count was threatened, Conkling offered legal counsel to the Democrats.

Theodore Roosevelt gave an interpretation of the election in New York reminiscent of Clay's explanation of his defeat forty years earlier: "If the Conkling wing of the Stalwarts had been true, if Burchard's terrible alliteration had not been sprung, if that 'soap dinner' at Delmonico's had not come off, and if the Prohibitionists had been as honest as they claimed, Blaine would have won" (Morison and Blum 1951–54).

The 1888 Campaign

In 1888, with Benjamin Harrison as its nominee, the Republican Party again courted the Irish vote. The *New York Star*, reporting a meeting of the party's executive committee immediately following the nominating convention, said that the committee regarded "capturing the Irish vote . . . as the big work of the campaign." A special committee was appointed to deal with this task, but its membership was not divulged, presumably because of the divisions among those who claimed leadership in the Irish community (*New York Star*, 14 July 1888). Party chairman Matthew Quay relied on the *Irish World* and its editor, Patrick Ford, for guidance in this aspect of the campaign, ignoring such Irish Nationalist figures as Dr. James Collins of Philadelphia, Professor Robert Ellis Thompson, John Devoy, and Alexander Sullivan.

The rejected Irish leaders found a sponsor, however, in Philadelphia businessman Wharton Barker and formed a campaign organization called the Irish-American Anti-Cleveland and Protective League. The title suggested a theme consistently used in the Republican campaign for Irish votes in this era, blending anti-British animus with support for a protective tariff. The Democratic policy of low tariffs, it was argued, stifled economic development at home and played into English hands by perpetuating American dependence on the British economy.

Emphasizing the importance of the league he was financing, Barker declared in a letter to vice presidential nominee Levi Morton that 90,000 of New York City's 250,000 voters were Irish. There, as well as in other states, he wrote, Irish voters had the power to determine the outcome of the election. "Without them the Republican Party is in the minority in all the doubtful states—and with them the Republicans have certain victory," Barker wrote (Barker Papers; *New York Times*, 17 December 1888).

The combined expenditure of the national committee and Barker's project to win the "Irish vote" amounted to $110,000, a very substantial sum in a campaign of the 1880s. By contrast, Republican spending at the national level for programs directed toward all other immigrant groups came to only $7,500 (Kehl 1981, 107–8).

Again in the late stages of this campaign a blunder affecting voters of Irish background occurred. The British ambassador to Washington, Lord Sackville-West, dispatched an incredibly naive response to an American of British origin who asked which of the presidential candidates was preferable from the British point of view. The ambassador's letter favoring Cleveland as more sympathetic to English interests fell into the hands of Republicans (who may have been behind the initial query) and was fully exploited by the party in appeals to the Irish-American electorate.

Cleveland's principal Irish advisers, Bostonians Collins and O'Reilly, were in a state approaching panic after the release of the Sackville-West letter and strongly advised the president to demand the recall of the ambassador. Cleveland followed this advice but nevertheless lost the election (Tansill 1940, 333).

How much any of this had to do with Harrison's victory and Cleveland's defeat in an election in which the Democratic plurality in the popular vote failed to produce a majority in the electoral college is impossible to say. The incident, however, seemed to confirm afresh the potentially decisive role of the Irish vote in national elections and the usefulness of an anti-British stance in attracting that vote.

Harrison gave some recognition to his Irish supporters by appointing Representative Joseph McKenna of California to the United States Circuit Court of Appeals and selecting Patrick Egan, former president of the Irish League, to be the minister to Chile. Such sparse spoils disappointed those who had labored in the campaign of 1888 in the expectation of reward that never came. Further, by 1892, the Republican administration found itself in hot water with a substantial segment of the Catholic press because of an issue that had been simmering throughout its term. It had discontinued the support granted by the government to a school system for Indians maintained by the Bureau of Catholic Indian Affairs. The director of the bureau, Father Joseph Stephan, in a confidential report which somehow found wide circulation, called the commissioner of Indian Affairs responsible for this action "bigoted" and President Harrison "no less bigoted" (Sievers 1952, 131).

The 1892 Campaign

Some fence-mending was undertaken by the Republicans in 1892 to mollify Irish and Catholic voters. Breaking two precedents, the party chose as its national chairman a man who was a Catholic and who was not a member of its national committee, Thomas H. Carter of Montana. The Republican platform, along with a reiteration of past declarations of sympathy for Irish nationalism, contained for the first time a broad disavowal of discrimination on the ground of religion or national origin as well as of color. It also recognized the growing Jewish population.

The platform assured minority groups that the "Republican Party has always been the champion of the oppressed and recognizes the dignity of mankind, irrespective of faith, color, or nationality; it sympathizes with the cause of home rule in Ireland and protests against the persecution of the Jews in Russia."

Another first was platform language recognizing nonpublic schools as "agencies and instrumentalities which contribute to the education of the children of the land." This word of approbation was coupled with a pledge of support for "the fullest measure of religious liberty" and opposition to "any union of Church and State." This formulation was meant to express rejection of any implication that a kind word about nonpublic schools might entail assistance for them from the public purse.

Harrison's running mate for the vice presidency, Whitelaw Reid, Greeley's successor as publisher of the always reliable Republican voice in New York, the *Tribune*, was particularly energetic in courting the Irish vote, even tempering the dispatches of the paper's London correspondent to avoid giving offense to Irish-Americans.

The defeat of Harrison in 1892 was greeted with satisfaction in the Catholic press, which tended to play up (and undoubtedly exaggerate) the part that the issue of the Catholic Indian schools had played in the outcome of the election. "Cleveland's victory," declared the *Catholic Herald* of New York, "was in truth the defeat of bigotry" (Sievers 1952, 131). Looking forward to 1896, Republicans could only conclude that their effort to make substantial inroads in the ranks of Catholics had produced few gains.

The Realigning Presidential Election of 1896

Shift in Voting Patterns

The loss of one hundred Democratic seats in the House of Representatives in the off-year election of 1894, reversing the party's victories of 1890 and 1892, clearly foreshadowed the historic shift in voting behavior that took place in the presidential election that followed. In the presidential balloting of 1896 nineteen states switched to the party they had rejected in 1892. The voting pattern showed a sharp sectional split, with East against West and South, as well as a split based on economic interest, with industry against agriculture and city dwellers against rural America.

Republican gains were most pronounced in the New England and Middle Atlantic regions. In New England only one county was carried by Bryan, and only one of its congressional districts sent a Democrat to Congress as Boston's Irish reelected John "Honey Fitz" Fitzgerald, who was to be the maternal grandfather of a future president. On the other hand, Bryan's sweep of states west of the Mississippi was complete except for Minnesota, Iowa, and California.

It was in urban areas, particularly in the East (which Bryan referred to early in the campaign as "enemy country") and in the midwest that the greatest shift of votes took place (see table 3-1). William McKinley carried forty-five of the fifty most populous counties in the nation. Of the five which Bryan carried, four were in the South. In the eighty-five largest cities, from which Cleveland received a plurality of 162,000 in 1892, McKinley ran 464,000 votes ahead of Bryan.

Confirmation of the hypothesis that many Catholics broke away from their ties to the Democratic Party in 1896 is furnished by returns from some less populous areas in the Midwest in which Catholics were concentrated. Kewaunee County in Wisconsin, heretofore carried only by Democrats in presidential elections, gave McKinley 53 percent of its vote after having cast a meager 20 percent for Harrison in 1892. In neighboring Brown County, which had voted for a Republican presidential candidate only once before,

TABLE 3–1. Democratic Percentage of the Presidential Vote in Selected Urban Areas, 1892 and 1896

Urban Area	*1892 (Cleveland)*	*1896 (Bryan)*
Boston (Suffolk County)	54	35
New York City	59	42
Philadelphia	42	26
Baltimore	57	38
Chicago (Cook County)	55	40
Louisville (Jefferson County)	59	35

McKinley received 59 percent of the vote, fifteen percentage points more than Harrison was given four years earlier.

Along with other voters, Catholics shifted in 1896, but only the crudest estimate of the extent of the shift is possible. It is likely that Bryan retained the support of a clear majority of Catholics. Yet in this contest the Democratic share of the presidential vote cast by Catholics shrank from the levels of preceding contests.

Explanations of Catholic Voting Behavior in 1896

Many of the influences that led non-Catholics to desert the Democratic Party in 1896 undoubtedly produced a similar response among Catholics. The economy was probably the major influence. The memory of the panic of 1893 was still fresh and its effects still strong. Economic misery and dislocation were linked in many minds to Democratic control of government. The Republican campaign promise of the full dinner pail was a powerful lure, at least to voters from the Atlantic to the nation's midsection.

In its platform and its nominee for president the Democratic Party tried to repudiate its recent past, but it is hard to convince disgruntled voters that a party associated with disaster can be trusted to lead the nation to a better future. Further, much of the nation was skeptical that remonetization of silver would cure the country's economic ailments. Both the nostrum the Bryan Democrats offered and the new leadership of the party disturbed conservative followers. Some of these leaders, particularly those drawn to the Democratic Party in 1896 from the Populist movement, sounded wild, reckless, and dangerous. Indeed, the Democratic convention showed its awareness of the danger of appearing too radical by balancing its ticket with a respectable businessman from Maine as its vice presidential candidate.

In the contest that took shape in 1896, Mark Hanna looked on the Catholic Church as one of the conservative forces of the nation and therefore an ally. The Church was firmly on record against socialism, and few American Catholics were identified with the Populist and Socialist causes that attracted a substantial following as the nineteenth century gave way to the twentieth. Throughout his career, Hanna expressed admiration for the Catholic church as a conservative bulwark protecting social and economic institutions against radical and violent change. Because of its influence with the new immigrants of southern and eastern Europe from whose ranks movements threatening economic disruption drew a following, he saw Catholicism as a useful ally to maintain order and stability—and perhaps to provide some help to the Republican Party. Hanna found particularly reassuring the fact that the labor organizations in which Catholics were prominent and which were encouraged by clergymen like Cardinal Gibbons, such as the Knights of Labor and the American Federation of Labor, were moderate in program and restrained in tactics.

William Jennings Bryan in personality and style typified the pietist Protestant preacher. As such he was not a candidate with whom Catholics, particularly the urban dwellers of the Northeast, could feel strong identification. Bryan's brand of Protestantism, including association with Prohibitionism, probably was a factor in the erosion of the Democratic vote among German Catholics of the Midwest. This erosion, as has been noted, was pronounced in Wisconsin, where a Catholic paper, *Columbia*, hitherto Democratic in policy, opposed Bryan. Paul Kleppner (1970, 322) explains the changed voting behavior thus: "To German Lutherans and Catholics, Democratic pietism was no more acceptable than the Republican variety had been for half a century. To defend their value systems these voters rejected Bryan's Democracy. They turned instead to the Republican party."

As the Republican Party abandoned, or at least muted, its anti-Catholicism, one of the barriers inhibiting Catholics from casting a Republican vote was lowered. The acid test, however, was the willingness of the party to condemn the APA. In 1894, the Republicans generally failed this test as the executive committee of the national committee turned aside the pleas of Patrick Egan and Committeeman Richard Kerens of Missouri for disavowal of APA principles. (*New York Times*, 5 October 1894). Similarly, the New York State Republican Convention, to the dismay of Theodore Roosevelt (Morison and Blum, 1951–54, 1: 401), failed to include in its platform the simple statement that no religious test should be required for public office (*New York Times*, 26 July, 1894; 19 September; 20 September).

Yet there were signs of a more open attitude on the part of Republicans toward Catholics. In New York, Levi P. Morton, candidate for governor, in his campaign speeches strongly endorsed the plank which his party platform had ignored. In Massachusetts, where both Republican senators, Lodge and Hoar, were opponents of the APA, the state party platform spoke out for "no distinction of birth or religious creed in the rights of American citizenship."

In the New York State constitutional convention of 1894 Republicans adopted a position that provided some measure of satisfaction to Catholic Church interests, even at the sacrifice of the principle of denying public funds to sectarian institutions. The draft of the constitution agreed on at the convention, which was Republican controlled, distinguished sectarian schools from church-sponsored organizations providing charitable and other social services. The constitution submitted to the voters prohibited expenditure of public funds for the former but permitted it for the latter. The Republican delegates to the convention, while overwhelmingly supporting the ban on aid to sectarian schools, by a vote of fifty to twenty-seven rejected a proposal to deny state support to charitable and social service institutions affiliated with religious groups (McSeveney 1972, 69–79).

The ban on aid to sectarian schools in the proposed constitution was a setback to a cause which churchmen had often sought to advance since the time of Archbishop Hughes. Nevertheless, the Catholic bishops of New York decided that they would not oppose ratification of the 1894 constitution. In fact, they signaled approval of the document by holding a dinner honoring delegates to the convention who had played leading roles in securing the half a loaf which the proposed constitution provided.

The position taken by the bishops of New York reflected a development of significance for the Republican Party. By 1894 many Catholic ecclesiastics had come to accept the fact that, except in a few localities, any form of government assistance for their schools was an unattainable goal. Evidence of this acceptance was revealed in a poll of Catholic prelates conducted by the magazine *Independent* at the beginning of the year. Of twenty-nine bishops who responded, only one reply clearly favored participation by religious schools in public "school funds." A suspension or downgrading of the demand for aid for Catholic schools eliminated an issue that was particularly troublesome for Republicans.

At the National Republican Convention of 1896, a struggle over the platform revealed that party leaders had no desire to confront the touchy religious school issue or to give offense to any Catholics who might vote Republican. In the process the party summoned the courage to defy the waning power of the American Protective Association. The three most recent Republican platforms preceding 1896 had avoided mention of amending the constitution to ban public support of sectarian schools. At the St. Louis convention which was to nominate McKinley, however, the APA resurrected this issue by proposing a platform plank endorsing a Blaine-type constitutional amendment. According to Senator Gear of Iowa, this proposal was at one point inserted in the draft of the platform prepared for submission to the convention. Word of what was afoot was conveyed by the McKinley camp to Archbishop John Ireland of St. Paul, who telegraphed a strong protest to Senator Thomas H. Carter of Montana. A platform provision of the type proposed, Ireland asserted, was uncalled for, would constitute a concession to the APA, and would foment religious animosity. The protest achieved its purpose; the platform presented to the convention and adopted by it contained no mention of church-state relations and no reference to anything resembling the Blaine Amendment (Desmond 1912, 87–90; O'Connell 1988, 263; King 1899, 263–68).

In choosing McKinley as its candidate in 1896, the Republican Party selected the only one among the potential nominees who had been rejected by the American Protective Association. In April of the election year the APA pronounced McKinley unfit to be president because of ties of various kinds (most very remote and innocent) with Catholics. The executive board of the organization declared that the Roman Catholic hierarchy "has through its leaders and followers massed its strength and resources to the support of Major William McKinley." Although the APA reversed its harsh judgment when it became likely that the Republican Party would nominate McKinley, grudging acceptance of the candidate did not erase memory of the earlier condemnation (Jones 1964, 142–44).

In 1896, aided by railroad magnate James J. Hill, Mark Hanna gave considerable attention to winning the vote of Catholics. In October, Hill's close friend, Archbishop John Ireland, issued a strong statement denouncing the Democratic platform. Released after Bryan had made a triumphal appearance in St. Paul, the statement was stage-managed as the prelate's response to a letter signed by twenty prominent Minnesota citizens requesting his views on the election contest. Ireland's views were given wide distribution by McKinley's campaign organization; some 250,000 copies were circulated in the three weeks before Election Day.

The *New York Times*, which in the 1880s complained bitterly about the boss-controlled Irish vote and in the 1980s was to complain about bishops' statements on abortion, greeted Ireland's campaign declaration with enthusiastic praise. Estimating that the archbishop's views "will increase the sound money vote in Iowa, Minnesota, Illinois, and Wisconsin by 50,000 or more," the *Times*, on 13 October 1896, added that he "like a patriotic American rebukes the attempt of Bryan and Altgeld to array class against class and the attempt of Tillman to array section against section." A fellow archbishop, Winand Wigger of Newark, dissented, calling Ireland in the *Freeman's Journal* of 17 October 1896, "an ardent Republican working for . . . his party . . . an extremist and an alarmist."

William Randolph Hearst sent an indignant telegram to Cardinal Rampolla, Vatican secretary of state, demanding to know whether Ireland's statement expressed an official position of the Church. The telegram went unanswered, but Hearst could have found the information he sought in the columns of the *Pilot*, 17 October 1896, which deplored Ireland's "strong invective against the Chicago convention and its candidates." Readers were assured that Ireland spoke "as a private citizen, not an Archbishop" and consequently was "entitled to as much respect as . . . any other private citizen of equal intelligence." "No Catholic," the article added, "will vote for this or that ticket because his ecclesiastical superior prefers one or the other."

Ireland's statement took aim at the platform adopted at the Democratic convention in Chicago in 1896 rather than at Bryan. Nor did it mention McKinley or the Republican Party. It disparaged free coinage of silver at sixteen to one, which Bryan made his central campaign issue, calling it "a delusion" which would destroy the American economy. Its major thrust, however, was directed at the radicalism which Ireland discerned in the Democratic program.

Never given to understatement, the archbishop accused the Democratic Party of embracing "the secession of 1861 which our soldiers believed they had consigned to death at Appomattox." This conclusion he drew from the platform's condemnation of the use of federal authority to override the wishes of a state, as Cleveland had done by using the Army to break the Pullman strike in 1894. Ireland might have found clearer justification for the charge he made in an inflammatory speech delivered at the convention by "Pitchfork" Ben Tillman of South Carolina. Tillman threatened that his state might again secede if the Democratic demand for silver coinage was denied.

Bad as the threat of secession was, the archbishop pronounced "worse . . . the spirit of socialism and anarchy . . . which has issued from the Democratic convention." Asserting that "the war of class upon class is upon us," he scored the Democratic doctrines of 1896 as an incentive to "reckless men" to "light up the fires of a 'Commune'" (O'Connell 1988, 424–26).

Ireland had long been a Republican and was no newcomer to the political fray when he expressed his sentiments in the presidential campaign of 1896. He had established personal ties to President Harrison and to other Republican leaders, notably in New York State. In 1894 he intervened in New York politics on two occasions. His first foray was as a lobbyist successfully helping to persuade Republican legislators to support the appointment of a Brooklyn priest, Sylvester Malone, as a regent of the University of the State of New York. Ireland's second intervention, in October as the state election drew near, was the issuance of a strong statement denouncing Tammany Hall and defending the Republican Party against the charge that it had a covert alliance with the APA (O'Connell 1988, 396–97). The charge that the statement was intended to counteract had considerable credibility in the light of the failure of the Republican state convention to repudiate the anti-Catholic organization.

Archbishop Ireland's view of the Bryan campaign was largely shared by a prominent lay Catholic, Bourke Cockran, a Tammany politician and a Democratic member of Congress. Cockran, like Bryan a great political orator, campaigned tirelessly against the radicalism of his party's candidate and program. He traveled to twenty states to deliver his message, and, evidencing the strength of his feelings about the stakes in the 1896 campaign, he paid all expenses from his own pocket.

Cockran asserted that the nation faced the gravest crisis it had gone through since 1860. It was, he declared, "a contest for the existence of civilization," between "the forces of order" and "the forces of disorder." To his mind, the Chicago convention which had nominated Bryan had launched a movement "to paralyze industry by using all the powers of government to take property from the hands of those who created it and place it in the hands of those who covet it" (McGurrin 1948, 150).

The 1896 campaign drew an extraordinary volume of partisan commentary and exhortations from the pulpits of the nation. As in past campaigns, the voices heard were principally those of Protestant divines. Despite Bryan's religious ties, the Protestant clergy for the most part rejected the Democratic-Populist candidate for reasons very similar to those expressed by Ireland and Cockran.

Two leading Catholic publications—the *Freeman's Journal* and the *Pilot*—were unmoved by the advice of clerics like Ireland and lay leaders like Cockran. The former paper, staunch in its support of Bryan, whom it called "the magnificent leader of the rejuvenated Democracy," declared monometalism, in its 17 October issue, to be the root cause of the nation's troubles. McKinley, it said on 7 November in its assessment of the outcome of the campaign, "owes his election to the money power, to the corporations, trusts, syndicates, and bondholders, and they will not let him forget what he owes them."

The *Pilot* pronounced the Republican victory "a triumph of gold, for gold, and by gold . . . on a well bought field." Its partisanship, however, was somewhat muted, and more than a little ambivalence crept into its election coverage. In its 17 October issue it evenhandedly complimented both Bryan and McKinley for conducting their campaigns on a high level while excoriating their "allies" for failing to do so. Among the "allies" were remnants of the APA who, according to the *Pilot*, were welcomed by Massachusetts Democrats and who were active in the Populist Party in support of Bryan.

The Elections of 1904 and 1908

In three campaigns for the presidency, William Jennings Bryan received a total vote remarkably stable from one contest to another, ranging from 6.5 million in 1896 to 6.4 million in 1900 and 1908. The vote cast for his Republican opponents, however, grew in successive races; Taft's plurality of 1.3 million in 1908 was more than double the margin by which McKinley defeated the Great Commoner in 1896. The strong base of support in midwestern and Rocky Mountain states which Bryan commanded in his first presidential race melted in later contests as silver and populism receded as regional vote-winning issues. In 1908, outside southern and some border states, Bryan succeeded in winning the electoral votes of only the silver states of Colorado and Nevada and of his home state of Nebraska. The decline in Bryan's vote in several states between 1896 and 1908 is shown in Table 3-2.

TABLE 3–2. Bryan's Percentage of Major Party Presidential Vote in Selected States, 1896, 1900, and 1908

State	*1896*	*1900*	*1908*
California	49	43	37
Colorado	86	60	51
Kansas	52	47	45
Michigan	45	40	34
Montana	80	59	48
South Dakota	50	42	37
Washington	57	44	36

The election of 1904, with Theodore Roosevelt running against an uninspiring Democrat who rejected Bryanism, was the high point of Republican fortunes until the 1920s. The plurality by which Theodore Roosevelt was elected was a precedent-breaking margin of more than 2.5 million votes. The breakaway of Catholic voters from the Democratic Party discernible in the presidential contest of 1896 was deepened and extended in 1904 and 1908. In a letter to Peter Finlay Dunne written shortly after the election of 1904, Theodore Roosevelt boasted of his success in winning the vote of Catholics:

> One of the things I am most pleased with in the recent election is that while I got, I think, a greater proportion of the Americans of Irish birth

> or parentage and of the Catholic religion than any previous Republican candidate, I got this purely because they know I felt in sympathy with them and in touch with them, and that they and I had the same ideals and principles. (Morison and Blum 1951–54, 4: 1042)

Encouraged by his presidential race, Roosevelt emphasized to Republican gubernatorial candidate Charles Evans Hughes in 1906 the crucial role of Catholic voters in New York: "One element we must not forget in this campaign is the great Catholic population of the State. In the old days Catholics used to feel obliged to vote the Democratic ticket. More and more they have tended to come over our way" (Morison and Blum 1951–54, 5: 442).

In 1908, Bryan, running against William Howard Taft, appears to have won the vote of a majority of Catholics in midwestern and western states. In the East, however—particularly in the major cities with a substantial Catholic population—Taft scored heavily, apparently outdoing even Roosevelt's vote four years before. In the nation as a whole, in the opinion of the leading historian of the Catholic Church in the United States, 1908 may have been the first presidential election in which a Republican presidential candidate received a majority of the vote cast by Catholics (Ellis 1956, 276).

Both Taft and Bryan attributed to Catholic voters a crucial influence in the outcome of the 1908 election. In postelection correspondence and interviews Taft credited Catholic support as an important factor in enabling him to carry such eastern Democratic strongholds as New York City and Hudson County, New Jersey (Hornig 1961, 536–37).

Bryan, for his part, was accused of harboring anti-Catholic prejudice—a charge he met with vigorous denial, as reported in the *New York Times*, 29 August 1908. Apparently to quash such reports and appeal to Catholic voters, Bryan chose as his campaign manager Norman Mack of New York, whom he mistakenly believed to be a Catholic. The correspondence Bryan received after the election offers considerable evidence that the followers of the Great Commoner felt that the defection of Catholic voters played a major part in their candidate's defeat. Ninety percent of the writers expressed this opinion. One wrote, "It was not the Republican party that defeated you. It was the Catholic Church. Mr. Taft was the Catholic candidate. . . . The South was loyal to you because its [*sic*] the Protestant American section of the United States, free from Catholic control" (Coletta 1964, 432–34).

The exceptionally strong support that both Roosevelt and Taft received from Catholics was attributable far more to the popularity of the two men than to their party. Unquestionably, the votes cast for the two were for many Catholics rare exceptions to the practice of voting a straight Democratic ticket.

Many Catholics were captivated by Teddy Roosevelt's forceful leadership and unabashed showmanship. And there were additional reasons for Roosevelt's specific appeal to Catholics which TR himself explained in these words: "They know I felt in sympathy with them and in touch with them, and they and I had the same principles and ideals." Roosevelt openly manifested this sympathy in many ways in his acts as a public official from police commissioner to president and as a private citizen. In the 1890s he had made clear his disdain for the APA when the Republican Party of New York refused to condemn the anti-Catholic organization. When he ran for governor in 1898, the *Freeman's Journal*, usually staunchly Democratic, noted as a point in his favor that he was opposed by the APA. When he ran for president, again the paper gave him vigorous support.

In the presidential campaign of 1904, Roosevelt had no stronger support from the press than that provided by Boston's *Pilot*, heretofore consistently Democratic in its endorsements. Noting TR's early repudiation of the APA, the *Pilot* declared on 10 September, "When we most needed him the brave and honest young Republican Theodore Roosevelt entered the den, dragged the monster into the light of day. . . . He was the only one who dared his political ruin by fighting for truth and justice, when time-servers would have cautiously passed it by."

In every issue through September and October and up to the week of election the *Pilot* carried several front-page articles as well as numerous editorials on the campaign, all lauding Roosevelt and denouncing the Democratic Party, platform, and presidential candidate. It appealed particularly to Irish sensitivity, publishing a series of articles under the caption "Roosevelt and the Irish" that credited the incumbent president with showing special solicitude toward the ethnic group that constituted most of the paper's readership. Accusing the Democrats of advocating a "free trade" policy and a timid foreign and military doctrine, the *Pilot* asked on 3 September, "Will the Irish vote be cast for British commercial, military and naval supremacy?"

Among other themes sounded in the *Pilot* in the course of the campaign was the charge that the Democratic Party had deserted its traditional principles to "take up with the radicalism of Populists and Socialists." In an editorial of 3 September, captioned "Theodore Roosevelt, Democrat," the paper asserted that "except for his party label," the Republican nominee was "an ideal American Democrat of the old-fashioned type." And it scornfully derided his opponent Alton Parker as a "blank" candidate.

In addition to the arguments which the *Pilot* used in its advocacy of Roosevelt, other considerations may have helped the cause with Catholic voters. TR cultivated a close and cordial relationship with several leading Catholic prelates, displaying his friendship with them in very public ways and giving them a kind of recognition accorded by no prior president and by no later one until another Roosevelt occupied the office. The two prelates with whom Roosevelt maintained the closest ties were James Cardinal Gibbons of Baltimore and Archbishop Ireland of St. Paul. In addition, TR counted as friends other members of the hierarchy, including John J. Keane, archbishop of Dubuque and first rector of the Catholic University of America, Bishop John Lancaster Spalding of Peoria, and Bishop Thomas O'Gorman of Sioux Falls, South Dakota. And he never failed to make a friend of the parish priest in Oyster Bay.

Appointment of Catholics to conspicuous federal offices was still rare when Roosevelt entered the White House. Grover Cleveland and Benjamin Harrison broke the ice, each appointing Catholics to the bench and diplomatic posts. McKinley, after listening to the plea of Archbishop Ireland that a Catholic be selected for a cabinet position, appointed Joseph McKenna attorney general, making him the third of his faith to hold a cabinet post and the first in almost half a century. Later McKinley appointed McKenna to the Supreme Court, braving complaints that this appointment meant that two Catholics would be sitting on the nation's highest tribunal.

In the 1904 campaign a pamphlet entitled *One of the Noblest of Presidents* by a Reverend T. A. Dwyer was circulated, particularly, according to Democratic critics, to priests. Enumerating a roster of Catholics holding federal posts from Attorney General Charles Joseph Bonaparte on down, it boasted that Roosevelt had brought into his administration more Catholics than had any of his predecessors. The *Catholic News* of New York revealed that Dwyer was not a priest and condemned the pamphlet as a deceptive "trick" (*New York Times*, 15 October 1904). Nevertheless, the facts cited were not challenged.

Much that Roosevelt and Taft did in settling the problems accompanying American control of the Philippines established the reputation of both as sensitive to the interests of the Catholic Church. Taft, as the first American governor general of the archipelago, dealt with a tangle of political and legal difficulties, including the replacement of Spanish bishops by Americans and the renovation of the educational system. The major issue was the disposition of the Friars' Lands, the large holdings granted by Spain to various religious orders. In 1903 an agreement was concluded by which the United States paid $7.2 million to the Church for the lands. This settlement with the Vatican was negotiated by an American commission headed by Taft. The American archbishop of Manila, Thomas Harty, in 1904 publicly announced his support of Theodore Roosevelt in the presidential contest (*Pilot*, 14 October). When Taft's turn to run for the presidency came in 1908, his service in working out amicable solutions to the problems affecting the Church in the Philippines undoubtedly was one factor disposing many Catholics to vote for him.

Effects of Realignment of the Electorate on Catholics

The realignment of voters beginning in the 1890s and extending into the 1920s changed the party balance in all sections of the country outside the South. By 1908, with the disappearance of silver as an issue, Bryan's strength had dissolved in western and midwestern states in which he had run strongly in 1896. The areas of the West which had been swept by Populism and the Bryan brand of Democracy became largely Republican.

In the East the shift of large Democratic constituencies to the Republicans had taken place in 1896. The 1908 election showed no significant recovery of Democratic strength in this region except in Massachusetts. As in 1896, Bryan fared poorly in urban areas in his subsequent races. Of the nation's twenty largest cities, Bryan carried only two in 1908—New Orleans and Kansas City, Missouri.

Four presidential elections swept by three different Republican candidates made it clear that a new political alignment had hardened. A solid majority of the nation was Republican and would remain so until the 1930s.

How did this realignment affect the burgeoning Catholic population? The great majority of Catholics remained Democrats. The vote received by Roosevelt and Taft from Catholics was in part an aberration—a tribute to leaders regarded as friendly to them and to their faith as well as a rejection of the alternatives offered by the Democratic Party in these particular elections.

For Catholic Democratic politicians the realignment opened up opportunities. As others deserted the Democratic Party, the Catholics who remained loyal moved up the ladder of leadership in many places (Hollingsworth 1963, 99–100). The base of support for the Democratic Party outside the South, particularly in cities, became more heavily Catholic. The national Democratic Party became more dependent on its urban Catholic henchmen, a fact that became evident in the roll calls of the party's national conventions. And, as the influence of the Catholic politician in the Democratic Party increased, his ambition led him to move upward from the narrow confines of local political activity to the level of the state. In the second decade of the twentieth century, the first Catholic governors were elected in Massachusetts and New York—David I. Walsh and Alfred E. Smith.

The vast majority of Catholics maintained their loyalty to the Democratic Party although some joined the movement around the turn of the century that enlarged Republican ranks, some did. One result was a changed attitude on the part of Republican personages and press. A striking piece of evidence of the change was the selection of James O'Grady as speaker of the New York State Assembly by the Republican members of that body in 1897. In campaigns Catholics were no longer regarded as out of the reach of Republican candidates. And the party's campaign strategy, as in the presidential elections from 1896 on and the New York gubernatorial election of 1906, was fashioned to attract such voters—or at least to avoid offending them. There was a changed attitude, too, among Catholics. As has been noted, influential and representative Catholic publications broke away from consistent endorsement of Democratic nominees for office and on occasion gave enthusiastic support to Republicans.

Data are lacking to permit any estimate of the number of Catholics of Republican affiliation in this period. One New Yorker who was both a Catholic and a Republican leader asserted in 1894 that seventy thousand of the state's voters were of his faith and party (McSeveney 1972, 78). This figure, although equaling only 9 percent of the vote cast for McKinley in the state in 1896, cannot be dismissed as completely insignificant. It was four times greater than the margin that made Theodore Roosevelt governor in 1898.

The Catholic Republican in New York at the turn of the century was likely to be of an upper socioeconomic level, relatively well educated, a professional or businessman, a second- or third-generation American, and, in many cases, a convert to Catholicism. At a somewhat later time Republicans were to find some Catholic adherents in the ranks of the new immigrants, notably Italian and French-Canadian in New England communities, where domination of the local Democratic Party by Irish leaders often shut out the ambitious of other ethnic extraction.

After the 1880s "Catholic" and "Democrat" ceased to be synonyms. Catholic Republicans became less of an oddity, although they were a distinct minority in both the religious and the political flocks to which they adhered. Nevertheless, Catholic Republicans were common enough to serve as testimony that the vote of Catholics was not a sure thing for any candidate bearing a Democratic label.

4

The 1928 Election and the Legacy of Al Smith

Whatever tendency Catholics had to drift away from the Democratic Party in the first quarter of the twentieth century disappeared in 1928 with the nomination of Al Smith for president. This first Catholic presidential candidate of a major party inspired a tremendous turnout of Catholics, many of whom cast their first votes in this election. His candidacy also drew to the polls large numbers inspired to vote against him. As a result of the heightened interest of both groups, almost 8 million more ballots were cast in 1928 than in 1924. This remarkable increase, 26 percent more than the turnout in the preceding presidential election, was not exceeded in any later contest in the twentieth century and was matched only in 1952.

The Roaring Twenties

The First World War left America victorious but disillusioned. None were more dismayed by the peace settlements than Irish-Americans, who had sought to free Ireland from British rule. They accused Woodrow Wilson, suspect as an Anglophile throughout his presidency, of betrayal because of his lack of interest in extending his principle of self-determination to Ireland. In the campaign to defeat the Treaty of Versailles, Senator Henry Cabot Lodge and his associates exploited the grievance of their Irish constituents to the full.

Although the United States rejected the League of Nations and the World Court, it was more than a bystander in the international arena in the 1920s. It took a leading role in the peace movement that produced agreements to reduce naval armaments of the major powers in 1921 and to ban resort to war by virtually the entire international community in 1928.

The "normalcy" that characterized the decade until 1929 brought a booming economy, for which Secretary of the Treasury Andrew Mellon was given a great deal of credit. While most Americans basked in prosperity, farmers complained that they had been left out as they struggled to adjust to shrinking foreign markets in the postwar economy.

Breaking with historic precedent that had made the United States a refuge for the "huddled masses" of Europe, the Congress imposed tight restrictions to curb immigration and to favor the admission of immigrants from northern and western Europe.

With the adoption of the Eighteenth Amendment to the Constitution, an old issue in state politics emerged on the national scene. Prohibition helped to promote sobriety but also fostered the rise of the mobster, the bootlegging trade, and a general upsurge in violent crime. From the time that Prohibition became the law of the land, agitation for its repeal was carried on, generating continued controversy and providing a burning issue throughout the decade.

From Stone Mountain in Georgia came a movement symbolized by white hoods and robes and a fiery cross, the Ku Klux Klan, preaching 100 percent Americanism, an old time religion, and hatred of Negroes, Catholics, and Jews. It plunged into politics, securing control of party organizations, naming candidates, and controlling officeholders in several states in the early twenties. In 1924 its influence split a badly fragmented Democratic National Convention. When in 1925 it mustered forty thousand members for a mammoth march in Washington, it was in decline. Like similar movements before it, it faded quickly, to be recalled in later years only when ambitious politicians like Hugo Black and Robert Byrd had to explain why they had once joined the Klan.

Catholics in the Twenties

No longer fed by vast numbers of immigrants, the Catholic population grew at a moderate rate compared with that registered in the earlier years of the century. The segment of that population that was of old stock—third generation or more—and considered itself as American as anybody else increased substantially. And, partly under pressures generated by the war, those of more recent immigrant stock were rapidly being Americanized. One indication of these pressures was the passage of legislation in several states requiring English as the language of instruction in all schools. In the 1890s, in Illinois and Wisconsin, similar laws had encountered so vigorous a protest that they were repealed soon after enactment.

The Catholic Church became more visible and more assertive on the national scene. The bishops established a permanent national agency in Washington to monitor and influence legislative and other governmental activity. An outgrowth of a coordinating body established to supervise Church activities relating to the military during the war, this agency was continued in peacetime as the National Catholic Welfare Conference with a broader function (Slawson, 1992). When the anticlerical government of

Mexico imposed harsh restrictions on the Church in the 1920s, the conference sought unsuccessfully to influence Republican administrations to persuade Mexico to relax its oppressive policy.

In 1926 the eyes of the nation turned toward Chicago, where 1 million people participated in a lavish International Eucharistic Congress sponsored by American Catholics. This was the twenty-seventh gathering of a congress of this type, bringing together ecclesiastical dignitaries from all parts of the world, but the first time such a spectacle had been witnessed in this country. It was held here to celebrate the sesquicentennial of the founding of the United States. At outdoor ceremonies of great pomp and splendor, the faithful of all ranks filled the vast expanse of Soldiers' Field, proclaiming that their Church had come of age in the United States. The attention given to this pageant by the press across the nation exceeded any hitherto accorded to a Catholic function. Among newsworthy events noted by the press was the action of the governor of New York as he bent a knee to kiss the ring of Cardinal Bonzano, the papal delegate to the Eucharistic Congress.

The governor of New York was Alfred E. Smith, four times elected to the office, the most prominent Catholic officeholder of the era. For at least half of the decade his supporters conducted a campaign to make him the first Catholic president. His candidacy, as has been noted, stimulated an extraordinary level of political activism among Catholics throughout the nation.

Well-established Democratic machines, heavily Irish Catholic in composition, held sway in several major cities, New York, Boston, and Jersey City being prime examples. Forty-two Catholics were members of the United States Congress in 1923 (thirty-five of them Democrats). The Senate included two Democrats named Walsh who distinguished themselves—one by vigorous investigation of corruption in the national government, the other by breaking the tradition that none but a Yankee could be a senator from Massachusetts.

During the Republican administrations of the twenties, appointment of Catholics to posts in either the executive or judicial branches of the national government was rare. Of 207 judges selected for the bench below the Supreme Court over twelve years, only 8 of the nominees were Catholics (Lubell 1956, 78). On the death of Chief Justice Edward D. White in 1922, however, President Harding nominated Pierce Butler, a Catholic like White, to the court as an associate justice.

The appointment, construed by some as recognition that there should be a "Catholic seat" on the court, infuriated a resurgent anti-Catholic movement then near its high point. This movement, with the Klan as its most conspicuous symbol, put Catholics on the defensive in several parts of the nation. A flood of publications recycling old familiar charges against Catholics sprang up. The Knights of Columbus Oath, a pledge allegedly taken by members of this fraternal order to do heinous injury to Protestants, was widely circulated even though it had been repeatedly exposed as fraudulent. In some states the Klan and its allies launched an attack on the Catholic school system. In Oregon legislation was enacted by referendum requiring all children to be educated in public schools—a requirement which the Supreme Court of the United States declared unconstitutional in *Pierce* v *Sisters of the Society of the Holy Name*, 268 U.S. 510 (1925).

Anti-Catholicism was bipartisan. In the North, particularly in the Midwest, the Klan was an effective force in the Republican Party. In the one-party South many young Democratic politicians found Klan membership helpful in advancing their careers. The most strident voice in Congress denouncing Catholicism was that of Senator Thomas J. Heflin, a Democrat from Alabama. The Democratic National Convention of 1924, following William Jennings Bryan's advice, refused, after a bitter floor fight and by the narrowest of margins, to condemn the Klan by name in its platform. At the Republican convention a proposal to denounce the Klan was quietly buried by the platform committee.

The Democratic Vote in 1928

To arrive at distinctive aspects of voting patterns in 1928 by comparison with another election, one is forced to compare the returns with those of 1920. For different reasons neither the presidential election immediately preceding the contest of 1928 nor the one following it affords a usable basis for comparison. The election of 1924 is an unsatisfactory base because the strong showing of the Progressive Party's presidential candidate, Senator Robert LaFollette of Wisconsin, in that year distorted the voting pattern to be expected in a contest in which the two major parties are unchallenged by serious opposition. In the presidential election following 1928, on the other hand, a new electoral cycle was well under way, with massive realignment of voters under the sting of the depression.

Nationwide in 1928, Al Smith polled 5,874,000 more votes than James Cox, the Democratic presidential candidate in 1920, had received. Herbert Hoover garnered 5,284,000 more votes than were cast for Warren Harding. In terms of percentage, Smith's vote was a gain of 79 percent, Hoover's an increase of 36 percent.

The vote cast by his fellow Catholics accounts for a substantial part of Smith's gain. Probably in no presidential election, before or since, have Catholics been so close to unanimity in their choice of a candidate as they were in 1928. Although lacking the kind of survey techniques developed in later years to determine voting behavior, Gallup estimated some years after the fact that 85 to 90 percent of voting Catholics cast their ballots for the Democratic nominee in that election.

In the two prior presidential elections in the 1920s Catholics appear to have deserted the Democratic banner in impressive numbers. Postwar disillusionment with the party in power during the conflict, peace and prosperity (at least in urban America) under the party in control in the twenties, hard times on the farm, and somewhat obscure and colorless Democratic candidates were all factors in this desertion by a group historically among the most reliable of Democrats.

The low point for a Democratic presidential candidate was 1920. In that election Harding, overwhelmingly victorious outside the South, seems to have made deep inroads into the Catholic vote. From the nation's twelve largest cities (most with a high percentage of Catholics in their population), the Republican candidate garnered a plurality of more than 1.6 million. In New York City all but one of the sixty-two assembly districts were carried by Harding. And, in only two of seventy-seven counties in northern and border states in which Catholics constituted a majority of the population did Cox secure more votes than Harding.

In his autobiography Cox attributed his defeat in part to opposition from "a militantly anti-Wilson Catholic oligarchy" (1946, 273). Al Smith, who lost his bid for reelection as governor in 1920 although running 1 million votes ahead of Cox in New York, believed that the voters of his state had responded to fears that the League of Nations would lead the country into future European wars as well as to resentment of the peace terms on the part of those of Irish, German, and Italian ancestry (Smith 1929, 197–98; *Gaelic American* 30 October 1920).

In 1928 a dramatic reversal of the vote was recorded in the nation's major cities harboring a substantial immigrant population. Samuel Lubell traced the shift in the twelve biggest cities in three presidential elections as a substantial net Republican plurality in 1920 dissolved completely by 1928 (table 4-1). The drastic change in voting behavior in 1928 led Lubell to conclude that "before the Roosevelt Revolution there was an Al Smith Revolution" heralding the end of the long-standing alignment of urban America with the Republican Party. (Lubell 1956, 34–35).

But not all of urban America joined the revolution. Such conversion of urban America to a Democratic stronghold as did take place was decisively influenced by the immigrant hordes who settled in the cities before World War I and who begat large numbers of children who turned into voters in the 1920s. The correlation between immigrant stock and the vote for Smith is well established. One study divided major cities into two categories, separating those with a population 50 percent or more of foreign stock from those with a population 50 percent or more native born of American parentage

TABLE 4–1. Aggregate Plurality in Presidential Elections in the Twelve Largest Cities, 1920–1932

Year	*Net Plurality*	
1920	1,638,000	Republican
1924	1,252,000	Republican
1928	38,000	Democratic
1932	1,910,000	Democratic

Source: Samuel Lubell, *The Future of American Politics* (New York: Harper, 1956), 34.

(table 4-2). Ten of the nation's twelve largest cities fell in the first group, with more than half of their population composed of immigrants or children of immigrants (Degler 1971, 137–41).

Table 4-2 highlights some of the significant differences between the two groups of cities. In terms of the increase in voter turnout and in the size of the Democratic vote, cities with the heaviest concentration of immigrants (Category A) far outpaced the cities with a stronger percentage of native stock in their population (Category B).

An examination of the individual cities composing each category gives added emphasis to the difference in voting behavior between the two groups in 1928.

In nineteen cities of the first category (Category A in Table 4-2) Smith's vote was in every case at least double that given to Cox eight years earlier. In eight of these cities (Milwaukee, Pittsburgh, Los Angeles, Chicago, New York, Buffalo, Philadelphia, and Boston), Smith's vote in 1928 at least trebled that cast for the Democratic candidate in 1920. In the thirteen cities of the second category (Category B in table 4-2), there was considerably less disparity between Smith's vote and that for Cox. In Atlanta, Birmingham, and Columbus fewer votes were cast for Smith than Cox had received eight years earlier. In the other ten cities Smith's vote ran from 70 percent more than Cox's (in New Orleans) to 14 percent more (in Akron and Louisville).

A comparison of the voting behavior in these two classes of cities clearly demonstrates the working of the immigrant factor in the 1928 election. In the cities with a large percentage of residents of immigrant stock, a startling increase in voter turnout was recorded—double that registered in cities in which native stock predominated. Further, in these "immigrant" cities the turnout increase was three times that of the nation as a whole.

The difference between the two groups of cities is also reflected in the distribution of the vote between the parties. In the immigrant cities, 4 million

TABLE 4–2. Aggregate Presidential Vote in Large Cities Categorized by Size of Immigrant Population, 1920 and 1928

	*Presidential Vote Category A Cities**			*Presidential Vote, Category B Cities***		
Year	*Democratic*	*Percent Democratic*	*Republican*	*Democratic*	*Percent Democratic*	*Republican*
1928	4,396,000	47.6	4,843,000	993,000	43.6	1,283,000
1920	1,389,000	26.6	3,856,000	734,000	44.2	925,000

Percentage Increase in Vote: 1928 Compared with 1920

Democratic	*Republican*	*Democratic*	*Republican*
+214	+26	+35	+39

Percentage Increase in Voter Turnout: 1928 Compared with 1920

Category A Cities	*Category B Cities*
76	37

* Category A = cities in which majority of residents were of foreign stock.
** Category B = cities in which majority of residents were of native stock.
Source: Carl N. Degler, "American Political Parties," in *Electoral Change and Stability in American Political History,* eds. Jerome M. Clubb and Howard W. Allen (New York: Free Press, 1971), 124–47.

TABLE 4–3. Democratic Percentage of Presidential Vote in Selected "Catholic Counties," 1928 and 1920

County	*State*	*1928*	*1920*
Costilla	Colorado	62.0	49.1
New Haven	Connecticut	50.5	36.5
Dubois	Indiana	64.7	53.1
Dubuque	Iowa	66.6	37.8
Ellis	Kansas	66.4	23.7
LaFourche	Louisiana	89.1	24.4
St. James	Louisiana	92.1	39.1
Stearns	Minnesota	71.4	10.6
Ste. Genevieve	Missouri	69.9	37.5
Greeley	Nebraska	59.0	46.7
Clinton	New York	59.2	31.4
Emmons	North Dakota	53.6	7.6
Stark	North Dakota	62.7	13.1
Brown	Wisconsin	63.7	30.5
Kewaunee	Wisconsin	71.9	18.6

more votes were cast in 1928 than in 1920, 3 million of which were registered in the Democratic column. This change gave Smith a gain of 21 percentage points when the share of the vote he received is compared with that obtained by Cox. In the native cities, on the other hand, Smith's share of the vote was a shade below that cast for Cox. In these cities Hoover's gain of 350,000 votes over Harding's total exceeded Smith's gain of 250,000 more than the vote received by the Democratic candidate in 1920.

The shift of the vote in the direction of the Democratic ticket was not limited to big cities. It occurred also in smaller communities and rural areas where Catholics were concentrated. (See table 4-3.)

Numerous studies have furnished detail on the tremendous outpouring of Catholics to vote for Al Smith in 1928. David Burner found (1968, 234–43) that Smith received an astounding 95 percent of the vote in Boston's Italian districts and more than eighty percent among the Irish of New York and the Poles of Chicago. J. Joseph Huthmacher (1959, 180) has documented the overwhelming vote cast for Smith in several Catholic communities of Massachusetts.

Not much more than one-third of Smith's vote, however, could have come from Catholics. Others not of his faith—relatively recent immigrants and others who felt a stigma of minority status in the society—were attracted to a candidate up from the city streets who would understand their struggle and their aspirations. Among such groups Jewish voters, who had been in the habit of voting Republican, were conspicuous. Smith carried with 78 percent of the vote the Jewish areas of Chicago in which Cox had received 28 percent. The traditionally Republican blacks of New York City gave Smith more than 40 percent of their vote after having cast only 3 percent for Cox in 1920.

Smith also made modest inroads among farmers and ranchers in parts of the Midwest and Rocky Mountain states. The failure of Republican administrations to relieve the distress of rural America led some prominent midwestern Republicans like Senators Norris of Nebraska and Blaine of Wisconsin to support the Democratic ticket. LaFollette declared himself a neutral in the 1928 contest but noted that the Democratic Party's views on several issues were close to his own. It is clear that many who cast their ballots for the Progressive party in 1924 expressed their continued dissatisfaction by voting Democratic in 1928. If the states are ranked in order of the magnitude of the margin by which the Democratic share of the presidential vote in 1928 exceeded that in 1920, six of the top ten states are in the Midwest (see table 4-4). In these six midwestern states LaFollette ran a strong race, capturing his home state of Wisconsin and outpolling the Democratic nominee, John

TABLE 4–4. Ten States Registering Largest Increase in Democratic Share of Presidential Vote: 1928 Compared with 1920

	Democratic Vote		*Percentage Point Increase*
	1928	*1920*	
1. Wisconsin	44.3	16.2	28.1
2. North Dakota	44.5	18.2	26.3
3. Massachusetts	50.2	27.8	22.4
4. Minnesota	40.8	19.4	21.4
5. New York	47.4	27.0	20.4
6. South Dakota	39.2	19.7	19.5
7. Rhode Island	50.2	32.8	17.4
8. Illinois	42.3	25.5	16.8
9. Connecticut	45.6	33.0	12.6
10. Iowa	37.6	25.5	12.1

W. Davis, in four of the others. It is clear from the returns of counties that had been strongholds of the Progressive Party in 1924 that the discontent of the farm population was still alive in 1928 and contributed, albeit modestly, to Smith's vote.

That there was much in the Democratic candidate's background, speech, and manner that was foreign to rural America was noted by his advisers on farm policy during the campaign. Analysts of the election in their postmortems also have pointed out that Smith did not fit well in William Allen White's America. (White 1926). Smith was reported to have asked at some point the jocular question, "What states are west of the Mississippi?" The question was in a class with Bryan's reference to the Northeast as "enemy territory" in 1896. An incident like this, even though it may have been apocryphal, effectively emphasizes one of Smith's limitations. His outlook, fashioned by experience confined to the politics of New York, was parochial. It was a handicap in carrying his campaign to inhabitants of places that may have appeared to be terra incognita to him. It is very likely that a different Democratic candidate would have had more success than Smith in mobilizing the discontent of rural America, and a different candidate certainly would have kept the solid South intact for the Democratic Party.

Al Smith would not, and could not, be remade into a candidate who could effectively reach across the cultural divide which separated him (along with many millions of Americans) from the majority of his countrymen. He was a New Yorker, a Catholic, Irish by ancestry (although later research suggested also Italian and German forebears), a wet, a Tammany Hall loyalist, a career big-city politician complete with brown derby and cigar. As such, Smith represented and energized as no one else of his era could have done a powerful emerging force in American politics—a substantial accomplishment which Lubell summarized in these words: "What Smith really embodied was the revolt of the underdog, urban immigrant against the top dog of old American stock" (Lubell 1956, 39).

Yet it should be recognized that at least half of the vote cast for the Democratic presidential ticket in 1928 must have come from voters who did not fit in any of the categories we have enumerated. As in every election, the tradition of party loyalty, though weaker than usual, had its effect, and millions of Protestant and religiously unaffiliated Democrats voted for their party, many overcoming misgivings about the candidate as they did so.

Democratic Losses

In twenty-one states, Smith's share of the vote fell below that which had been cast for Cox in 1920 when the Democrats hit their lowest point in two-party presidential races since Reconstruction. Fourteen of these states were southern or border states, and the decline in the percentage of the vote cast for the Democratic candidate was greatest in this region, dropping by as much as twenty-six percentage points in Florida and twenty-three points in Texas. Even in two states which Smith carried, Georgia and Alabama, a severe falloff in the Democratic vote occurred. In two other states, South Carolina and Mississippi, which Smith carried handily, the decline in the Democratic share of the vote was relatively modest, less than five percentage points. In Louisiana (with a large Catholic population) and in Arkansas (with its Senator Joseph T. Robinson as the vice presidential candidate) the Democratic ticket received a higher percentage of the vote than in 1920—substantially higher in the case of the Bayou state. In the midwestern states of Indiana, Kansas, and Ohio, and in the western states of Arizona, Colorado, New Mexico, and Oregon, the share of the vote accorded to Smith failed to match that given to Cox by margins ranging from one percentage point (in Oregon) to six points (in Kansas).

In the South Democratic losses were most severe in the cities (New Orleans excepted) and particularly in metropolitan areas experiencing heavy in-migration from the North. In the Midwest and the Far West it was in small towns and farm areas that the drop-off in the Democratic share of the vote was heaviest. In all regions losses were greatest where immigrants were few, where Protestant churches (especially Baptist, Methodist, Lutheran, and fundamentalist sects) predominated, and where the Ku Klux Klan had flourished.

The Issues of 1928

On a few questions of public policy there was clear disagreement between the two presidential candidates in 1928. Prohibition, which had bedeviled the nation since its enactment, was by far the most important. There were also differences—less clear-cut—regarding the use of the tariff to protect domestic industry, as well as a sharper difference with regard to public ownership of electric power facilities.

But it is doubtful that any of these matters, except for Prohibition, weighed heavily in the minds of any large number of Americans as they made their voting decisions. The dominant issue was Governor Smith's Catholicism. To the Catholics who flocked to the polls in unprecedented numbers and in close to unanimity of opinion, the question they answered when they cast their vote was whether the door to the White House should be closed to Catholics because of their religion. To many non-Catholics who voted for Hoover, the question was whether a Catholic—or at least this Catholic—could be trusted to respect some of the nation's basic principles and uphold the rights of his countrymen who were not of his Church.

The religious issue raised in the campaign of 1928 embraced a wide range of objections to Catholics and their Church, running from the serious and the scholarly to the absurd and the scurrilous. Objections of the former type appeared when the *Atlantic Monthly* in the spring of 1927, in anticipation of the outcome of the Democratic convention of the following year, published an "Open Letter to the Honorable Alfred E. Smith." The article, written by Charles C. Marshall, a New York lawyer and Episcopal layman, challenged the eligibility of any Catholic to hold the presidency and perhaps any public office in the United States, alleging conflict between the religious duty of a Catholic and the civic duty of an American. The charge that Catholics had dual and inconsistent loyalties had been raised from the earliest period of the nation's history and consistently denied by the American hierarchy. Nevertheless, pronouncements of councils, popes, and other ecclesiastics on Church and state down through the years continued to trouble sincere and tolerant Protestants and to raise doubt about the conduct to be expected of a Catholic president.

The response to Marshall's attack, published under the caption "Alfred E. Smith, Catholic and Patriot, Replies," answered in specific and unequivocal terms each of the concerns that had been raised in the "Open Letter." Summarizing his creed as that of "an American Catholic," Smith affirmed his devotion to freedom of conscience, to the First Amendment guarantee of freedom of religion, to separation of church and state, to the public school, and to the equality of all churches before the law as a matter of right. He firmly rejected any claim of "power in the institutions of my Church to interfere with the operations of the Constitution of the United States or the enforcement of the law of the land." And to quiet fear that as president he might intervene to end the persecution of the Church in Mexico, Smith asserted his belief "in the principle of non-interference . . . in the internal affairs of other nations." As legislator and as governor, Smith pointed out, he had established a record that should have put to rest the concerns that troubled Marshall. He had taken an oath of office nineteen times in all, and, he declared, he had never encountered any conflict between his official duties and his religious beliefs (Smith 1927, 721–28).

Although Smith believed that the service which he and many other Catholics had rendered to their country made the questions in Marshall's article unnecessary and insulting, he conceded that this controversy was conducted on "a high plane." The bulk of the attack directed against him on religious grounds by others, however, deserved no such characterization. All the old familiar allegations against Catholic doctrine and practice, against popes and clerics, against the Jesuits and other orders of priests and nuns were resurrected.

A charge which often appeared in the anti-Catholic campaign literature of 1928 accused members of the Church-sponsored fraternal organization, the Knights of Columbus, of taking a secret oath to exterminate non-Catholics. As reported in several publications such as the *Fellowship Forum*, this oath pledged that, sparing "neither age, sex, nor condition," the Knights were to "hang, waste, boil, flay, strangle, and burn alive these infamous heretics [the Protestants] . . . rip up the stomachs and wombs of their women and crush infants' heads against the wall, in order to annihilate forever their execrable race." Among the weapons of annihilation recommended in the oath were "the poison cup, the strangulation cord, the pistol, and the poniard" (Burner 1968, 204). That such nonsense could have gained credence even among the most bigoted and uninformed residents of twentieth-century America is hard to believe. The Knights of Columbus made a vigorous effort to puncture this falsehood by offering a reward to anyone who could produce evidence that the oath was genuine and by successful libel suits against several people who circulated the spurious oath.

Equally incredible tales, many recycled from past anti-Catholic campaigns, were spread in a torrent of publications largely associated with the Klan and certain fundamentalist sects. Weapons, it was said, were stockpiled in Catholic churches; land had been purchased for a papal residence on Maryland's eastern shore to be occupied upon the inauguration of a Catholic president; the Holland Tunnel under the Hudson River, which Smith had opened, would serve as a link in an underwater connection between the Vatican and the United States.

Intertwined with the campaign against Smith that frontally attacked his religious affiliation was a stream of vicious abuse of a personal character directed against the candidate and Mrs. Smith. The caricatures of Al and Katie that were circulated echoed the themes that *Harper's Weekly* had used to lampoon the Irish immigrant in the nineteenth century.

The issue of Prohibition undoubtedly played some part in the voting pattern of 1928. It was a question on which the views of the presidential candidates were in conflict. The difference between them was easy to grasp. One was "wet," and the other was "dry." The cultural clash in the election was reinforced by the division along religious lines about "the noble experiment," Hoover's description of Prohibition. The Eighteenth Amendment had been placed in the Constitution largely because of the persistent effort of several major Protestant Church bodies. "Scarcely a Protestant minister in the country . . . outside the Protestant Episcopal Church and the Unitarian fold," one writer observes, "failed to endorse prohibition. To millions of Protestants, both ministers and laymen, the crusade to drive liquor from America was the greatest moral issue in their lives" (Miller 1956, 150).

No campaign in the nation's history has sparked as extensive a mobilization of major Protestant denominations in the election process or as conspicuous a participation by their clergy as did the electoral battle of 1928. The mobilization of the churches began in July with a conference at Asheville, North Carolina, called by the dominant figure in the movement, Bishop James Cannon of the Methodist Episcopal church and by a prominent Baptist, A. J. Barton. By Election Day it had reached congregations in all parts of the nation (Cannon 1928, 376–77). The church-related press of the Methodists, Baptists, Lutherans, Presbyterians, and Congregationalists campaigned vigorously for Hoover, breaking away from the neutrality they had observed in past national elections and to which they returned in 1932, even though that contest was to decide the fate of Prohibition.

Although emphasizing Smith's wetness, the Protestant press did not ignore the religious considerations which they believed provided valid reasons for voting against the Democratic candidate. The nondenominational *Christian Century* took pains to absolve from the charge of bigotry those who found Smith's Catholicism a reason for voting for Hoover. The publication explained its logic in the following passage:

> The increase of Catholic influence in American society threatens certain institutions which are integral to our American system. With a Roman Catholic in the White House the influence of the Roman Catholic system will be enormously increased in American social and political life. Therefore . . . this voter declines to assist in its extension by helping to put its representative at the head of the government. In so declining, and in using whatever influence this voter may have to persuade others likewise to decline, he is not acting as an intolerant person, or a bigot, but as an intelligent and faithful American citizen. (Miller 1956, 158)

On occasion the *Christian Century* put its views in less judicious language, appealing to xenophobic anti-Catholicism. Protestants, it declared on 18 October 1928 "cannot look with unconcern upon the seating of a representative of an alien culture, of a medieval Latin mentality, of an undemocratic hierarchy, and of a foreign potentate in the great office of the President of the United States."

Methodist Bishop Adna W. Leonard of Buffalo struck a similar note, mincing no words in calling on the "Nordic, Protestant, English-speaking world" for "Anglo-Saxon unity against foreigners, particularly the Latins . . . who trample on our flag" (quoted in Silva 1962, 16). Recalling Smith's greeting to the papal delegate to the International Eucharistic Congress in 1926, Bishop Leonard declared, "No Governor can kiss the Papal ring and get within gunshot of the White House" (quoted in Moore 1956, 21).

Catholicism was the dominant issue in 1928. The most careful and sophisticated study of the election, written by Allan J. Lichtman, reported, "Of all possible explanations for the distinctive political alignments of 1928, religion is the best. . . . Religious considerations preoccupied the public, commanded the attention of political leaders and sharply skewed the behavior of voters" (Lichtman 1979, 231–32). Lichtman's opinion was shared by other scholars, journalists, and practicing politicians, notably by the Democratic national and local leaders polled after the election by newly elected governor Franklin D. Roosevelt. It is important to understand what Lichtman is saying. His analysis concludes that the difference most commonly found in the behavior of the electorate when the 1928 election is compared with several that preceded it was a shift of Protestants to Hoover and a shift of Catholics to Smith.

This is not to say that Al Smith would have won had he been of a different religion or that any other candidate whom the Democrats might have chosen could have won. Nineteen twenty-eight was a Republican year. With prosperity at home and a placid world environment, with an electorate generally satisfied and strongly Republican, there was no powerful pressure for a change of government. Had the Democrats nominated a Protestant in 1928, he would in all probability have shared the fate of the Protestants the party chose as its candidates in 1920 and 1924. Indeed, the fact that Al Smith could win the Democratic presidential nomination without any great struggle was in itself evidence that party professionals held no strong hope of victory in 1928.

The Republican Party and the Religious Issue

In his speech accepting the Republican nomination, Herbert Hoover voiced a general endorsement of religious tolerance, and he said nothing in the course of the campaign to encourage the outpouring of anti-Catholic venom that characterized many of the attacks on his opponent. The bulk of the attack on Smith on religious grounds emanated from sources other than the Republican Party. It was led by clerical personages, particularly of Methodist and Baptist persuasion.

The dominant figure in the attack was James Cannon, Jr., bishop of the Methodist Episcopal Church South and chairman of an organization called Anti-Smith Democrats. It was he who mobilized a variety of Protestant churches to elect Hoover in the aftershock that set in with the realization that "the Democratic party had, like the City of New York, come under the direction and control of Roman Catholics" (Cannon 1928, 376–77).

Not that Republican Party officials were above this fray. There is abundant evidence to establish their complicity in the movement to exploit anti-Catholic feeling in at least several southern states. Specific actions of this kind on the part of national committee members and Republican candidates for office in Alabama, Louisiana, North Carolina, Oklahoma, and Virginia have been amply documented.

A principal source of the anti-Catholic material that was circulated was a publication named the *Fellowship Forum*. Among its owners were the Republican national committeeman from Virginia and the Republican candidate for governor of West Virginia. Oliver Street, Chairman of the Republican campaign in Alabama, distributed 200,000 copies of a circular titled "Governor Smith's Membership in the Roman Catholic Church and Its Proper Place as an Issue in This Campaign." It asserted, as did many other pieces of campaign literature, that "it has been the everlasting unwritten law of this nation since its creation . . . that only a Protestant shall be President of the United States." The "bar against Catholics," it declared was "absolute," apparently nullifying the constitutional ban on any religious test for public office (Williams 1932, 223).

This type of campaigning had some sanction from national party leaders. Shortly before the election the Democrats produced a letter on Republican National Committee stationery written by a top campaign official, Senator George Moses of New Hampshire. The letter transmitted to a North Carolina editor an anti-Catholic column (which Moses called "hot stuff") for distribution to the press in the state without implicating the Republican Party. A circular authored by a Republican Party official in Virginia, Mrs. Willie W. Caldwell, calling on the women of America to save the nation from being "Romanized and rum-ridden," prompted the press to query Republican Party Chairman Hubert Work about this appeal. The queries drew from the chairman a Delphic utterance, "There are two sides to every question."

In due course, four days after the *New York Times* published a critical editorial entitled "Hoover Should Speak Out," the Republican candidate himself reacted with his strongest statement on the subject of religion as an issue. Referring to Mrs. Caldwell's opus, Hoover expressed "indignation at any such circulars" (while suggesting the offending document might have been forged), "Religious questions," he declared, "have no part in this campaign. I have repeatedly stated that neither I nor the Republican Party want support on that basis" (Williams 1932, 221).

The *New York World* commented that Hoover, instead of giving attention to the activity of a relatively obscure local figure, should have put a halt to the campaign carried on by an official of the Justice Department, Mabel Walker Willebrandt. Mrs. Willebrandt's major role was the stimulation and exploitation of opposition to the Democratic ticket among Protestant religious organizations. Undertaking an ambitious schedule of speeches before such groups throughout the campaign, Mrs. Willebrandt urged her audiences to organize and get to the polls. Speaking to a convention of 2,000 Methodist pastors in Ohio, she reminded them that they had 600,000 members in their churches, "enough to swing the election." She added, "Every day and every ounce of your energy are needed to rouse the friends of Prohibition to register and vote" (Lichtman 1979, 91).

Mrs. Willebrandt contended that she warned her religious audiences not of the danger of installing a Catholic in the White House but solely of the consequences of electing a candidate connected with liquor and Tammany corruption. Nevertheless, the *Chicago Tribune,* which supported Hoover, asserted in an editorial on 22 September 1928 that "by any construction of her language, she appealed to religious prejudice." And the Democratic *New York World* for 1 October 1928, accusing her of provoking "religious strife," called on Hoover to "suppress" her and "reaffirm the principle that in the United States Church and State are still disassociated" (Williams 1932, 221–22) The Republican national chairman was eager to keep his distance from the lady, calling her a "free agent" even as his committee scheduled her appearances.

What judgment should be made about the Republican Party's responsibility for the anti-Catholic campaign of 1928? If the party's candidates and officials did not, for the most part, inspire it or participate directly in it, they profited from it and made only perfunctory effort to disown it.

At the height of the campaign, one of Hoover's supporters, Bernard Baruch, whose counsel was sought by several presidents during his long career as an elder statesman, expressed his amazement "at the virulence and persistence of the attacks on Governor Smith's religion and the appeal to other religions." In a letter addressed to Hoover on 16 October 1928, he continued "I believe that if you realized their possible grave effects of a permanent nature on respect for all religion in this country you would find some way to avoid these attacks, prevent some of these appeals, and use your high standing to temper these results."

In reply, Hoover complained of "virulent activities on the Catholic side" reported to him "from all over the country." "If we were to expose 10% of the material sent to us it would shock the country," he wrote on 19 October. He turned aside Baruch's plea with the observation "There is no controling the extremists on either side" (19 October 1928, in Prepresidential Correspondence, Herbert Hoover Library, West Branch, Iowa).

After the election the *Nation*, which had supported Smith, editorialized that Hoover owed his victory to "Prejudice, Bigotry, Superstition, Intolerance, Hate, Selfishness, Snobbery, and Passion. . . . It is idle to say he did not wish their aid. . . . To them Herbert Hoover is in lasting debt." Instead of giving these malevolent forces the "rebuke . . . the scorning and scourging which should have been theirs," Hoover, the *Nation* alleged, tacitly accepted their help (quoted in *Catholic World,* 28 December 1928).

Similarly writing before the passion of the contest had had time to cool, the Jesuit weekly *America* on 1 December 1928 called the 1928 campaign "the most fearful outpouring of anti-Catholic slander this country has ever known" and asserted, "From first to last every agency of bigotry in this country worked for the success of the Republican party. From first to last, not one decisive word against any of these agencies was spoken either by Mr. Hoover, or by anyone entitled to speak for the party."

A disinterested scholar years later rendered a similar judgment on Republican culpability. Allan Lichtman (1979, 67) wrote,

> The evidence shows that Republicans mounted no campaign against anti-Catholic agitation, even within their own ranks. The party organization neither disciplined those who pandered to religious bigotry nor attempted to police their activities. Until forced by circumstance, Herbert Hoover refused to denounce religious bigotry forcefully. . . . Fragmentary evidence further suggests that the Republican leadership deliberately set out, covertly, to exploit Protestant opposition to the election of a Catholic president.

Enduring Effects of the 1928 Election

To the great mass of Catholics the campaign of 1928 was a shock and its outcome a bitter disappointment. That their hero had gone down to defeat was not the only reason for grief. The campaign had made clear the barriers that separated them from millions of their fellow Americans. They had known of the existence of anti-Catholicism, but, until the floodgates of intolerance were opened with the nomination of Al Smith, they had not known its extent and depth. It was a shock to learn that they were regarded with suspicion and even contempt and that their devotion to the country they had lovingly served in war and peace was widely questioned.

Many Catholics shared the opinion of the *Catholic World* that Smith's "religion was the deciding factor in his defeat," a view expressed by even the scholarly John A. Ryan. They dismissed the issue of Prohibition as "a convenient camouflage for religious prejudice" (*Catholic World*, 28 December 1928; Lichtman 1979, 89). And many interpreted the outcome of the election as an endorsement of the "unwritten law" barring Catholics from the presidency, of which much had been heard in the campaign.

This interpretation of the determinative influences behind the outcome of the 1928 election cannot stand up to close scrutiny. Powerful as anti-Catholic sentiment was in amassing the vote cast for Hoover, it was not the strongest reason for Governor Smith's defeat. No Democrat opposing Herbert

Hoover, the candidate of the dominant party of the era, would have won the presidency in that year of prosperity at home and tranquillity abroad. As Ruth Silva (1962) concluded in her scholarly study of voting behavior in 1928, Smith was a strong candidate and probably the best vote-getter that his party could have offered in that year. There is no reason to believe that a Protestant candidate would have fared better than had Cox and Davis in their unsuccessful campaigns.

Determinative or not in the election results, the strong expression of anti-Catholic sentiments in the 1928 campaign left lasting wounds. A widely shared sentiment was expressed by Father John A. Ryan of Catholic University in his postelection analysis: "As a Catholic I cannot be expected to rejoice that some millions of my countrymen would put upon me and my co-religionists the brand of civic inferiority" (1928, 381).

Historian David J. O'Brien asserts that the experience of 1928 "served to perpetuate and accentuate the isolation and insecurity of American Catholics" and retarded their progress (1968, 45–46). Richard Hofstadter found that the election "with its religious bigotry and social snobbery" inflicted "a status trauma" on Irish-Americans still perceptible in the mid-1950s (1963, 86).

The 1928 campaign also had lasting effects beneficial to the Democratic Party in the elections which followed. It was the beginning of a movement that brought to the polls millions hitherto outside the arena of political activity. The new voters came particularly from the families of the pre-World War I immigrants and from women, still somewhat hesitant to exercise the right to vote guaranteed by the Nineteenth Amendment to the Constitution (Andersen 1979, 7–10; 32–38). That the new voters included a disproportionate number of Catholics is suggested by survey findings that, of those who cast their first vote in 1928 although they had reached voting age by the year of an earlier election, 53 percent cast their votes for Smith (Campbell et al. 1960, 155). These Catholics and others introduced to the franchise in Al Smith's campaign gave overwhelming support to Franklin D. Roosevelt in four elections and, with relatively minor defections, maintained their loyalty to the Democratic Party in presidential contests through 1948.

As a result of the 1928 campaign, the Republican Party acquired anew its reputation of unfriendliness to Catholics which had faded with Roosevelt and Taft in the early years of the twentieth century. In responding to actions of his supporters who blatantly appealed to prejudice, Hoover was cautious and uncertain. In his autobiography he called "the religious issue" the "worst plague in the campaign." Nevertheless, he chided his opponent for "unwittingly fanning the flame" by addressing the subject of anti-Catholicism in a speech in Oklahoma City instead of ignoring it (Hoover 1951–52, 2: 208). To many this blame-shifting sounded like ascribing guilt to the one who sounded the fire alarm rather than the arsonist who lit the flame.

In the 1920s, antedating the Hoover-Smith campaign, a series of events had served to keep alive the anti-Catholic reputation of the Republican Party. In some states—notably Colorado, Indiana, and Ohio—the Ku Klux Klan had exercised a strong influence in the party. In 1924, whereas both Democrat Davis and Progressive LaFollette condemned the Klan, the other presidential candidate, "Silent Cal" Coolidge, lived up to his nickname, saying nothing about the organization while enjoying the endorsement of its leaders (Burner 1968, 134).

In the era of Democratic dominance beginning in the 1930s, the South returned to the fold after the temporary aberration in its voting behavior in 1928. From 1932 through the World War II years southerners were as solid in their support of the Democratic Party as they had been in the half century before 1928.

For victory in national elections, however, the Democratic Party needed more than this reliable southern base. Catholics were an indispensable part of the added ingredient. These voters united by urban residence, underdog status, economic interest, religious ties, and a recollection of Republican indifference or hostility toward them were an important element of the New Deal coalition that elected Franklin Roosevelt to the presidency and Harry Truman after him. For more than twenty years the Catholic population was overwhelmingly attached to the Democratic Party. This attachment was cemented by many influences, including a catastrophic "Hoover depression" and a new president who inspired confidence that he would rescue the victims of the disaster. But also, in no small part, it was the legacy of Al Smith, who brought an army of newcomers to the electorate as loyal Democrats.

The New Deal Years

The expansion of the electorate generated by Smith's candidacy in 1928 continued for the next dozen years. Voter turnout in the presidential election of 1940 exceeded that of 1928 by 11 million—an increase of 28 percent—despite the slowdown in the population growth rate to a mere 7 percent in the decade of the 1930s. At the end of the decade the electorate included a higher percentage of Catholics than in the mid-twenties, owing particularly to the introduction of new voters with southern and eastern European roots.

With the inauguration of Franklin D. Roosevelt, Catholics also began to emerge in significant numbers as officeholders in the federal government. For the first time since the administration of Theodore Roosevelt, Catholics were nominated for cabinet posts. In the circle of influential advisers to the president and of appointees to high office were names like Farley, Corcoran, Murphy, and Kennedy. As Democrats returned to power in Washington, a bewildering array of alphabetical agencies came into existence to administer the programs of the New Deal, affording patronage opportunities far beyond the largesse available to preceding administrations. The pool of job applicants with the credentials of party loyalty and public service in state and local government undoubtedly contained a disproportionate representation of Catholics. And with people like James A. Farley, Roosevelt's campaign manager in 1932, ensconced in a position to influence the distribution of rewards, discrimination against Catholics was not likely to occur.

In the 1930s Catholics graduated in force from the state and local levels of politics to the national arena. One important indicator of their changed status can be found in an analysis of the religious affiliation of appointees to the federal judiciary. Of the judges chosen by three Republican presidents in the 1920s, only 4 percent were Catholics. In contrast, in the 1930s and 1940s, Catholics were selected for 25 percent of the federal judicial posts filled during the Roosevelt and Truman administrations.

Like Theodore Roosevelt, Franklin D. Roosevelt cultivated a personal relationship with the most influential members of the hierarchy. He had close ties to Cardinal Mundelein of Chicago and, secondarily, to Cardinal Hayes of New York and his successor, Cardinal Spellman. Mundelein's biographer, noting Roosevelt's "remarkable talent for feigning intimacy" with people he was using, wrote that the Cardinal "served Roosevelt as friend, occasional confidante, Catholic mouthpiece, and even messenger boy." As his major service, Mundelein by "pro-Roosevelt speeches and activities certified for Catholic voters that Roosevelt was a safe, non-Communist political leader" (Kantowicz 1983, 234–35).

Perhaps the most striking service performed by the Cardinal in the role of messenger boy was his unsuccessful attempt to persuade James A. Farley to stay out of the contest for the Democratic presidential nomination in 1940, thereby removing an obstacle to Roosevelt's bid for an unprecedented third term in the White House. Farley later wrote that he responded to the plea by remarking that in his thirty years in politics Mundelein was "the first person in the Church who has ever attempted to influence me on a political matter" (Farley 1948, 175). The remark must have surprised the Cardinal, described by his biographer as having been "neckdeep in politics throughout the 1930s" (Kantowicz 1983, 222).

There was, in the words of one scholar, "a fortuitous similarity between much of the New Deal's reform legislation and the social and economic teachings of the Church" (Flynn 1968, ix). A document issued in 1919 entitled the "Bishops' Program for Social Reconstruction" foreshadowed certain elements of the program of the Roosevelt administration, including legislation establishing a minimum wage, insurance protecting the aged and the unemployed, and recognition of labor's right to organize.

In a campaign address in 1932, Roosevelt linked his economic philosophy to that which Pope Pius XI had enunciated a year earlier in his encyclical *Quadragesimo Anno*. And, as the New Deal unfolded, several administration spokesmen and many Catholic theorists, led by John A. Ryan, author of the bishops' 1919 program, pointed out how it meshed with the social doctrine of the Church. The program offered by the president to combat the desperate condition of a floundering nation was received by Catholic spokesmen with enthusiastic approval (Flynn 1968, 36–60).

In four elections Franklin D. Roosevelt received an overwhelming share of the Catholic vote. In 1936, developments threatening to turn Catholic voters away from the Democratic candidate aroused some concern among the party's strategists. Two prominent Catholics who had supported Roosevelt in 1932 were defecting—Al Smith supporting the Republican nominee, Alf Landon, and Father Charles E. Coughlin forming a third party offering a congressman from North Dakota, William Lemke, as its presidential candidate. Although both Smith and Coughlin had commanded a large following in earlier years, their opposition to Roosevelt had a negligible effect on voting behavior in 1936. The influence of Smith is hard to measure; Coughlin's can be estimated in light of the fact that his candidate received less than 2 percent of the vote cast for president.

In 1932 Coughlin had used his radio pulpit to tell his listeners that their choice in the election was between "Roosevelt or Ruin." In 1936 he denounced Roosevelt as a "great liar and betrayer." There is reason to believe that Coughlin's unprecedented activism in the 1936 campaign and the intemperance of his oratory with its undertone of anti-Semitism redounded to Roosevelt's advantage with Catholic voters (Grant 1990, 42–47). To many, the prominent involvement of the radio priest in the campaign against the president was unseemly. Further, the partisan activity of the most widely known Catholic clergyman prompted a countercampaign on the part of several Catholic figures and publications unwilling to allow an impression to form that Father Coughlin spoke for the Church. The highlight of this show of Catholic support for the president was a radio address entitled "Roosevelt Safeguards America" delivered to the nation by Monsignor John A. Ryan (Flynn 1968, 217–27). The abnormal volume of pro-Roosevelt comment and activity by Church personages intended to affect the voting behavior of the nation's Catholics made the 1936 election unusual. This ecclesiastical electioneering was not repeated in Roosevelt's subsequent campaigns.

Father Coughlin's was not the only Catholic voice raised during the 1936 campaign in criticism of the policies of the Roosevelt administration. The chief concerns of other critics, however, focused on matters of foreign policy such as the diplomatic recognition extended to the Soviet Union and the American reaction to Mexico's treatment of the Church rather than on Roosevelt's domestic program.

The opposition to Roosevelt expressed by some leading Catholics aroused a meager response from Catholic voters. Gallup polls suggest that Roosevelt was supported by close to three-quarters of the Catholics who voted in 1936 and by about 70 percent in 1940. When the president ran for his third term, a modest erosion of the vote he received from Catholics from its high point in 1936 is reflected in these figures. The decline in his vote can be accounted for largely by the impact of the war, particularly on those voters of German, Irish, and Italian background whose ethnic sensibilities were still strong. A protest against a policy that pointed toward involvement in the war is discernible in a pronounced vote shift away from Roosevelt in 1940 where Germans had settled (as in Stearns County, Minnesota, and Outagamie County, Wisconsin) or Irish or Italians (as in Queens County, New York).

What is remarkable about the voting behavior of the Catholic population throughout the thirties and forties is how steadfast it remained in its lopsided attachment to the Democratic candidate in presidential elections. By a two-thirds majority, Catholic voters supported Roosevelt in his campaign for a fourth term in 1944, and at least 60 percent voted for Truman in 1948 in his contest against three serious opponents.

Looking back two decades from the election in which Harry Truman confounded the pundits, one finds major changes in the role of Catholicism in political life. The alienation that Catholics felt as a result of the 1928 campaign was in great part dissipated. For this, Franklin D. Roosevelt deserves special credit, for it was his administration that opened a welcoming door to Catholics, giving "them recognition as a major force in society" (Lally 1962, 48; Ladd and Hadley 1978, 49–53).

5

Catholics After World War II: They Liked Ike

A new world grew up in the ashes of the Second World War. The United States became an active world power, the dominant member of a United Nations feeling its way toward international cooperation, the leader in the reconstruction of Europe and Japan, the major, if not the only, barrier to Communist expansion, and the principal warrior in the conflict to defend South Korea against aggression. A substantial share of the country's resources was committed to tasks related to concerns outside our borders in order to maintain the military strength and promote the economic development of the Free World. The Cold War, the struggle to preserve the sphere of freedom against an expansive Communism, became the focal point of foreign policy. And fear that the subversive forces of Communism in our own country would weaken our defenses and imperil our freedom introduced a new issue into domestic politics.

The economic system was converted from war making to the production of goods for peacetime use with relatively minor friction. The output of the economy soared. Thanks to opportunities opened up through the GI Bill of Rights, college campuses swarmed with students, and the educational level of the population bounded upward. Slowly, amid protest and strife, racial barriers began to crumble in the nation's armed forces and schools and eventually in most of society's institutions.

After twenty years of low birth rates, returning veterans and their wartime brides generated a baby boom which drew attention to the state of the nation's educational facilities and caused alarm about a classroom shortage.

Housing the newly formed families also became a concern. The suburbanization of the nation, typified by the mass-produced developments known as Levittowns, gathered steam, helped by programs to enable veterans to become homeowners and, in the fifties, by the interstate highway program.

American Catholics in the Wake of the War

Catholic families did their part in contributing to the postwar baby boom. As a result of higher birth rates and, to a considerably lesser degree as a result of a relaxation of the stringent limits on immigration, the Catholic population increased at a pace even greater than the increase in the total head count.

Young Catholic families joined others of their generation in establishing homes in developing suburbs, leaving the urban ethnic neighborhoods of their childhood to slowly wilt away. With this migration one aspect of Catholic separatism from non-Catholic Americans gradually vanished.

Catholics participated, too, in the rush to the schools. Because of the GI Bill of Rights, which virtually eliminated any economic barrier to a college education for qualified veterans, untold numbers of young men became the first of their family to receive a degree and to enter occupations beyond the reach of their fathers.

As a result of broadened opportunities in education and employment, the postwar years were for the nation's Catholics a time of impressive upward movement. The gains registered were described in one scholarly study as "dramatic," effecting by the 1960s a reversal in the relative standing of Catholics and Protestants "in most aspects of status" (Glenn and Hyland 1967, 85).

The educational benefits of the GI Bill of Rights were granted without discrimination to those who chose church-related colleges and universities as well as students at secular and public institutions. In a sense this policy of including educational institutions with a religious affiliation in the program for veterans was a continuation of a wartime practice of widespread use of such schools for the training of ROTC cadets.

As religious colleges and universities began to receive a substantial inflow of funds from public treasuries, the courts were fashioning new restrictive interpretations of the doctrine of separation of church and state, placing constitutional barriers in the way of government action to assist children attending church-related elementary and high schools. The philosophical underpinnings of two decisions of the Supreme Court—*Everson v. Board of Education*, 330 U.S. 1 (1947) and *McCullom v. Board of Education* 333 U.S. 203 (1948)—were roundly criticized by many Catholic scholars and led the bishops in 1952 to issue a warning against a secular humanism that would "divorce religion from education . . . [and] remove all influence of religion from public life."

One effect of a growing school population and federal educational benefits to veterans was a vast enlargement of Catholic institutions of higher education. At the same time the system of elementary and secondary Catholic schools expanded under the pressures of the postwar baby boom. When the Congress turned its attention to legislation to provide federal financial assistance to the nation's elementary and secondary schools in the 1940s, Catholic Church leaders sought to include for nonpublic schools funds for "auxiliary services"—types of aid such as nonreligious textbooks and transportation which had been ruled constitutional by the Supreme Court. This effort triggered a bitter battle which doomed all congressional action of a general character aiding elementary and secondary education until the latter half of the 1950s. The argument about the Barden bill, the school aid measure, which drew in representatives of a number of denominations as well as educators and such personages as Eleanor Roosevelt and Cardinal Spellman, became particularly tainted by bias and invective on both sides (Lash 1973, 150–61; Gannon 1962, 314–22).

Near the end of 1951, President Truman announced his intention to change the nature of the representation which the United States had maintained at the Vatican since 1940. In place of a personal representative of the president—the practice instituted by Roosevelt when he sent Myron Taylor to Rome—formal diplomatic relations were to be established with the Vatican, and General Mark Clark was to be the first ambassador of the United States to the Holy See.

The nomination of General Clark to serve in this post stimulated another debate in which religious antagonism surfaced. The *Christian Century* on 31 October 1951 accused President Truman of capitulating "to papal pressure for recognition and to his own greed for votes" and pointed to the protest from the leaders of the major Protestant churches and "thousands of pulpits from Maine to California." With the organization Protestants and Other Americans United for the Separation of Church and State and Paul Blanshard, the prolific author of books warning against Catholic power, leading the charge, the president's proposal was a casualty in a battle in which once again Catholics were accused of a dual loyalty inconsistent with American citizenship.

The Election of 1948

Although his party was splintered into three factions in the campaign of 1948, Harry Truman confounded the polls and the pundits by defeating Thomas E. Dewey as well as Strom Thurmond and Henry Wallace in the contest for the presidency. But despite this victory, the seeds of a major realignment of an important part of the Democratic Party's faithful constituency were sown as Alabama, Louisiana, Mississippi, and South Carolina—states which had stuck with the party even in 1928—were carried by Thurmond under the banner of the States' Rights Party. In no election thereafter down to the end of the century was any Democratic presidential candidate to carry the once solid South—all eleven of the states that formed the Confederacy (see table 5-1). In seven of the last eight presidential elections of the twentieth century—all but that of 1976—the desertion of white voters deprived the Democratic candidate of a majority of the votes cast in the South. The

TABLE 5–1. Democratic Presidential Vote in Southern States: Three Eras, 1932–1996

Democratic Majority		*Party Equality*		*Democratic Minority*	
Year	*Percentage of Vote*	*Year*	*Percentage of Vote*	*Year*	*Percentage of Vote*
1932	81	1948	50	1968	31
1936	81	1952	52	1972	29
1940	78	1956	48	1976	54
1944	72	1960	51	1980	44
		1964	50	1984	37
				1988	41
				1992	41
				1996	47

election of 1948 marked the beginning of this major realignment in presidential voting.

White southerners broke long-standing party ties in 1948, but another element of the Democratic coalition retained its historic loyalty. By a margin of two to one, Catholic voters registered a preference for Truman over Dewey. The factors which led to widespread desertion from the Democratic Party by Southerners—the racial issue brought to the fore by the civil rights planks of the Democratic platform and by the candidacy of Strom Thurmond—failed to turn Catholics away from Democratic ranks.

On the other hand, it seems likely that the revolt against Truman by the left-wing elements marshaled by Henry Wallace helped to cement the allegiance of Catholics to the Democratic ticket. Wallace had broken with his party on issues of foreign policy and specifically on the response to Soviet expansionism. By a series of actions Harry Truman had established his credentials as a staunch anti-Communist. The Truman Doctrine and the aerial lifeline to Berlin in defiance of a Soviet-East German blockade were sufficient evidence of the president's stand even without his campaign oratory scornfully rejecting "Henry Wallace and his Communists." Wallace's candidacy highlighted Truman's anti-Communism and diverted attention from policies potentially troublesome to Democrats symbolized by the Yalta Agreement. In 1948, confident of victory, Dewey was loath to raise such issues, which, four years later, were to be exploited in the Eisenhower campaign.

The Eisenhower Victory of 1952

In 1952 the twenty-year reign of the Democrats in Washington was brought to an end. Thirteen million more votes were cast in the presidential election of that year than had been recorded in 1948. So massive an increase in turnout—26 percent—had not been matched since 1928, when religious passion produced an upsurge of the same magnitude. Nor was it equaled in any subsequent election in the twentieth century. Clearly the public was aroused more than it had been in any election of the previous twenty-four years, even those held as depression devastated the nation or as war raged in Europe and American involvement in the conflict came closer.

Eisenhower's triumph in 1952 shattered the voting coalition that had given the Democratic Party possession of the apparatus of the national government for two decades. It gave the Republican Party control of the White House and, narrowly, of the Congress. The presidential ticket scored the most broadly based victory in Republican history. Sweeping every state outside the South, it even cracked the solidity of Dixie as Eisenhower carried four southern states. Midwestern farmers, who had provided crucial support for Harry Truman in 1948, returned to the Republican fold with a vengeance. And the Republican ticket also made substantial inroads among such traditionally Democratic groups as union members and low-income families.

The Catholic Shift in the Fifties

Prominent among the traditionally Democratic groups which shifted most dramatically toward the Republican presidential ticket in 1952 were the Catholics. Dewey had received only thirty-five percent of their vote, Eisenhower won almost fifty percent.

Protestants, a majority of whom had voted for Dewey in 1948, also gave the Republican ticket a greater share of their vote in 1952. The shift among Protestants was, however, only about half the magnitude of that registered by Catholics. The nation's Protestants cast two-thirds of their vote for Eisenhower in 1952. This result was impressive, but Protestants had favored Republican presidential candidates consistently before and after the worst years of the depression. Catholic voting behavior in 1952, on the other hand, was a sharp departure from the usual past pattern. The returns indicated that one of the staunchest Democratic constituencies had broken loose from its moorings.

This conclusion was confirmed by Gallup's analysis of Catholic voting behavior by ethnic group in 1952. One finding, unsurprisingly, indicated that Catholics of German ethnic background were most enthusiastic in their support for Eisenhower, giving him more than 70 percent of their vote. Irish and Polish Catholics divided their vote evenly between the two presidential candidates, and 60 percent of those of Italian background supported Stevenson (Harris 1954, 87–101). It is likely that these results reflect a significant change in voting behavior, although reliable comparable data for previous elections are not available to give precision to the magnitude of the change.

The Democratic Response to Erosion of Catholic Support

Among the "pros" in the Democratic ranks, particularly party leaders in major cities, like Chicago's Jake Arvey, concern that the party would suffer a major desertion of Catholic voters in November was voiced early and often in the 1952 campaign. These party leaders recommended that a Catholic be chosen for the chairmanship of the Democratic National Committee. In response, Stevenson selected for the post Stephen Mitchell, a friend without experience in national politics but one who passed the religious test and was believed to be "close to" Cardinal Stritch of Chicago (Martin 1976, 616–18).

At least one of the intellectuals in the Stevenson entourage shared the concern of the pros. By memorandum Arthur M. Schlesinger Jr. warned the campaign chiefs of a threatened defection of Irish Catholics "because of McCarthy, Hiss, the divorce, and the absence of leading Catholics from . . . headquarters and the campaign plane." He recommended "a full-dress anti-Communist speech," use of well-known Catholic figures like James Rowe and Senator Pastore of Rhode Island in prominent campaign roles, and issuance of a letter explaining Stevenson's position on the aborted Truman initiative of appointing an ambassador to the Vatican (Martin 1976, 681–82). This last recommendation was intended as a means of repairing damage Stevenson was thought by some to have suffered with Catholics because of impromptu remarks he had made rejecting Truman's proposal as a violation of the principle of separation of church and state.

As the campaign unfolded, no appeal tailored to Catholic voters in particular was evident. Stevenson declined Cardinal Spellman's invitation to attend the annual dinner of the Alfred E. Smith Memorial Foundation at the Waldorf Astoria, a gathering of New York's wealthiest and most influential Catholics. Eisenhower was present to deliver a foreign policy speech which the *New York Times* found "skillful and penetrating." Stevenson did speak on the campus of Notre Dame in mid-October, and late in the campaign the fact that fifty-six members of that university's faculty had endorsed the Democratic candidate was given extensive publicity in newspaper advertisements as well as in an address by James A. Farley in what was billed as a climactic rally in Madison Square Garden. The impact of this endorsement by so many

Fighting Irishmen was somewhat undercut by Notre Dame's president, Theodore M. Hesburgh, who, affirming the university's neutrality in the presidential contest, criticized the professors who had endorsed Stevenson for their use of the university's name. He also pointed out that the endorsers constituted only 12 percent of the faculty (*New York Times*, 27 October 1952; 30 October 1952).

One of the strangest events in a campaign that never ran with smooth efficiency was the decision to suppress a strong statement of support for Stevenson signed by 141 prominent Protestant ministers of various denominations after the clergymen had agreed to permit the use of their names. The statement was withdrawn by Volunteers for Stevenson after distribution to the press but before its release date. Interpreting the withdrawal as a concession to avoid offense to Catholic sensibilities, the *Christian Century* in a biting editorial of 26 November entitled "Is Protestant Support a Liability?" speculated that "the Democratic party command is made uncomfortable by having Protestants around."

The Sorensen-Bailey Analysis of the 1952 Election

At the Democratic National Convention of 1956 in an attempt to convince the delegates to nominate John F. Kennedy for vice president, a memorandum was circulated by John Bailey, party chairman for Connecticut, attributing Stevenson's defeat in his first campaign for the presidency largely to the defection of Catholics. Prepared by Kennedy's principal staff assistant and speechwriter, Theodore Sorensen, and widely distributed before the convention to selected party leaders and friendly members of the press corps, it was attributed to Bailey in a transparent effort to mask its real origin in the candidate's office.

The memorandum asserted,

> Catholics in 1952, roughly 25 percent of the voting population, went approximately 1 out of 2 for the Republican candidate. . . . In 1948 they had gone 2 out of 3 for the Democratic nominee. . . . Though they had constituted approximately one-third of the Democratic vote in 1948, they were only 28 per cent of Stevenson's vote and constituted 21 per cent of Eisenhower's. . . . Approximately 30 per cent of Catholics for Eisenhower were "shifters" . . . "normally Democratic Catholics." . . .
>
> . . . If Stevenson could have held in 1952 *only* those Catholics who had voted for Truman in 1948 but for Ike in 1952—or if he could recapture them in 1956—this would . . . *add 132 electoral votes to the Democratic column, enough when combined with the Solid South to provide a majority of electoral votes*!

The memorandum not only identified the states that would provide the added 132 electoral votes but specified with precision the percentage of Eisenhower's 1952 vote in each which came from normally Democratic Catholic voters: New York (11 percent), Pennsylvania (11 percent), Illinois (9.3 percent), Massachusetts (15.3 percent), Connecticut (14.4 percent), and Rhode Island (18.9 percent).

Buttressed by a citation of the vote Al Smith had received in Catholic strongholds, the memorandum arrived at the conclusion that these errant Democrats could be recaptured by placing a "well-known Catholic" on the ticket in 1956 (Sorensen 1960, 68–72).

At one point Stevenson seemed to give some consideration to the argument made in the memorandum, but eventually he came to the conclusion that it advocated too risky a step in view of the extent of prejudice still rampant in the nation. A Catholic running mate, he wrote, "is only to be considered if the boldest steps are necessary" (Martin 1977, 342). Stevenson left the selection of the vice presidential candidate to the Democratic convention, and with the convention's decision to nominate Estes Kefauver, the thesis of the memorandum was not put to a test. Had it been, John Bailey and Theodore Sorensen, author of the memorandum, would in all probability have been revealed as false prophets, and a rising political figure might have capped his career in public life with the title senator from Massachusetts rather than president of the United States.

Factors Affecting Catholic Voting Behavior

The Republican campaign of 1952 was encapsulated at the time in three alliterative words meant to emphasize the failings of the Truman administration—Korea, Communism, corruption. Each was a shorthand expression of concerns which persuaded many Americans to vote against the party in power, but the three are not a sufficient explanation of the impressive turnout nor of the result. In addition to these negative considerations, voters—particularly Independents and Democrats—found a powerful positive reason for voting Republican once the nominations had been made. Eisenhower had an appeal to these groups not matched by Robert Taft, his principal rival for the nomination, or any other conceivable candidate.

Korea

Korea was by far the dominant concern of the voters in 1952, and as the year went by, concern mounted. So the Gallup poll reported on the eve of the election, finding that 52 percent of the public listed Korea among the country's most important problems, double the number who had held that opinion in January. Stevenson was probably correct in his postelection judgment that "the most important contribution to the Republican victory was the impression that General Eisenhower . . . could settle the Korean War promptly" (letter to Claude G. Bowers, 12 December 1952; Johnson 1972–79, 231).

The *Christian Century* of 26 November 1952 ventured the opinion that Catholics, predominantly of the working class, had deserted the Democrats in large numbers in the election because hardship connected with the war affected them more severely than it did groups of higher status. This opinion is plausible, but it is hard to find evidence that Korea influenced the vote of Catholics more powerfully than the vote of other groups.

In dealing with the war in Korea the Republican campaign in 1952 focused on a series of alleged misjudgments on the part of the Truman administration. The withdrawal of American troops from the Korean peninsula in 1949, the Republicans argued, was based on misjudgment of North Korea's readiness to resort to force as well as of South Korea's ability to defend itself. The speech delivered by Secretary of State Dean Acheson in January 1950 proclaiming to the world that Korea lay "outside our defense perimeter" was cited as another example of misjudgment on the part of the administration giving a false signal to our adversaries. Republican orators argued that this drawing of a boundary line limiting the American defense perimeter was tantamount to an assurance to North Korea that an attack on the South would not provoke intervention by the United States. Five months after this speech North Korea attacked.

The issue of Korea in the 1952 campaign was less whether the country could have avoided getting into the war then how to get out. As was to happen later in regard to Vietnam, the public lost whatever enthusiasm it had initially for pursuing the conflict. The United Nations forces appeared to have become bogged down in a stalemate in which casualties continued as peace talks dragged on inconclusively. A public which wanted the war to end but (unlike many at the time of Vietnam) was not ready to accept defeat eagerly responded to the campaign declaration, "I will go to Korea," willing to trust Eisenhower to find an acceptable end to yet another war.

The Communist Issue

A second theme of the Republican campaign, anti-Communism, was one to which Catholics appear to have been particularly responsive. Stevenson noted "tremendous disaffection among the Irish Catholics because of 'Communists in government'" (Johnson 1972–79, 231). The *Brooklyn Tablet*, the organ of the Diocese of Brooklyn and a favorite of conservative Catholics, framed the reason for disaffection in broader terms, telling its readers in mid-October,

> Communism is the issue of the day. Abroad the atheistic forces directed from within the Kremlin have enslaved nations and peoples. . . . They have ruthlessly and contemptuously trampled on every Christian concept of freedom and human rights. At home the agents of atheistic Communism have infiltrated our Government, our schools, our labor unions, our intellectual and even religious fortresses.

Catholics were used to hearing about the threat of Communism. In 1937 in the encyclical *Divini Redemptoris*, entitled *On Atheistic Communism* in its English version, Pope Pius XI reviewed the string of utterances from the Vatican condemning Communism going back to 1846. Indeed, the pope asserted, "The Papacy has called public attention to the perils of Communism more frequently and more effectively than any other public authority on earth." At the time of this encyclical, the pope declared, an attack on "Christian civilization," directed from Moscow, was being carried on by "the most persistent enemies of the Church." To the faithful he addressed a warning against collaboration with Communism "in any undertaking whatsoever."

In the aftermath of World War II, the expansionist policies of Moscow demonstrated in the imposition of Communist governments throughout Eastern Europe, the coup in Czechoslovakia, the Berlin blockade, the support of Communist parties in Italy and elsewhere, and widespread Soviet espionage caused grave alarm in the Free World. As Western Europe, Canada, and the United States were forming NATO as a shield against further Communist aggression in Europe, a new shock came with the Communist military victory over the Nationalist forces of Chiang Kai-shek in China.

Reaction to the threats posed by Communism was strong in the United States—in some respects stronger than in countries more exposed to the military power of the Soviet Union. The federal government embarked on an offensive against subversion—a program to root out disloyal employees in the federal service, legislation passed over President Truman's vetoes to require registration of Communist-related organiations and to keep subversives out of the country, and, above all, vigorous use of the investigative power to expose disloyalty. The actions taken by the federal government were replicated by the states. In 1949 alone the legislatures of fifteen states enacted anti-Communist laws (Prendergast 1950, 556–74).

Catholics were in the forefront of the anti-Communist movement. As satellite governments in Poland, Hungary, and Yugoslavia embarked on a program of suppressing the Church, Catholic spokesmen in the United States responded with a heightened counterattack. It was conducted in the pulpit and the press and through myriad Church organizations, notably the Knights of Columbus and the Catholic War Veterans. European churchmen such as Archbishop Stepinac of Yugoslavia and Cardinal Mindszenty of Hungary, imprisoned by the Communist regimes which ruled their countries, became well known in the United States as their names were given to newly built American Catholic schools.

Captive Nations and the Appeal to Ethnic Voters A dynamic element was added to Catholic anti-Communist ranks by the enactment of the Displaced Persons Act of 1948 under which more than 400,000 refugees from the countries of Eastern Europe were admitted to the United States between 1948 and 1955. Among the displaced were many equipped to give leadership to Americans of their national origin—people of upper social and economic strata, cultured and well educated, highly motivated by patriotic fervor and resentment of the loss of station, wealth, and power which they had suffered.

Their hope and objective was the restoration of freedom to their homelands. The policy of containment of Communism enunciated by George Kennan and pursued by the Truman administration fell short of their hopes, for containment seemed to signify acceptance in perpetuity of Soviet domination of once independent peoples. What they sought was liberation of the captive nations which had been brought under Soviet domination. The goal was endorsed in 1950 when Congress with bipartisan support adopted the Captive Nations Resolution in what was to become an annual exercise for the next forty-two years. In the following year Congress included in the defense appropriation bill funding the war in Korea a provision to finance a force of volunteers from the captive nations as part of NATO's military arm. The provision sponsored by Republican Representative Charles Kersten of Wisconsin enjoyed more enthusiastic support on the Republican side of the aisle than the Democratic, and no action was taken by the Truman administration to make it effective.

Liberation became a theme of the Republican campaign in 1952 by inclusion in the platform and endorsement by the candidate. In a mid-August press conference and again in an address to the American Legion later in the month, Eisenhower pledged to pursue a policy of liberation "by peaceful means" of the "people now behind the Iron Curtain in both Europe and Asia" (*New York Times*, 14 August 1952; Theoharis 1970, 144–46). Even some Republicans were skittish about espousing a policy which, despite the assurance that only peaceful means would be employed in its execution, might provoke even sterner Soviet repression of its satellites and end up in armed conflict. Stevenson played on such concerns, warning that "the General's proposal would lead, not to the liberation of captive peoples, but to their obliteration—not release, but to war (*New York Times*, 1 November 1952).

The hope that a vigorous anti-Communist stance blaming the Democrats and their Yalta Agreement for the plight of Eastern Europe and pledging liberation of the captive nations would reap a harvest of votes from ethnic groups inspired Republican campaign strategists to establish in the National Committee an office somewhat camouflaged under the title Special Activities Division.

Seeking ethnic votes was not a new pursuit for the Republican Party. In its first campaigns almost a century earlier it had courted the German vote, a tactic which Lincoln adopted by secretly purchasing control of a German language newspaper. Then it was seeking the support of German Protestants. In 1952 the Special Activities Division clearly had as its major target ethnic Catholics alienated from the Democratic Party. The honorary chairman chosen for the Division was John A. Danaher, scion of a family of prominent Democrats in Connecticut who in 1938 became the second Catholic Republican to serve in the United States Senate by popular election. With branches embracing Italians, Hungarians, Poles, Germans, and Ukrainians, this division contributed to the campaign by bombarding the foreign language press with releases and operating a busy speakers' bureau. Its message was that the policies of Democratic administrations had enabled Communists to reap their gains in Europe and Asia as well as to infiltrate sensitive posts in the United States.

The Influence of Senator McCarthy For four years from the time Senator Joseph McCarthy burst upon the national scene in Wheeling, West Virginia, in 1950 with his count of the Communists he alleged had burrowed into the State Department, his name tended to dominate news reports on domestic Communism. The term "McCarthyism" entered the national vocabulary as one of the most damning pejoratives known to politicians and the press.

That McCarthy helped to sway some Catholic voters, particularly among the Irish of Boston and New York, toward candidates of the Republican Party in 1950 and 1952 is very likely. The Democratic high command was sufficiently disturbed by his apparent influence to commission polling to determine the extent of the disaffection the senator was generating or exploiting in the ranks of the party's Catholic followers (Crosby 1978, 240–43). The poll indicated that the impact of McCarthy's message was substantial among the Catholics of Massachusetts.

Perhaps for this reason John F. Kennedy in his early years in the House and Senate maintained a cautious stance toward his fellow Irishman from Wisconsin, who enjoyed the status of friend of the family. McCarthy avoided any appearance in Massachusetts as Kennedy ran against Henry Cabot Lodge for the Senate in 1952, and Kennedy uttered no criticism of McCarthyism. On his way to the White House, one of the most serious obstacles Kennedy was to encounter was the belief of liberals like Eleanor Roosevelt that he had shirked service in the battle against McCarthy. He had condemned diplomats of the postwar years who had "lost what our fighting men had gained"; he had told a Harvard audience that "Joe may have something" in alleging Communist infiltration of unions and government agencies; he had presented himself as a more reliable anti-Communist than Henry Cabot Lodge, his opponent for the Senate in 1952; and, as a senator in 1954, he had failed to vote or even indicate his position on the resolution which the Senate adopted censuring McCarthy (Crosby 1978, 213; Reeves 1982, 442–44).

Despite the high visibility which the media gave to McCarthy in his heyday, there is no reason to believe that his influence on the presidential vote in 1952 was anything but minimal. Eisenhower would have won overwhelmingly without the effort Joe McCarthy made in the campaign. Evidence that Eisenhower had no need of McCarthy's support can be drawn from the results in Wisconsin. As Eisenhower carried the state with a plurality of almost 360,000 and Republican Governor Kohler won reelection by more than 400,000 votes, McCarthy defeated his Democratic opponent by a margin of only 140,000.

In view of the intensity of anti-McCarthy sentiment among some influential segments of the public, support from the Wisconsin senator had mixed consequences for Eisenhower. A survey of polls and of the Catholic press led the president of the Catholic Historical Association to find "a preponderance of pro-McCarthy sentiment among Catholics" but a sharp and definite split of opinion. While Catholic publications like the *Brooklyn Tablet* and *The Sign* strongly supported McCarthy, others such as *Commonweal* and *America* were among his most vigorous critics. The member of the hierarchy most outspoken in his criticism of McCarthy was the liberal auxiliary bishop of Chicago, Bernard Shiel. Shiel told a convention of the United Auto Workers in 1954 that McCarthy's activities were "phony," "a burlesque," flouting America's "democratic procedures and sense of fair play" (DeSantis 1965, 28–30).

Donald Crosby concluded after examining eleven surveys of public opinion that "Catholic McCarthyites outnumbered the anti-McCarthy Catholics" and that the senator's "popularity with Catholics was slightly stronger than with the rest of the population." Yet the approval rating among Catholics which McCarthy attained in these polls exceeded 50 percent only three times—all in surveys taken at the end of 1953 and during the first three months of 1954 (Crosby 1978, 242–43).

Corruption

All the standard surveys of sentiment taken during the 1952 campaign concur that corruption in government was a major concern of the public. From 1950 on, a series of scandals involving officials, notably in the Internal

Revenue Service and the Reconstruction Finance Corporation, tarnished the reputation of an administration suspect because of Harry Truman's old ties to the Pendergast machine in Kansas City. The Michigan Survey Research Center observed growing doubt among the voters about the honesty of federal officials after 1950. Although none of the accusations involved crimes comparable to those of the Harding administration's Teapot Dome, it found they "had a much greater political impact." It concluded that "the moral lapses of the Truman Administration, real and fancied, had a strong influence on the electorate" (Campbell et al. 1960, 525). In the campaign corruption was subsumed as an issue as part of "the mess in Washington"—a phrase frequently employed by Republican orators which was sweeping enough to cover whatever special grievance the voter might be nourishing.

The Appeal of Eisenhower

Perhaps the most influential consideration affecting voting behavior in 1952—and particularly the behavior of those who switched from casting Democratic votes in 1948—was Dwight D. Eisenhower himself, a man whose personality, character, and reputation had made him extremely popular with Americans. No stronger testimonial of the vote-pulling power which practical politicians attributed to the man who had led American troops to victory in Europe could be imagined than the frantic efforts of leading Democrats of all shades of opinion to draft Eisenhower as their party's presidential nominee in 1948. Those who participated in the effort, ranging from leaders of Americans for Democratic Action to Dixiecrat southerners, launched their campaign without knowing their candidate's views on any policy issues or, indeed, without any assurance that he was a Democrat. What was known from a Gallup poll taken in the spring of 1948 was that Eisenhower was regarded by more people as better fitted to be president than anybody else. Twenty-four percent of the public made this judgment of Eisenhower; Harry Truman was the choice of 11 percent.

In the immediate postwar years Eisenhower was the nation's unique hero. He was relatively unscarred by the negatives associated in the public mind with politics and Republicanism, for he was not a politician and not strongly identified as a Republican. And at a time when the leading issue was a quick and honorable end to the Korean War, who could be better equipped to find the way out of the morass than the military commander who had led the nation to victory over Hitler's Wehrmacht?

The 1956 Election

In 1956 Eisenhower was reelected even more handily than in his first campaign. The Republican presidential ticket increased its share of the vote from

55.4 to 57.7 percent, winning with a record-breaking plurality of 9.5 million. In the states west of the Mississippi, particularly on the farms, however, its vote slipped from the heights of 1952.

In southern states Eisenhower made gains, particularly among the still small band of black voters. After voting for Stevenson in 1952, Louisiana (the southern state with the highest percentage of black and Catholic voters) moved into the Republican column in 1956. The Supreme Court's decision in *Brown v. Board of Education* 347 U.S. 483 (1954), declaring racial segregation in public schools unconstitutional, and the threat of massive resistance to the Court's ruling by southern Democrats apparently gained black votes throughout the South for the Republican presidential ticket without a major loss of white votes—but also without widespread gain among northern blacks.

That Catholic voters were moved by the same influences as their non-Catholic neighbors is clear in the voting statistics of the Midwest. In rural counties populated heavily by Catholics throughout Wisconsin, Minnesota, Nebraska, Missouri, and the Dakotas, Eisenhower's vote declined modestly from its 1952 level, as it did among farmers in the region generally. The decline in the farm vote affected the electoral vote of only one state, Missouri, which switched from Eisenhower in 1952 to Stevenson in 1956.

In the nation as a whole, however, Catholic support of Eisenhower increased in 1956. The Republican presidential ticket made its most striking gains in the Northeast and in heavily Catholic areas. The two leading surveys of voting behavior, although differing in their figures as they had in 1952, agreed that Eisenhower's share of the vote cast by Catholics was five percentage points higher than it had been four years earlier. According to the Michigan Survey Research Center, 54 percent of the Catholic voters voted for Ike; according to Gallup, it was 49 percent. Either estimate makes 1956 a noteworthy election. Not only did a majority of Catholics—or close to a majority—vote for a Republican presidential candidate, but Eisenhower's gain of five percentage points among Catholic voters over 1952 was more than double the increase in his vote from the electorate as a whole.

In 1952 the Republican presidential ticket carried 72 of the 102 counties in the nation in which Catholics formed a majority of the population, in 1956 it carried 83 such counties. In the 36 largest cities, mostly Democratic strongholds since 1928 or earlier, Eisenhower received 51 percent of the aggregate vote, and he carried 25 of them. In 1952 he had won 17 of these cities. Dewey, by contrast, had carried only 4 in 1948. Among the "most Catholic" cities which provided Eisenhower with a plurality in 1956 were Chicago, Buffalo, Baltimore, Milwaukee, New Orleans, San Francisco, and Jersey City. In New York City and Boston the Republican presidential ticket came close, receiving 49 percent of the vote in the former, 46 percent in the latter.

So impressed was Samuel Lubell with these results in urban centers that he gave an affirmative answer to the question "Can the GOP Win Without Ike?" the title of his analysis of the 1956 vote. "The Democratic majorities in the cities have been slashed so drastically," he explained, "that the Republicans must be rated as favorites to win the White House in 1960" (Lubell 1957, 31).

This prediction underestimated the strong attraction to John F. Kennedy which Catholic urban dwellers were to feel in 1960, and it overestimated the extent to which a vote for Eisenhower in 1956 signified an attachment to the Republican Party. There were clear signs in both 1952 and 1956 that the Republican presidential candidate was far more popular than his party. In both elections Eisenhower had run well ahead of Republican candidates for other offices.

The election of 1952 produced Republican majorities in Congress, but in 1954 Democrats regained control of both houses. In 1956 despite Eisenhower's impressive victory, his coattails exerted limited influence when voters came to choose among candidates for the legislative branch. Republicans made no gain in the Senate and suffered a loss of two seats in the House of Representatives. The 1956 election was the first since 1848 in which the party of the winning presidential candidate failed to achieve control of at least one house of Congress.

Although the presidential candidates and the outcome in 1956 were the same as in 1952 and both elections were in a sense referenda on the stewardship of the party in power, the issues were quite different. With the armistice ending conflict in Korea the threat of military action ceased to stir public anxiety. With the installation of the Eisenhower administration and the downfall of Joe McCarthy, concern about Communism as a domestic danger abated. No great scandals blemished the record of the Eisenhower administration in its first term, and the alleged corruption of the Truman years faded from memory. In 1956 the character of Eisenhower and the peace and prosperity which the nation then enjoyed were dominant factors in the minds of voters as they went to the polls. In the final days of the campaign, events abroad—the brutal suppression of the Hungarian uprising by Soviet troops and the Anglo-French-Israeli invasion of Egypt—appear to have worked to the advantage of the Republicans by emphasizing the continuing relevance of foreign and military policy experience in the White House (Campbell et al. 1960, 53; Divine 1974, 161–80).

Republican Defeat in 1958 and the Response

In the off-year election of 1958 the Republican Party suffered a severe setback—a net loss of 13 seats in the Senate, 48 in the House of Representatives,

5 governorships, and 686 seats in state legislative bodies. These results set off a flurry of activity to determine (in the words of the pollster commissioned by the Republican National Committee to probe the disaster) "what ails the Republican party and what can we do about it." At the same time, National Committee Chairman Meade Alcorn, at the prompting of President Eisenhower, appointed a group of leading Republicans from public and private life to formulate a fresh statement of party aims and policies. The group, called the Committee on Program and Progress, was chaired by Charles Percy, president of Bell and Howell and future United States senator.

Little practical guidance for rebuilding the weakened party was offered by the report of the pollster, Claude Robinson, to whom the Republicans often turned for advice in the 1950s. The report stressed the chronic handicap borne by Republican candidates in being perceived as representative of wealth and privilege, and it recommended greater effort to organize such voting groups as "businessmen, farmers, and negroes." Strangely, despite the relatively successful effort made in the two Eisenhower campaigns to win votes from Catholic ethnics, the potential for support from such a source was not mentioned.

The report of the Committee on Program and Progress proved to be more useful. Percy, as chairman of the Platform Committee of the 1960 Republican Convention, found in this report planks ready made for insertion in the Party's 1960 document.

The Committee on Program and Progress issued, under the title *Decisions for a Better America*, a statement that was comprehensive and specific in its policy proposals—and in some, in fields such as civil rights, relatively bold for its time. Emphasizing in its treatment of foreign affairs the struggle with Communism and calling emphatically for "emancipation" of the Captive Nations, it did not ignore campaign themes used to attract Catholic voters. It voiced hopes that seemed unrealistic at the time. Twenty years before events occurred in Europe which were to give the ring of prophecy to its statement, it asserted that "the innate desire in all men for freedom" could release satellite nations from Communist control and also "overpower tyranny in the Soviet Union and China."

The Republican Party Entering the Sixties

The 1958 election was not the first signal of the weakness of the Republican Party. In 1954, running without Eisenhower on the ticket, Republicans lost the narrow margin of control of both houses of Congress which they had won in 1952. A comparison of the two presidential elections of the fifties with earlier elections provides clear evidence that Eisenhower was far more popular than his party. Throughout the twentieth century prior to 1952, Republican presidential nominees on average had received a vote 6 percent greater than the aggregate vote cast for Republican candidates for the House of Representatives—a relatively small difference in view of the number of seats conceded to Democratic aspirants without a contest. Eisenhower, by contrast, ran far ahead of the Republican House candidates collectively—by almost 20 percent in 1952 and 25 percent in 1956. In the latter year one in five who voted for the Eisenhower-Nixon ticket failed to vote for a Republican for the House. And, as noted earlier, the 1956 election was the first since 1848 in which the party of the winning presidential candidate failed to achieve control of at least one house of Congress.

For the electorate as a whole the decade of the fifties ended with the proportion of Republicans, Democrats, and Independents almost the same as at the beginning (table 5-2).

TABLE 5–2. Party Affiliation of Voters in the 1950s (As Percentage of Total)

	1952	*1956*	*1958*	*1960*
Democrat	46	43	48	45
Republican	28	30	29	31
Independent	23	24	20	22

Source: University of Michigan Survey Research Center.

Despite two terms of a Republican presidency, no realignment of the electorate at large took place during the Eisenhower years. The victories of 1952 and 1956 were primarily personal triumphs of a popular war hero who captured the trust and respect of the public and not victories of the party whose label he bore.

The party alignment of the Catholic population during the 1950s, as tracked by the University of Michigan Survey Research Center, underwent its own evolution. From the beginning of the decade through Eisenhower's second electoral victory in 1956, there was some slight growth in the percentage of Republicans and a decline in the percentage of Democrats. This trend was found in both the entire population and in the Catholic component. As the 1960 election came closer, however, the trend among Catholics verged sharply from that registered for the total electorate.

TABLE 5–3. Party Affiliation of Catholics in the 1950s (As Percentage of Total Catholic Electorate)

	1952	*1956*	*1958*	*1960*
Democrat	56	51	55	61
Republican	18	21	17	16
Independent	7	11	9	9

Source: University of Michigan Survey Research Center.

Between 1952 and 1960 the percentage of the total white population identifying as Democrats delined marginally while the percentage of Republicans increased modestly.

The change among Catholics is reflected in the following ratios: in 1952 Catholic Democrats outnumbered Catholic Republicans 3 to 1; in 1956, 2½ to 1; in 1960, by almost 4 to 1 (table 5-3).

There is no mystery in the strong and abrupt change of party attachment on the part of many Catholics in preparation for the 1960 election. They became Democrats to elect John F. Kennedy to the presidency. Their enlistment in the party was a leading indicator of how their votes would be cast in November.

6

Kennedy and the Return of the Prodigals

Unitarian Theodore Sorensen prepared an unusually frank and direct document to persuade Democrats to nominate John F. Kennedy for vice president in 1956. His thesis was that the religion of the young senator from Massachusetts could provide the ingredient needed to restore the party's control of the White House. The Democratic Party was defeated in 1952, the document asserted, because of the loss of "its political base among the Catholics and immigrants of the large northern cities." It went on to say that "one of every four voters is a Catholic" and that the Catholic population is concentrated "in pivotal states with large electoral votes . . . several of which are inevitably necessary for a victory in the Electoral College." As the vice presidential nominee, Kennedy would bring his errant coreligionists in these crucial states back to the Democratic fold, for, "a high percentage of Catholics of all ages, residences, occupations, and economic status vote for a well-known Catholic candidate or a ticket with special Catholic appeal."

Conceding that Kennedy's religion would be a handicap with some segments of the electorate, the document identified three groups likely to be offended but minimized the severity of the prospective losses. The first was southerners, but they were so overwhelmingly Democratic that even "if one of three Democrats stayed home (or even voted Republican) . . . due to a nominee's religious affiliation, few, if any, Southern electoral votes would be lost." The second group was "Republicans who would not support the Democratic ticket under any circumstances." And the third group likely to be disaffected was "Northern liberal intellectuals" (in quotes in the Sorensen memorandum) who would nevertheless vote for Adlai Stevenson "without regard to the Vice President's religion" (Sorensen 1965, 82–4).

Religion in Kennedy Campaign Strategy in 1960

As soon as the votes had been counted in 1956, the campaign to put John F. Kennedy in the White House in 1960 began. And there was probably never a time when the theme of the Sorensen-Bailey memorandum was forgotten by campaign strategists. But, building a campaign for the presidency guided by the lessons of Catholic support for a Catholic candidate which the memorandum drew from election history entailed serious problems. Any candidate—and especially a Catholic—who appealed to his coreligionists for their votes risked the loss of the votes of those unsympathetic to his church. Wisdom cautioned against an appeal that was obvious, blatant, or premature, or that directly involved the candidate. Kennedy, Sorensen reports, instructed his staff "never to talk in terms of Catholic voting strength—1960 was not 1956." This time it was the presidency, not the vice presidency, that was the goal, and "all talk of a Catholic voting bloc—to which the 1956 Bailey [sic] Memorandum had contributed—would only encourage Protestant voting blocs" (Sorensen 1965, 127).

The first requisite for the Kennedy campaign in 1960 was to distance the candidate from those aspects of Catholicism most likely to generate suspicion of, and opposition to, his candidacy among non-Catholics. Before entering the presidential race with a declaration of his candidacy, Kennedy took steps to make clear his independence of the Church. This was the thrust of an article published in *Look* in March 1959 (Knebel 1959). In it Kennedy affirmed his support of separation of church and state. On constitutional grounds he expressed opposition to proposals to provide aid to church-related schools, a stand consistent with his record in the Senate but a reversal of his position as a member of the House of Representatives in the 1940s. He also reiterated the opposition to sending an ambassador to the Vatican which he had expressed in 1956 (reversing a position he had taken in 1954). He based his position, however, not on constitutional principle but simply on a desire to avoid recurrence of the bitter controversy that had erupted when President Truman had proposed appointing Mark Clark ambassador to the Holy See in 1951.

A second task, important in winning a Democratic nomination, was to establish Kennedy's credentials with the liberal establishment, still sentimentally attached to Adlai Stevenson but unwilling to risk defeat a third time. In this task Arthur Schlesinger Jr. and a group from the Harvard faculty performed valuable service, although they were not successful in winning Eleanor Roosevelt's support. In part, as the Sorensen-Bailey memorandum had recognized, distaste for some positions generally associated with Catholics and their Church underlay the reservations many liberals entertained toward a Catholic presidential candidate. These reservations tended to give way after assurance of the candidate's independence of the Church and its hierarchy and of his staunch support of public schools and separation of church and state. In the case of John Kennedy, however, there was much more that had to be refuted or explained away—including his father's alleged attitudes toward Nazis and Jews, his relationship with Joe McCarthy, the strident anti-Communist rhetoric of his early political career, and his 1950 contribution to Richard Nixon's campaign for the Senate against Helen Gahagan Douglas. The last was a persistent rumor, denied by Kennedy's supporters in 1960 but later confirmed by Nixon (Nixon 1978, 75).

One other group which the Sorensen-Bailey memorandum expected would be alienated by the nomination of a Catholic for the presidency was the voters in southern states. Although the memorandum minimized the consequences of defection among southerners, the Kennedy strategists in 1960 viewed the potential losses in the South very seriously. In order to hold the South, and particularly the Lone Star State, Lyndon Johnson was selected to be the vice presidential nominee, even over the protests of Bobby Kennedy and at the risk of precipitating a revolt of the party's liberal wing.

The Nation as the Sixties Began

As Eisenhower completed his eighth year in the White House, he was still an immensely popular president. His average approval rating for the year 1960, according to Gallup, was 61 percent. No later president of the twentieth century was to be rated as highly in his last year in office—except John F. Kennedy in the year of his assassination. Sorensen concedes that Eisenhower, had he been the Republican nominee for a third time, would have been reelected handily. As testimony of the esteem in which the nation held the outgoing president, the word went out to Kennedy campaigners to avoid making any attack on Ike by name (Sorensen 1971, 3464–65).

The nation had enjoyed eight years of peace. It had prospered over these years, although with some economic setbacks that seemed to coincide with congressional elections. The march of Communism had been halted except for the Castro victory in Cuba, a development that appeared at the time more embarrassing than threatening. The Communists of North Vietnam showed no inclination to use force to add to the territorial gains they had won in 1954 from the French, and a tiny training detail of fewer than three hundred Americans in South Vietnam appeared to be providing all the military support needed to stabilize the country under the Diem regime.

Despite the withdrawal of the occupying Allied military forces from Austria, Soviet control over its satellites in Eastern Europe was in no way relaxed in the 1950s. Congress and the president annually observed Captive Nations Week by calling for the restoration of freedom to peoples under Communist control without apparent effect. The Cold War went on. Signs of a thaw such as the "spirit of Geneva" and Nikita Khrushchev's visit to the United States were overshadowed by the growth of Soviet military power and the willingness to use it displayed with ferocity on the streets of

Budapest, reinforced by minatory rhetoric from Moscow that the Communists were out to "bury" us. When the Soviet Union sent Sputnik into space before the United States was able to demonstrate a similar capacity, the effect on the American people was more devastating than that of any other event beyond our shores in the fifties. The feat was widely taken as confirmation of claims that this country had lost first place in the world in many respects.

The bright hopes of the Republicans at the beginning of the decade had not been realized despite eight years of control of the executive branch. Eisenhower was no partisan. He had no strong interest in party affairs and had little respect for many Republican leaders. He gave half-hearted endorsement to efforts to modify the party's philosophy in the direction of an ambiguous "Modern Republicanism" but granted them no sustained support at times when his influence was at its peak. As the fifties ended, the Democratic Party was preferred by a majority of the voters, and the Republicans were no stronger than they had been when the decade began.

The Catholic Population in 1960

Catholics and their Church were the object of more intense public attention and scrutiny in 1960 than ever before in the nation's history. The campaign of John F. Kennedy for the presidency generated a surge of interest on a scale last seen in 1928, rallying both a greatly enlarged group smarting from the stigma of exclusion of a Catholic from the nation's highest office and also reawakening a dwindling band determined to perpetuate the exclusion.

The Catholic population, numbering 40 million in 1960, had doubled since 1928, exceeding the growth rate of the rest of the nation. Catholics had risen in the socioeconomic scale, becoming a larger proportion of the nation's college graduates, of upper income families, and of professional and managerial classes. In politics, they had achieved considerable success, particularly through the Democratic Party, outnumbering members of any other religious persuasion in the United States Congress and holding the governorships of such large states as California, Ohio, and Pennsylvania.

Having lost their immigrant mindset with its acceptance of a lower status and experiencing upward mobility in an era when discrimination was increasingly coming under attack, many Catholics saw the 1960 election as a chance to strike a symbolic blow against barriers to their advancement and that of their children. As Catholics entered the mainstream of society, hostility toward them had abated substantially but had by no means disappeared. Even in 1959 a Gallup poll found that one-fourth of the public responded that they would not vote for a qualified Catholic for president if their party were to nominate one of that faith.

In 1958 a new pope was chosen who was to exercise a profound influence on the Catholic Church, its position in the world, and the relationship of American Catholics to members of other faiths. In 1960 there was still no indication of the changes which John XXIII was to bring about as he preached *aggiornamento*, an updating, of the Church as a necessary reform and summoned the bishops to bring it about.

The Religious Issue in the 1960 Campaign

The Democratic Approach

For the Kennedy campaign the problem related to religion was to stem vote loss because of it, especially among Southerners and Liberals—two of the three groups identified in the Sorensen-Bailey memorandum of 1956 as most inclined to reject a Catholic candidate. Catholics needed no special urging to vote for the candidate whose victory would spell the end of the last political barrier in the way of those of their faith. To add to the strong vote certain to come from members of his church, Kennedy needed only to see to it that Catholics were made fully aware of the anti-Catholic propaganda in circulation.

Before his nomination, through an article in *Look* and an address to the American Society of Newspaper Editors, Kennedy had dissociated himself from potentially damaging positions. He had, in Sorensen's words, "met the religious issue head on, emphasizing his record on separation of church and state, on independence from ecclesiastical authority, and against public aid to parochial schools" (Sorensen 1971, 3458).

The most dramatic and successful action Kennedy took to quiet fears about the effect Catholicism might have on his performance as president was his appearance before the Greater Houston Ministerial Association in September. He addressed this skeptical audience after an ad hoc campaign organization called Citizens for Religious Freedom had all but declared any Catholic disqualified from serving as president. Headed by the Reverend Norman Vincent Peale, rector of the Marble Collegiate Church in New York and author of *The Power of Positive Thinking*, this Protestant group pronounced the Catholic Church "a political as well as a religious organization" bent on breaking down the wall of separation between church and state and on denying freedom of conscience to those outside its fold. The group's statement also expressed strong doubt that any Catholic president could "withstand the determined efforts of the hierarchy of his church" to undermine these bulwarks of American democracy (George 1993, 201–3).

As the storm broke over the declaration issued by Dr. Peale and his associates, Kennedy assured the ministers in Houston of his belief in the "absolute" separation of church and state and in the public school and pledged to uphold religious liberty for all. He expressed opposition to any effort by any religious body to "impose its will directly or indirectly upon the general populace or the public acts of its officials." He declared that he would grant no public funds or political preference to any church or church school and would not seek or accept instructions from ecclesiastical authority. He had, he said, opposed sending an ambassador to the Vatican as well as providing "unconstitutional" aid to parochial schools, without defining unconstitutional aid, and without revealing that his position on both of these matters appeared to have shifted since his early days in Congress. Among the symbolic gestures employed to minimize a Catholic coloration of his campaign, Kennedy broke with a Democratic tradition of long standing by selecting a Protestant, Senator Henry "Scoop" Jackson of Washington, to serve as the official director of the enterprise to win the White House.

As in 1928, although on a smaller scale, a campaign attacking the Democratic presidential candidate because of his religion was carried on repeating the old allegations, including the spurious Knights of Columbus oath. Although Democratic organizations formally associated with the campaign refrained from seeking to link Nixon to the anti-Catholicism which surfaced, an auxiliary group, the Committee on Political Education of the AFL-CIO, did not show similar restraint. Through a brochure entitled "Liberty or Bigotry" and a chorus of spokesmen in labor's strongholds in the nation, it accused Nixon of sharing the prejudices against minority groups held by extreme political elements like the Ku Klux Klan. This attack was strongly criticized. The Michigan State Fair Campaign Practices Committee composed of three clergymen (one a Catholic) denounced the brochure as an exercise in "bigotry in reverse." In an editorial of 16 October 1960 the *Michigan Catholic* called it "Back Alley Tactics." It seems probable that this type of attack on Nixon boomeranged.

The Republican Approach

In 1960 the Republican party followed a far different course from the one it pursued in 1928 in dealing with the religion of the Democratic presidential candidate. When Al Smith was that candidate, Republican participation in the campaign exploiting religious bias was scarcely veiled. When John F. Kennedy ran, the Republican campaign officials made a good-faith effort to avoid seeking votes on such grounds.

Immediately after his nomination by the Republican convention, Nixon declared that he would not talk about religion during the campaign. On 16 August Nixon's campaign managers, Leonard W. Hall and Robert H. Finch, laid down the following guidelines for participants in the campaign:

1. No person or organization conditioning their support on religious grounds will be recognized in this campaign.
2. There should be no discussion of the "religious issue" in any literature prepared by any volunteer group or party organization supporting the Vice President, and no literature of this kind from any source should be made available at campaign headquarters or otherwise distributed.
3. Staff and volunteer workers should avoid discussing the "religious issue" either informally or casually since this might be construed as some kind of deliberate campaign (Republican National Committee 1961, 48).

Independent sources absolved the Republican Party of involvement in exploitation of religious prejudice in the campaign. Charles P. Taft, chairman of the Fair Campaign Practices Committee, on the eve of the election summarized the results of his organization's investigation into "many reports of Republican complicity in the anti-Catholic effort" by saying, "We have not found a single instance that justifies the suspicion that any responsible Republican figure or organization is doing anything but trying to stop the exploitation of religious issues." (Republican National Committee 1961, 49).

In a similar vein, the executive director of the committee, Bruce L. Felknor, surveying fifteen hundred pieces of "rabid and unfair anti-Catholic propaganda" collected by the organization during the 1960 campaign, concluded that "Richard Nixon merits hearty applause" for the standard he adhered to in the electoral contest. Nixon, Felknor wrote, "was determined on, he insisted on, he would not permit any deviation from, a rigid and unexceptioned policy of leaving the religious issue out of his campaign" (Felknor 1966, 56–58).

Cardinal Richard Cushing of Boston, the ecclesiastic closest to the Kennedy family, added to this chorus of approbation after the election, "unhesitatingly" calling Nixon "the Good Will Man of 1960." Nixon, Cushing was quoted as saying in the 12 January 1961 issue of the *Baltimore Evening Sun*, "never exploited the religious or any other issue that would tend to divide the American people." Kennedy himself, according to Sorensen, "at all times . . . acquitted Nixon and Nixon's party of any responsibility for the growing tide of intolerance." Whether Sorensen agreed with his candidate is not completely clear, for he also wrote, "the Republicans were . . . handling the religious issue very shrewdly," raising "the issue by deploring it" (Sorensen 1965, 193).

Both the public record and private correspondence offer ample evidence that Nixon did all that could be reasonably expected to discourage those who sought to win votes for him by attacks on Catholicism. When Dr. Norman

Vincent Peale and his colleagues in Citizens for Religious Freedom expressed their fear that papal influence would override a Catholic president's duty to the country, Nixon came to Kennedy's defense. Deploring the injection of a religious issue and pledging that no one doing so would be permitted to participate in his campaign, Nixon, as reported by the *New York Times* on 12 September 1960, said, "I have no doubt whatever about Senator Kennedy's loyalty to his country" or his readiness to put the Constitution above any other consideration.

The timing of Nixon's repudiation of the Peale group's manifesto could not have served his opponent's cause better if it had been arranged by Pierre Salinger, for it was released on the day of Kennedy's appearance before the Greater Houston Ministerial Association. Also on that day—September 12—one hundred Protestant clergymen of several faiths issued a statement responding to Peale's organization by deploring exclusion of any aspirant from public office because of his religion. All in all, the day's events were highly effective in overcoming doubts about the risks of electing a Catholic to the presidency—and not solely because of the skillful plea which Kennedy made to his clerical audience.

During the campaign Nixon construed very strictly the rule he had laid down banning use of any appeal suggesting exploitation of religion. He repeatedly turned aside offers made by the Reverend Billy Graham to provide a public show of support, including an article for publication in *Life* magazine endorsing Nixon's candidacy, even though no mention of religion was planned (Ambrose 1987, 546–47, 602–3).

At one stage in the campaign, Representative William E. Miller of New York, chairman of the National Republican Congressional Committee, speaking "as a Catholic and out of a sense of outrage," accused "those running the Kennedy campaign . . . [of] deliberately keeping the religious issue alive and inflamed—apparently in the hope that this will produce more votes for Senator Kennedy from among our fellow Catholics." Miller's charge was featured in a pamphlet sponsored by the New York Young Republicans for Nixon and Lodge entitled "BIGOTRY IN REVERSE or How the Kennedy Supporters Are Using His Religion for Political Purposes." In the final days of campaigning, when polls indicated a very close race, Nixon rejected the unanimous recommendation of his staff that he exploit such a theme by accusing his opponents of using Kennedy's religion to win the vote of Catholics (Nixon 1962, 365–67).

Voting Behavior in 1960: The Religious Gap

An analysis of the vote in the Kennedy-Nixon contest by scholars at the University of Michigan Survey Research Center concluded, "there can be little

TABLE 6–1. The Religious Gap in Voting Behavior, 1960

	Kennedy Voters		*Nixon Voters*	
Voting Group	*Catholics*	*Protestants*	*Catholics*	*Protestants*
Entire group	78	38	22	62
Men	77	41	23	59
Women	78	35	22	65
Age 21–29	78	41	22	59
Age 50+	77	34	23	66
East	77	28	23	72
South	75	47	25	53
Cities 50,000–500,000	82	34	18	66
Farms	86	45	14	55
Professional/business	69	27	31	73
White-collar	75	32	25	68
Skilled labor	81	44	19	56
Unskilled labor	83	52	17	48
Union members	85	52	15	48
College graduate	65	27	35	73
Grade school	83	45	17	55
Voted for Ike in '56	62	15	38	85
Voted for Adlai in '56	97	84	3	16
Republicans	18	3	82	97
Democrats	95	77	5	23
Independents	72	28	28	72

Source: American Institute of Public Opinion. *The Gallup Poll*, 1692–94.

doubt that the religious issue was the strongest single factor overlaid on basic partisan loyalties in the 1960 election" (Converse et al. 1961, 1269–70).

The effect of religious affiliation on the choice voters made between the presidential candidates in 1960 is put in relief in table 6-1, based on polls conducted by the Gallup organization. A mammoth gap is shown between Catholic and Protestant voters in groups with such common characteristics as union membership, educational level, occupation, and region of residence. Approximately 80 percent of Catholic voters supported Kennedy while about 62 percent of the Protestants voted for Nixon. Nixon's strongest showing among Catholics was found in the ranks of the college educated, of professionals and business persons, and (obviously) of Republican adherents. Yet among three of these four groups, Kennedy outpolled Nixon by a margin of more than two to one. Almost one in five Catholic Republicans voted for the Democratic presidential ticket. Of the Catholics who voted for Eisenhower in 1956 and returned to the polls in 1960, 62 percent supported Kennedy in a switch of gigantic dimension.

Kennedy fared considerably better with Protestant voters than Nixon did among Catholics. From Protestant union members and from the unskilled, he received a slim majority. He gained more than 45 percent of the vote cast by southern Protestants, Protestant farmers, and by Protestants with only a grade school education. Protestants who voted in both 1956 and 1960 were far less inclined than Catholics to switch parties in their presidential balloting. Of Eisenhower's Protestant supporters in the earlier race, 15 percent chose Kennedy in 1960; of Protestants who voted for Stevenson, 16 percent voted for Nixon.

Researchers at the University of Michigan classified Protestant Democrats into groups based on frequency of church attendance. Their findings showed a clear correlation between this characteristic and defection to vote for Nixon, somewhat stronger among southern than northern Protestants. Forty percent of Democratic Protestants in the South who were regular churchgoers chose Nixon. The defection rate declined as the rate of church attendance dropped until it became negligible among Democratic Protestants in the North who never attended a religious service (Campbell et al. 1966, 89).

In addition to a religious gap, modest gaps on the basis of gender and age can be discerned in Gallup's polling in 1960. Both are found among the Protestant, but not the Catholic, electorate. Nixon received a stronger vote from Protestants over fifty years of age than from younger cohorts. And Protestant women gave him a larger share of their vote by six percentage points than did Protestant men.

A comparison of the presidential vote in 1960 with that of either four or eight years earlier reveals no shift on the part of any group from one party to the other even approaching the movement of Catholic voters from Eisenhower to Kennedy. In 1960 Kennedy received almost 50 percent of the vote of the entire electorate, eight percentage points more than the 42 percent Stevenson garnered in his second bid for the presidency. Catholic voters gave Kennedy about 80 percent of the vote they cast, roughly thirty percentage points higher than the Catholic vote for Stevenson in 1956. Protestants showed no overall change in the distribution of their vote between the major parties. According to Gallup, 38 percent of Protestant voters supported Kennedy, a figure imperceptibly different from the 37 percent casting ballots for the Democratic ticket in 1956.

Whether Kennedy's religious affiliation was on balance a help or a handicap in his quest for the presidency is a question that cannot be answered with a high level of confidence. One scholarly study concluded that, because of his religion, Kennedy suffered a net loss of 2.2 percent in the popular vote nationwide (Converse et al. 1961, 1264–75). The method on which this conclusion rests—positing a "normal" Democratic vote and attributing to religious motivation any variation of the actual vote from this norm—is shaky. Further, even if this calculation is accepted, since the president is chosen on the basis of the electoral college vote, not the popular vote, it fails to provide a conclusive answer to the question.

A plausible case can be made that Kennedy's religion was more of a help than a handicap in winning electoral votes for reasons set forth in the Sorensen-Bailey memorandum. The Catholic population was concentrated in eastern and midwestern states rich in electoral votes—all except Indiana, Ohio, and Wisconsin carried by Kennedy. In several of the largest states, like New York, Pennsylvania, and Illinois, Kennedy's margin of victory was provided in big cities with a large Catholic vote. These cities yielded Democratic pluralities sufficient to overcome deficits in the rest of the state. In the twelve large cities in the nation with the highest percentage of Catholics in their population, the Democratic share of the vote in 1960 far exceeded that won by Stevenson in 1956. In New Orleans, for example, Kennedy received twenty-four percentage points more of the vote than had Stevenson; in Buffalo, twenty-three percentage points more; in Boston, twenty-one; in Newark, twenty.

On the other hand, in the South, where anti-Catholic voting presumably was most widespread, the defection of voters from the Democratic ticket because of religion still left Kennedy with a substantial cushion of support. Kennedy won eighty-one of the electoral votes cast by the region's eleven states; Nixon gained thirty-three from three states, and Byrd earned fourteen from dissenting Democrats.

A sage and witty adviser to several presidents, Bryce Harlow, addressed a post-election memorandum analyzing the campaign of 1960 to leading Republican officials. Noting the regional difference between northern and southern voters in attitudes toward Catholicism, he offered as one reason for Nixon's defeat "a maldistribution of bigots" in the nation.

The conclusion that Kennedy's religion, on balance, provided some marginal advantage in his quest for the presidency found support from one group of scholars. Their study concluded that the net effect of religiously motivated voting in 1960, whatever its influence on the popular vote may have been, was to provide a gain of ten electoral votes for the Democratic ticket (Pool et al. 1965, 115–18).

Differences Between Elections of 1928 and 1960

The reasons that John Fitzgerald Kennedy succeeded in an enterprise in which Alfred Emmanuel Smith had met failure are fairly obvious. Among the many differences in the nation wrought in the thirty-two years separating the two elections, the reversal of the role of the major parties was the most basic political change. Smith was the nominee of the minority party, the deeply split loser in national elections since 1918. The Democratic Party in 1960, by contrast, had enjoyed majority status in the nation for almost thirty years. Recognizing that Democrats outnumbered Republicans, Kennedy made an appeal to party loyalty a major theme of the standard campaign speech he delivered at every opportunity.

During these years the Catholic population had multiplied and prospered. It had doubled from 20 to 40 million, from 16 to 23 percent of the national head count, and even more as a percentage of the electorate. The total voter turnout in 1960 was 90 percent higher than in 1928. Far greater was the increase in the Catholic electorate—perhaps 130 percent above the 1928 level. Catholic voters gave Kennedy roughly 10 million more votes than they cast for Nixon. Smith, though probably gaining from his coreligionists a higher percentage of their vote than Kennedy was to receive, may have reaped a plurality of only 5 million over Hoover from the smaller band of Catholic voters of his era.

In 1960 anti-Catholicism was far less pervasive, far less open, and far less influential than it had been in the 1920s. Both Catholics and Protestants had leveled many of the barriers that had separated them in earlier times. The Ku Klux Klan, still an active and potent political force in the 1920s, had been reduced to a few stragglers unwelcome in both parties. When Smith ran, only Rabbi Steven Wise, Presbyterian Moderator Henry Van Dyke, and some Episcopalian clergymen were prominent in his defense against attack on religious grounds. When Kennedy ran, Norman Vincent Peale's abortive mustering of Protestant churchmen to oppose him foundered because of the vigorous condemnation it drew from respected clergy, particularly of mainline Protestant churches. The *Christian Century*, which had denounced Smith as the "representative of an alien culture . . . and of a foreign potentate" in 1928, in 1960 announced its neutrality in the presidential contest after Kennedy's appearance before the Ministerial Association in Houston.

Between 1928 and 1960 the ranks of those who would not vote to put any Catholic in the White House had thinned. And the ranks of those who still felt that way and were at ease with their decision were even thinner. Taking advantage of the changing mood, the Democratic campaign sought to exploit the spirit of fair play by equating a vote for Kennedy to a vote against prejudice.

One other factor differentiating the two election contests lies in the Democratic candidates themselves. Al Smith was accorded by the Catholics of his day a rare kind of adulation and by millions of others respect for his distinguished service as governor of New York. But he could not successfully reach across a cultural divide separating him from the majority of his countrymen. Minds were not open to his appeal because he came from a big polyglot city and its political machine, because he spoke in the accents of New York's lower East Side (and sometimes ungrammatically), because his education was limited to eight grades at St. James School in Manhattan, because as a "wet" he stood for the liquor interests, because he was thought (erroneously) to be of relatively recent Irish immigrant stock, and because he belonged to the wrong social class as well as the wrong church.

The suave, cultured, Harvard-educated, Cape Cod-bred, handsome, impeccably tailored, Pulitzer Prize-winning heir to great wealth, comfortable in Palm Beach or Scarsdale or the Court of St. James, nominated by the Democratic Party in 1960, resembled the nominee of 1928 only in the religion he professed. Even in this respect there was at least a shade of difference. In his gubernatorial office Smith kept a picture of the pope. Kennedy, who, in the words of one friendly historian "wore his religion lightly" (Fuchs 1967, 182–83), displayed no religious symbols in the Oval Office.

By 1960 the age of television as a political campaign instrument had arrived. Kennedy's style, appearance, speech, and manner were well adapted to the medium. In the debates, which were crucial to his victory, he demonstrated mastery of the device that introduced him in an intimate way to more Americans than had been reached by any prior presidential candidate. We can only speculate about the effect TV might have had in the Smith-Hoover campaign had it been available.

Lingering Effects of the 1960 Election

One important result of the Kennedy victory was the elimination of the so-called religious issue in national campaigns. For Catholics it spelled the end of an odious tradition that seemed to bar one of their faith from the presidency. Even the Catholics who voted for Nixon—perhaps 3.5 million in all—seem to have felt some sense of triumph. For non-Catholics concerned about the dangers of installing a Catholic in the White House, Kennedy's presidency completed the task of dispelling their fears, a task well advanced by the time the campaign was concluded. Theodore White noted this result of the election, writing "No American prejudice faded, I think, faster than the religious prejudice that vexed and underlay the election of 1960" (White 1978, 494). Historian Jay P. Dolan wrote the following appraisal of the Kennedy candidacy and presidency:

> Catholics at long last were comfortably integrated into American society. For Catholics Kennedy became a symbol of success; wealthy and well-educated, he had achieved the dream of every American: the presi-

> dency of the United States. His popularity enabled Catholics to stand a little taller, because one of their own had become an authentic folk hero during his lifetime and after his tragic death was quickly assigned to the company of American legends. (Dolan 1985, 422)

The myth that Washington for "one brief shining moment" had been Camelot, invented jointly by Jackie Kennedy and Theodore White, gave the 1960 election and the presidency of John F. Kennedy a luster that glowed more brightly with the passing years after the assassination in Dallas. The Kennedy era brought several tangible benefits to the Democratic Party, giving it a hero to place beside Jefferson, Jackson, and FDR in the party's pantheon. Youthful voters, especially activist and idealistic young people, flocked to the Democrats. And Catholics, especially the families of workers and the middle class who had been lured away by Eisenhower, rejoined the party of their forebears. They had been prodigals, but Kennedy's charisma brought them back to their father's house.

In winning the vote of some 80 percent of the Catholic electorate, John F. Kennedy had apparently put an end to Republican hopes to continue to make inroads into this group. A part of the vote he received was a protest, however, and with his election, the reason for the protest began to melt away. As another decade began, it became clear that Kennedy's success in reconnecting the mass of Catholics to the Democrats was temporary.

Unlike the campaign and election of 1928, the contest of 1960 did not leave Catholics believing that the Republican Party was a hostile force. Nixon's insistence on avoiding exploitation of the religious issue avoided the Catholic backlash that followed Hoover's campaign. After 1960 there were no bitter memories to deter Catholics from voting for Republican candidates or even joining—or rejoining—the ranks of Republican Party members.

Finally, it was to the benefit of Republicans that an issue that had operated to steer Catholics away from the party was definitively settled in 1960. In its postelection report the Republican National Committee observed that "many Catholics voted for President Kennedy . . . to end a custom which seemed to bar one of their faith from the highest office in the United States. . . . Now that the barrier has been removed, we can expect that a false issue has been eliminated from the political arena" (Republican National Committee 1961, 47).

7

Catholics in the Turbulent Sixties and Seventies

The 1960s, which began with the nation at peace at home and abroad, developed at mid point into a time of strife and violence. In 1965 the country became engaged in a major war in Vietnam which was to cost it dearly in blood and treasure and generate a disruptive conflict among Americans. Young people of the most privileged class made battlegrounds of the campuses of leading universities from Columbia to Berkeley. The slums of major cities erupted in riot and arson. Racial ghettoes were seething, and the Koerner Commission pronounced its bleak verdict that the country was becoming "two societies, one black and one white—separate and unequal."

Black society increasingly took up residence in big cities and white society in the suburbs and exurbs. With this change political power in urban America shifted as the task of governing cities was made more difficult by mounting problems and declining resources.

Patterns of behavior that had been rare became commonplace as the social consensus on moral standards seemed to evaporate. Uncounted young people—and some not so young, like Timothy Leary—protested the dominant culture and mores by dropping out of society and adopting a lifestyle of rootlessness, indolence, and drugs. Suffering considerable abuse for his findings, Pat Moynihan pointed out the disintegration of family structure in the black community as the incidence of illegitimate children in fatherless homes reached unprecedented levels (U. S. Department of Labor 1965; Rainwater and Yancey 1967). Similar conditions, though of lesser magnitude, were to be found in the white community, and pundits chortled that the "Ozzie and Harriet" family was hopelessly out of date.

Political assassination, rare in the nation's history and unknown for thirty years, became familiar as John Kennedy, Robert Kennedy, and Martin Luther King were struck down in the sixties and an attempt was made on the life of President Ford in the following decade.

The proceedings of the Democratic National Convention of 1968 in the Chicago Stockyards were overshadowed by events outside the auditorium.

As Cleveland's Mayor Carl Stokes was delivering an address seconding the nomination of Hubert Humphrey for president, network television cut away from the convention podium to show a pitched battle in the streets between police and protesters. And in the ensuing campaign the appearances of the candidates, particularly Humphrey's, were frequently disrupted by mobs howling obscenities.

It would be wrong, however, to remember the sixties as simply a bleak and destructive era of conflict. It was also the era when Congress enacted the comprehensive social legislation of Lyndon Johnson's Great Society and the civil rights laws which were to open the electoral process to black America and lead to the installation of thousands of black officeholders in all parts of the nation.

In 1972 the Democratic Party came under new management. The protesters of 1968 assumed control, facilitated by reforms instituted to give greater representation to women and minorities. One striking evidence of change was the unseating of the elected Illinois delegation headed by Mayor Richard J. Daley in favor of a group selected by a dubious process but Richard J. considered under the party's new rules to be more representative of the state's Democratic voters than that chosen in the Democratic primary.

The emergence of new issues threatening to dismantle the historic coalition supporting the Democratic Party was recognized by Richard Scammon and Ben Wattenberg in their book *The Real Majority* (1970, 20, 63), in which they wrote,

> Many Americans have begun casting their ballots along the lines of issues relatively new to the American political scene. For several decades Americans have voted basically along the lines of bread-and-butter economic issues. Now, in addition to the older, still potent economic concerns, Americans are apparently beginning to array themselves politically along the axes of certain social situations as well. These situations have been described variously as law and order, backlash, anti-youth, malaise, change, or alienation. These situations . . . constitute a new and potent political issue. We call it the social issue. . . .
>
> That the Democrats have held the allegiance of most of the "plain people" has been the critical fact in American presidential politics for more than a third of a century. That is why the Democrats have won so often. Now, upon the shoals of the Social Issue, there seems to be the possibility of a rupture in that pattern.

The Catholic Church under Stress

In the 1960s divisions began to surface in the Catholic Church which were startling to older Catholics accustomed to unity and obedience. The proportion of self-identified Catholics faithfully attending Sunday mass declined in a trend that was to continue down into the 1990s. The proportion accepting Church teaching on such matters as divorce and artificial birth control plummeted. Perhaps most shocking to an older generation was the defection of large numbers from the priesthood. This loss compounded the problem of replacing an aging clergy from the thinning ranks of young men entering seminaries. At the same time the number of nuns declined, a development which, along with economic pressures and changes in the religious and racial composition of urban America, forced the closure of a large number of Catholic elementary and high schools, particularly in large cities.

Catholics were used to outside attacks on their beliefs, their Church, and its representatives. But now they heard a rising chorus of open criticism and complaint from within. It came from all sides—on one hand from those who argued that reform was too limited; on the other, from those who deplored changes which they regarded as Protestantizing their Church.

Two events that occurred in Rome had much to do with arousing dissent. One was the sweeping reform movement initiated by the Second Vatican Council assembled by Pope John XXIII in 1962 and completed under Paul VI in 1965. Although approved by the great majority of American Catholics, changes in forms of worship and other innovations attributed to Vatican II were upsetting to many devout members of the Church. Older Catholics in particular regretted the passing of venerable rites, the Latin mass, and symbols familiar since their childhood.

A second event that stirred up discord was the promulgation by Paul VI of the encyclical *Humanae Vitae* in 1968 reaffirming the Church's view that the use of artificial means of birth control violated the moral law. According to Andrew Greeley (1990, 91–105), this rejection of contraceptive measures, apparently used as commonly by Catholics as by others, has been the major cause of conflict within the Church in the last decades of the twentieth century.

Dissent erupted also over clerical celibacy and the status of women in the Church. Priests and nuns left their calling for marriage and secular pursuits, leaving pulpits without preachers and classrooms without teachers. Not all dissidents followed the same course. Some quit the Church; some became lax in religious practices; some became anticlerical; a few carried on campaigns to change Church practices on such matters as clerical celibacy and ordination of women. All suffered a diminution of reverence for the Church and of willingness to heed its authorities.

The Catholic Church was not alone in suffering discord in the late sixties and seventies. During these years Protestant denominations, too, experienced strife in their ranks and in addition, most saw their congregations dwindle. For the Catholic Church, on the other hand, the losses in membership it sustained because of dissent were more than offset by new adherents.

Few were the Catholics who did not welcome the election of John F. Kennedy to the presidency. It was a release from what John A. Ryan had called second-class citizenship after Al Smith's defeat in 1928. It proclaimed the passing of the tradition barring Catholics from the White House and signified repeal of that "unwritten provision" of the Constitution limiting Catholics to lesser offices in the national government.

An apparent by-product of the Kennedy victory was a belief in both parties that there was a solid Catholic vote to be won by placing a Catholic on a presidential ticket. Republicans nominated William Miller for vice president in 1964. The Democrats awarded second place on their ticket to four Catholics—Muskie, Eagleton, Shriver, and Ferraro between 1968 and 1988. None of these experiments led to electoral success for either party.

With the decision of the Supreme Court in *Roe v. Wade* 410 U.S. 113 (1973), a new issue appeared on the national political agenda. The ruling of the Court's majority that the Constitution guaranteed the right to abort a fetus and that governmental power to regulate that right varied for each trimester of a woman's pregnancy baffled many students of constitutional law. It also precipitated a conflict in Washington and in every state and territorial capital from Augusta to Agana.

The conflict generated considerable bitterness and aroused the bishops of the Catholic Church and leading ecclesiastical figures of several other denominations, most of an evangelical orientation, to vigorous political action. They regarded abortion at any stage of pregnancy as the taking of human life—in short, in most cases, as murder. In the minds of those who called themselves pro-life, abortion posed the dominant moral issue of the time. The zeal it generated was not unlike that which swept many churches about the question of slavery in the mid-nineteenth century.

After JFK: Elections of the Sixties

In 1964 Catholics voted for Lyndon Johnson almost as overwhelmingly as they had for John F. Kennedy four years earlier. The candidacy of Barry Goldwater with a Catholic running mate failed to tap the reservoir of conservatism presumed by some Republican campaign strategists to lie in the Catholic community. Whether the election was a test of public opinion on conservatism versus liberalism or on any other basic philosophical principles is doubtful. The outcome hinged instead on the comparison that voters made between men—Goldwater on one hand, Johnson (and Kennedy) on the other. Goldwater was judged brash and reckless, likely to plunge the nation into conflict abroad (even to start a nuclear war), ready to dismantle Social Security as well as other measures protecting the aged and the unfortunate, and willing to front for racists resisting the march toward equality. By contrast,

Johnson was the man who would not "supply American boys to do the job that Asian boys should do," cautious and safe in foreign policy, compassionate and tolerant in domestic affairs.

The benefit that accrued to Johnson by being perceived as Kennedy's heir was substantial, particularly among the Catholic population. At election time in 1964 the memory of the violent and untimely death in Dallas was still fresh, and John F. Kennedy had become hero and martyr to his coreligionists and many others throughout the world. A vote for Johnson, many Catholics and others felt, was a tribute to the fallen president and a vote for a continuation of the New Frontier and Camelot. Johnson was well aware of the advantages of linking himself to Kennedy, a perception he fostered from his maiden presidential address to Congress until he abandoned the race for another term in 1968. In his last meeting with Robert Kennedy, then about to launch a campaign for the White House, Johnson declared he had always considered his years as president not the Johnson administration but the Kennedy-Johnson administration (Johnson 1971, 542).

The following presidential election was contested in a political environment far different from that of 1964. By 1968 it was impossible to continue the fiction that American forces in Vietnam, increased in four years from 23,000 to 500,000, were there to advise the South Vietnamese. The Tet uprising as a new year began for the Vietnamese seemed to demonstrate to a weary and confused America that there was no light ahead in Southeast Asia, only an interminable tunnel into which American lives and treasure would be poured without ever achieving victory. The public's patience wore thin as it had in the face of stalemate in Korea, but this time open disorder broke out. America's most privileged youth became antiwarriors and went on a rampage. The antiwar movement tore up some of the nation's most prestigious campuses and disrupted traffic in Washington and other cities with marches protesting the actions of the U.S. government (never of North Vietnam or the Vietcong).

At the same time violent disorder for reasons other than the war engulfed the cities in a wave of murder, mayhem, arson, and looting. Beginning in 1965 with the Watts riots in Los Angeles, not a year passed without widespread disturbances in the black ghettoes of major cities, which reached a crescendo in 1967 with 164 riots and 83 dead. With the assassination of Martin Luther King in 1968, bloodshed and destruction came to the nation's capital, and troops were stationed at the meeting place of Congress for the first time in a century. Almost two decades later, Pat Moynihan, then a Democratic member of the Senate, recalled the condition of the nation in 1968 as approaching anarchy or civil war (Ambrose 1989, 403).

In this setting the confusing presidential campaign played out. Lyndon Johnson declared himself out of the race but too late to permit several potential candidates to launch a campaign with any prospect of success. Briefly the field was left to two Catholics, the intellectual ex-seminarian Eugene McCarthy and the heir apparent of the Kennedy family, Bobby. Of the two, Robert Kennedy, struck down by an assassin at the hour of his greatest primary victory, would probably have been the choice of Catholic voters as well as of the total electorate. His death made it possible for Hubert Humphrey to win the Democratic nomination for the presidency in the tumultuous Chicago convention without entering a single primary.

Adding to the confusion was the entry of George Wallace into the race. His candidacy was the most serious third-party movement in twenty years—more threatening to the major parties than Strom Thurmond's bid in 1948—for Wallace had demonstrated power to win a substantial share of the vote in several northern states as well as in the South. Because of the Wallace candidacy there was a real possibility that an inconclusive vote in the electoral college would leave the selection of the president to the House of Representatives.

Surveys after the Republican convention found Nixon, favored by 43 percent of the electorate, substantially ahead of his two opponents. By 21 October, as support for Wallace outside his southern bastions steadily evaporated, it was clear that the race had become a two-candidate contest, with Humphrey gaining but still eight percentage points behind Nixon in the Gallup poll. By Election Day the two leading polls agreed that Nixon's lead had shrunk to two percentage points. The actual returns reflected a photo finish in the popular vote: Nixon, 43.4 percent, Humphrey, 42.7.

Postelection surveys found that one-fifth of the voters had switched from one candidate to another in the course of the campaign. Hubert Humphrey was the beneficiary of this churning and George Wallace the victim. Between Labor Day and Election Day Humphrey's standing in the Gallup poll rose by 40 percent, whereas Wallace suffered a net loss of one-third of those who had originally declared an intention to vote for him. Nixon's strength hardly budged throughout these eight weeks that were the height of the campaign season. In early September, 43 percent of the voters favored the Republican ticket, Gallup reported; by 2 November, 42 percent.

In the mind changing that occurred in 1968, Catholic voters appear to have vacillated to the same degree as the nation at large, 19 percent changing their voting intention during the campaign. Eight percent of the Catholics who went to the polls switched from Nixon to another candidate, and 7 percent abandoned their intention of casting a vote for Wallace. This bloc of 15 percent of the group vote ended up overwhelmingly in Humphrey's column (Republican National Committee, 1969).

Catholics and "The Emerging Republican Majority"

One interpretation of the 1968 election offered by Kevin Phillips found in the results evidence that a Republican majority was emerging. Phillips asserted that 1968 marked "the beginning of a new Republican cycle comparable in magnitude to the New Deal era which began in 1932" (Phillips 1969, 23). The Republican majority, he explained, was being fashioned by "a populist revolt of the American masses . . . elevated by prosperity to middle-class status and conservatism . . . against the caste, policies and taxation of the mandarins of Establishment liberalism" (470).

But in fact a Republican majority had not emerged, and the election returns made a less than convincing case that a new Republican cycle had begun. True, Wallace voters added to Nixon voters constituted a heavy majority of those who went to the polls in 1968, but there were many obstacles to putting the two groups together, including the continued ambition of the maverick ex-Governor of Alabama, who saw "not a dime's worth of difference" between the Republican and Democratic Parties. Nevertheless, there was a basis in Republican successes in the South, particularly in 1964, to support an argument that Wallace's followers could be turned into Republicans.

Whatever might be said about Republican prospects in the South, however, constructing a Republican majority in the nation would require more than the vote that could reasonably be expected from Dixie. The other large group of voters whose support, combined with that of southerners, would produce the emergence of a Republican majority and launch the new Republican cycle was the Catholic population. But it is hard to find in the returns of the election to which Phillips timed his book a basis for regarding Catholics as fertile ground for the seeds of a Republican revival. Nixon was the choice of only one-third of the Catholic voters. This was no better a result than Dewey had registered in 1948. It looked impressive only when compared with the one-fifth share of the Catholic vote that Nixon had secured running against Kennedy or with the fortunes of Republican candidates in the years of depression and war.

Although Hubert Humphrey received only 42 percent of the vote cast by the electorate at large, he was the choice of 60 percent of Catholic electors. George Wallace garnered only 6 percent of the vote cast by Catholics, less than half of his 13 percent share of the total vote recorded in the election.

This distribution of the vote provides some basis for conclusions about what was and what was not on the minds of the Catholic voters when they went to the polls. The unimpressive vote which they gave to Wallace argues that race was a minor factor in their voting decisions. Despite his efforts to sound broader economic and social themes in his campaign, George Wallace was still the man who had tried to block the schoolhouse door and the candidate for voters most strongly resistant to changes in the status of African-Americans in society.

The substantial vote cast for Hubert Humphrey in 1968 reflects the continued attachment of a strong majority of Catholics to the Democratic Party. This attachment had been reinforced by memories of two martyred members of the Kennedy family. In addition, Humphrey had credentials attractive to the Catholic electorate—a record of concern for middle- and lower-class America and an anti-Communist stance dating back to his entrance into politics in Minnesota, as well as an ebullient personality. Finally, many Catholics found Humphrey an appealing candidate because of the enemies he had made—those who rioted at Chicago and plagued his campaign appearances with disruptive tactics.

The Republican Effort to Woo Catholics

Since the 1950s Catholic voters, to the extent that they were targeted by the agencies of the Republican Party at the national level, were the concern of those handling ethnic affairs, and the appeal made to them was the message of anti-Communism. When Ray C. Bliss, always a skeptic about the effectiveness of courting ethnic groups on the basis of issues and themes geared to their parochial interests, became chairman of the Republican National Committee in 1965, he allowed the unit responsible for this task, then called its Nationalities Division, to expire. After rebuffing frequent requests from Representative Edward Derwinski of Illinois for the reestablishment of the division, Bliss consented to resurrect it in March of 1968 as another national election approached. In the presidential campaign of 1968, however, activity directed toward ethnic voters, like many other aspects of the campaign, was managed chiefly by Volunteers for Nixon-Agnew rather than the National Committee. The Nationalities Division, with Governor John Volpe of Massachusetts as its honorary chairman, was given a modest budget of $90,000.

The downgrading of the Nationalities Division reflected a change in Republican strategy. The centerpiece of the party's campaign to win Catholic voters became education in place of anti-Communism. The Republican platform of 1968 called for inclusion of "non-public school children" in programs of federal assistance to education. It further recommended circumventing legal obstacles imposed in some states blocking federal aid to such children by using the device of making federal payments to beneficiaries directly rather than through state agencies. The model for such a system had been set by Congress in 1946 when it included private and parochial school children in the School Lunch Program through this method.

This platform pledge went beyond previous Republican offers of aid to children in private and parochial schools which had been limited to tax relief for those who paid the school bills. The proposal of tax relief first appeared in an official Republican pronouncement in 1962 when a committee of Senate and House members drafted a Declaration of Republican Principle and Policy to serve as an off-year election platform. Melvin R. Laird, committee co-chairman, inserted in the declaration the promise of "tax relief . . . for those who bear the burden of financing education for themselves and others." This pledge, along with all others made in the Declaration of Republican Principle and Policy, was incorporated by reference in the 1964 Republican platform drafted by a committee again chaired by Laird.

The Democratic platform of 1968, unlike the Republican, had nothing to say about nonpublic schools. The potential issue which this silence presented was ignored by both parties in the presidential campaign.

The 1972 Election

In 1972 Nixon achieved a kind of victory rare in American elections. Winning 60.7 percent of the popular vote and losing the electoral votes of only Massachusetts and the District of Columbia, he achieved a triumph comparable to Roosevelt's landslide in 1936 and Johnson's in 1964.

In 1972, a mammoth shift occurred in the voting behavior of Catholics. The Gallup poll found that Nixon's share of the vote cast by Catholics rose from 33 percent in his first successful presidential race to 52 percent in his second. For the first time since its polling began, the Gallup organization reported that a Republican presidential candidate was the choice of a majority of the nation's Catholic voters. The Michigan Survey Research Center found an even stronger shift toward the Republicans, declaring that Nixon received 60 percent of the vote cast by Catholics. Even Gallup's more conservative figures indicate a startling increase of almost 60 percent in Nixon's share of the Catholic vote from 1968 to 1972, far exceeding his 40 percent increase in the share of the vote he received from the entire electorate.

During the campaign George McGovern expressed to journalist Theodore White his concern about losing working-class Catholics. "Our main problem," he said, "is the blue-collar Catholic worker. You just didn't know what would reach them" (White 1973, 312). Election returns demonstrated that McGovern had failed to solve his main problem. Blue-collar Catholic ethnic groups broke loose from their attachment to the Democratic Party. In contrast to the heavy support they gave to Hubert Humphrey in 1968, only

46 percent of their vote went to McGovern. Irish blue-collar workers, with a meager 34 percent voting for McGovern, led the wave of deserters from the Democratic standard. Blue-collar voters of Italian and eastern European ancestry were next in line giving Nixon a majority of their vote. Of all Catholic blue-collar ethnics, only Latinos, 81 percent of whom stuck with McGovern, remained loyal to the Democratic Party.

The returns from sections of major cities in which Catholics were still concentrated offered abundant confirmation of the switch in the Catholic vote. Polish Ward 36 in Chicago voted 66 percent for Nixon; Italian Ward 26 in Philadelphia (with the encouragement of Democratic Mayor Frank Rizzo) did the same; Nixon received 56 percent of the vote of New York's Borough of Queens—as great a proportion as had been cast for Eisenhower twenty years earlier. Among the big cities with a large Catholic population the only apparent exception to the trend was Boston, where only one-third of the voters chose Richard Nixon.

Catholics and the Silent Majority

Throughout his political career Richard Nixon sought to include Catholics in building a base of support. A Sulpician priest, John Cronin, did occasional duty as his unofficial adviser, notably at the time of the investigation of Alger Hiss. The Nixon staff always had Catholics in important positions—more, Nixon opined in 1960, than were on the Kennedy staff. And as president, Nixon broke precedent by installing in a White House staff position a Catholic priest, Jesuit John McLaughlin.

In the fall of 1969, when Nixon began to rally a band of supporters to counter the Vietnam protesters, he turned his attention to the Catholic population as a major source of recruits for the "silent majority." Just before Christmas he prodded an apparently sluggish Republican National Committee to action, "again" directing it "to concentrate on getting Catholic support for the Administration" (National Archives, Nixon Materials, memo of Harry Dent to John R. Brown, 22 December 1969).

Earlier in the year several White House staff members, notably the two Pats—Moynihan and Buchanan—were emphasizing the importance of attending to the concerns of Catholics. In response to a suggestion from Moynihan that a staff member be designated liaison officer to Church personages, Peter Flanigan was given this responsibility. Moynihan made the suggestion after a dinner meeting with Bishop Joseph Bernardin and other representatives of the U.S. Catholic Conference at which policies of the new administration were discussed. At this meeting Moynihan reported receiving an unfavorable reaction to rumors that Nixon might appoint an ambassador to the Vatican. His dinner companions preferred that the administration deal with Rome through them, Moynihan explained (Nixon Materials, memo of Moynihan to Nixon, 6 March 1969). Pat Buchanan proceeded to establish his own links with the official Church, volunteering to act as the president's contact with newly elevated Cardinal Terence Cooke of New York, whom he found to be well disposed toward the administration and deeply concerned about the "acute crisis in Catholic education" (Nixon Materials, memo of Buchanan to Nixon, 11 April 1969).

In 1970 the decisive influence of Catholic voters of New York in electing the Conservative Party's candidate James Buckley to the United States Senate and eliminating the incumbent Republican Charles Goodell, who had been a major irritant to the White House, further impressed upon Nixon the importance of the Catholic vote. As he considered his prospects in the election of 1972, however, the president was pessimistic that Catholic voters would prove reliable if he were pitted against a Democrat professing their faith. Nixon's concern was based on his memory of two defeats, to Kennedy in 1960 and to Pat Brown for the governorship of California in 1962.

But in the fall of 1971, Charles Colson brought good news. His polling showed Nixon would run ahead of either Muskie or Kennedy among Catholic voters. Reporting "significant inroads into the Catholic vote," he wrote that Nixon registered among Catholics "the biggest increase in popularity over our 1968 figures of any voting category" (Nixon Materials, memo of Colson to Buchanan, 20 October 1971).

There were ups and downs in presidential popularity with the Catholic constituency. In preparation for a meeting between Nixon and Cardinal Cooke on 20 January 1972, Flanigan composed a memorandum to Nixon entitled "Catholic Voting Attitudes." Expressing concern about recent poll data suggesting erosion of support for the administration among Catholics, the memorandum declared "we should continue to give special emphasis in our campaign and legislative strategy to winning back these votes" (Nixon Materials, memo of Flanigan to Nixon, 20 January 1972).

Campaign Issues Affecting Catholics

The greatest concern of the Catholic hierarchy in 1972 was the maintenance of the Church's school system. Rising costs, declining religious vocations, and relocation of Catholic families from urban neighborhoods were forcing closure of parish schools throughout the nation.

Since 1962, Republican platforms and other policy statements had offered some kind of government aid for children attending nonpublic schools, most commonly in the form of tax relief. In the fall of 1971, however, a sharp difference of opinion emerged in the White House about the wisdom of advocating assistance to Catholic education. Roy Morey of the

Domestic Council staff raised questions about the effectiveness and the risks of "the Parochial aid issue," which, he argued, "may not be that important to Catholics" but which would be likely to alienate "Protestants and 1.8 million public school teachers."

Pointing out that twice as many Catholic children were in public schools as in the Church's schools, Morey argued against any strategy of appealing to Catholics as Catholics and proposed instead an approach based on more general social, cultural, and economic issues—"taxes, crime, basic values, patriotism, and equality of opportunity" (Nixon Materials, memo of Morey to John Erlichman, 20 September 1971).

Polls could have been cited to confirm fears that aid to parochial schools was a risky issue. A Gallup poll in August 1972 asking voters whether they would be more or less inclined to vote for a candidate favoring aid for parochial and private schools showed an equal division of opinion among the total electorate but a pronounced disagreement between Catholics and Protestants on the question (table 7-1).

Table 7–1. Public Opinion on Government Aid for Non-Public Schools, 1972

In August 1972 the Gallup poll asked the question:

Would you be more or less inclined to vote for a candidate favoring aid for parochial or private schools?

It analyzed the results in terms of three groups: total population, Catholics, and Protestants.

	More Inclined	*Less Inclined*	*No Opinion*
Total population	43	42	15
Catholics	70	21	9
Protestants	34	49	17

The task of responding to the Morey memorandum was entrusted to Pat Buchanan. It was Buchanan's point of view that prevailed in the platform adopted by the 1972 Republican National Convention, which declared:

> Our non-public schools, both church-oriented and non-sectarian, have been our special concern. The President has emphasized the indispensable role these schools play . . . and he has stated his determination to help halt the accelerating trend of non-public school closures. We believe that means which are consistent with the Constitution can be

> devised for channeling public financial aid to support the education of all children in schools of their parents' choice, non-public as well as public. One way to provide such aid appears to be through the granting of income tax credits.

In the campaign Nixon's message to Catholics emphasized the Church's schools. "In your fight to save your schools, you can count on my support," he told the Knights of Columbus.

But it was not the only message. The platform's plank on schools was combined with more general themes less likely to engender division along religious lines—dealing with crime, taxes, patriotism, and the rest. The platform also endorsed voluntary prayer in schools and other public places, and it condemned busing for racial balance while pledging to end de jure school segregation.

Busing to achieve school integration was regarded by White House advisers as perhaps the greatest single grievance of the Silent Majority. Colson thought it "the only issue" in the spring as George Wallace was demonstrating strength in northern as well as southern primaries (Ambrose 1989, 542). From the Democratic side came some support for this judgment. Surveying the Democratic platform, Ben Wattenberg said, "They have just lost Michigan to the Republicans today with their busing plank. No one seemed impressed by the fact that in Macomb County they voted against busing in a referendum last fall by fourteen to one" (White 1973, 161). The county mentioned, a suburb of Detroit, is home to working-class Catholics.

In the presidential campaign of 1972, abortion was a peripheral issue. Not until four years later, after the Supreme Court had rendered its controversial decision in *Roe v. Wade*, did it emerge as a major concern in a contest for the presidency. In several states, however, abortion had seized the attention of voters in 1972. In Michigan, North Dakota, and parts of Massachusetts, referenda aimed at the modification of legal restrictions on the procedure were on the ballot. In New York, Pennsylvania, California, Connecticut, and Rhode Island, legislative bodies passed laws affecting abortion. The laws generally were intended to tighten restrictions, but in most cases they were negated by gubernatorial vetoes or judicial disapproval.

Nixon defined a position on abortion when, as commander in chief of the armed forces, he limited access to the practice for service personnel and their families by requiring military hospitals to observe whatever restrictions were established by the states in which they were located. In March 1972 the Commission on Population Growth and America's Future, which Nixon had appointed, filed an explosive report recommending (among other measures) public financing of abortion and repeal of laws restricting the practice. On 13 April these recommendations were denounced by the Catholic bishops in a statement calling abortion "an unspeakable crime." On 5 May the president rejected his commission's proposals declaring abortion "an unacceptable means of population control" (*New York Times*, 6 May 1972).

Also in a letter to Terence Cooke the president commended the cardinal for his effort to establish a less permissive regulation of abortion in New York than existing law, which permitted the practice through twenty-four weeks of pregnancy. "I would like to associate myself with the convictions you deeply feel and eloquently express," Nixon wrote (*New York Times*, 11 May 1972). In all probability, as White House spokesmen averred, this letter was not meant for release to the press, for it opposed the position taken by Governor Rockefeller, manager of the Nixon campaign for reelection in New York.

Whereas Republican spokesmen labeled McGovern the candidate of abortion (as well as acid and amnesty), the Democratic strategy was to keep abortion out of the campaign. Exercising their strong control of the Democratic National Convention, the McGovern forces mustered 58 percent of the delegates to vote down a motion to insert in the platform an endorsement of unrestricted abortion. During the campaign, when questioned or attacked on abortion, McGovern asserted that its regulation should be left in the hands of the states—the same position (he insisted) that Nixon held (*New York Times*, 25 September 1972). But McGovern, unlike Nixon, made no effort by word or gesture to associate himself with the position of the bishops on abortion.

As 1972 came to an end, momentum on the question of abortion appeared to be with its opponents. In several state legislatures their views had prevailed even though often frustrated by governors or courts. They scored decisive victories in the referenda in Michigan and North Dakota; in a referendum in part of Massachusetts, results were mixed and the verdict unclear. At that time the pro-life cause found an eloquent advocate in Senator Edward Kennedy, who declared that "legalization of abortion on demand is not in accordance with the value which our civilization places on human life. . . . Human life, even at its earliest stages, has certain rights which must be recognized—the right to be born, the right to love, the right to grow old" (*Pilot*, 11 November 1972).

The Social Issue in the 1972 Campaign

In writing *The Real Majority*, Scammon and Wattenberg intended to guide the Democrats away from a course leading to defeat in 1972. Ironically, while ignored by McGovern, the book made a deep impression on Nixon and Colson. To them it suggested a winning campaign plan.

McGovern's attention was focused on constructing a majority out of elements very different from those to which *The Real Majority* pointed. The coalition expected to produce a Democratic victory, McGovern explained to Tom Wicker of the *New York Times*, was to be an amalgam of "the poor and the minorities and the young people and the anti-war movement" (Kirkpatrick 1973, 59). The real majority, Scammon and Wattenberg pointed out, was un-poor, un-black, un-young, and strongly patriotic. Typified by the Dayton housewife of a working-class family of middle or somewhat lower income, the group included a large number who normally voted for Democrats and a large number of Catholics. It was not made up of flower children, campus radicals, and black power activists. It did not feel oppressed by the dominant culture and was not in rebellion against the establishment.

The Republican platform of 1972 sounded the general theme of the campaign to win over the targeted Democrats. "In this year 1972," it declared, "the national Democratic party has been seized by a radical clique which scorns our nation's past and would blight her future." The McGovern party was depicted as the party of the counterculture out to destroy all that the Silent Majority held sacred.

Jeane Kirkpatrick, then a Democrat, interpreted the election as "a cultural class struggle with Richard Nixon cast as leader of the masses and George McGovern as the spokesman of an embattled revolutionary elite." "Cultural values," she wrote, "displaced pocketbooks as the chief determinant of presidential voting" (Kirkpatrick 1976, 59). Charles Colson agreed, concluding that the election "for the first time in American history turned on social issues." Another commentator called the campaign "the beginning of the Reagan revolution in 1980" (Balzano 1991, 276–78).

Vietnam and the Election of 1972

Despite the emphasis McGovern placed on the Vietnam war as he sought the presidency, many analysts of the 1972 campaign have tended to minimize the importance of this issue as an influence on voting behavior and on the outcome of the election. The difference between the positions taken by the two major candidates was sharply defined. Although of less concern to voters in 1972 than it had been in the previous election, policy toward Vietnam remained a major issue. In one poll taken in 1968, 50 percent of the voters named Vietnam as the nation's greatest problem. By 1972, the number naming Vietnam had dropped to 25 percent, but no other problem on the national agenda was cited by more voters than the continuing conflict in Southeast Asia.

By the time of the election the withdrawal of American ground forces from Vietnam was almost complete, and the draft had been ended. The specific difference between the positions taken by the two candidates on what McGovern made his chief issue was whether American efforts to enable our South Vietnamese ally to survive after our withdrawal should be totally abandoned. Nixon argued for what he called an "honorable peace," an agreement to end the fighting, to return Americans held as prisoners, and an American resolve to support South Vietnam's independence by air power if the North violated the agreement. In the closing days of the campaign Henry Kissinger announced that such a peace was at hand perhaps convincing some voters that this outcome was not an unrealistic hope. McGovern promised a total, unilateral, and irreversible pullout of American power from the conflict within ninety days after he took office. Asking no promises of North Vietnam, he was ready to assume that American prisoners would be returned.

The policy choice toward Vietnam offered by the two candidates had an important bearing on the stance taken in the 1972 campaign by George Meany and by the AFL-CIO and on the outcome of the election. Early in the year Meany made a wrenching decision. In spite of his attachment to the Democratic Party and his hope that Nixon would be rejected in his quest for reelection, Meany said, "I don't want to see him defeated by somebody who is advocating surrender. . . . I will not go with a fellow running for President of the United States who advocates surrender in Southeast Asia." In a later comment more directly aimed at the McGovern campaign, Meany complained that "the way these guys are going, by the first of September, who knows, they may be advocating not only surrender but give Hanoi Texas as a gift" (Robinson 1981, 321).

Even though the ultimate outcome was to be only a delayed application of McGovern's policy, in 1972 this outcome was not regarded as inevitable—and certainly not as an acceptable policy choice—by the majority of the public. There may have been general regret that the nation's armed forces had been committed to the conflict, but a clear majority still favored support for the non-Communist forces after American withdrawal and opposed a Communist takeover of South Vietnam (Rosenberg et al. 1970, 48).

But to think that the issue of Vietnam in 1972 was seen by voters as only a choice between two conflicting military/diplomatic policies is to miss its impact on millions of Democrats who voted for Nixon. The issue of Vietnam merged with the social issue to turn many deeply patriotic Americans against the Democratic ticket. To such voters McGovern was the representative of antiwar forces that had brought violence to streets and campuses, burned draft cards and the flag of their country while parading behind the banner of the Viet Cong, and expressed their loathing of America's service personnel, whom they condemned as murderers of women and children. McGovern came close to joining this chorus when he compared attacks made by the United States Air Force in Vietnam to Hitler's worst atrocities.

All this deeply offended many Catholics, along with others whom devotees of the New Politics might consider superpatriotic. None took greater offense than those whose sons were in uniform. None responded to the tactics of the antiwar movement with greater indignation than the ethnics of middle and lower economic status. The shock and disgust with which one such group reacted—the Italian-Americans of a section of Brooklyn—is recorded in the sociological study *Canarsie* (Rieder 1985, 156–57). In this Little Italy the burning of the American flag was regarded as a sacrilege equivalent to the desecration of a chalice used in the mass.

McGovern's Contribution to Nixon's Victory

The contribution that McGovern and those who took power in the Democratic Party made to the Nixon victory in 1972 was enormous. In a meeting with key advisers to plan his campaign, Senator McGovern contrasted his position with that of others seeking the Democratic presidential nomination, saying he would "be to the left of them all." His hope of victory rested on a great outpouring of youth at the polls in this first election since the ratification of the Twenty-Sixth Amendment lowering the voting age to eighteen throughout the nation. The young, McGovern thought, would trust him, and "the most left-leaning candidate" would also be "the most reconciling candidate" (White 1973, 43). Often during the campaign McGovern sounded this theme, calling himself "a bridge over troubled waters," ready to lead dissident youth back into a society refashioned to make it worthy of their respect.

The most left-leaning candidate was too far from the mainstream for millions of Democratic voters, 42 percent of whom (according to the University of Michigan Center for Political Studies) cast their votes for Nixon. The young on whom McGovern had counted so heavily failed to come through. The turnout of the newly eligible voters eighteen to twenty-one was well below that of older age groups, and these youngsters favored McGovern over Nixon by a less than overwhelming margin of 54 to 46 percent.

In late August Ted Van Dyk, charged with the development of issues for the campaign, sent a memorandum to McGovern urging him to change course by "returning to traditional Democratic themes." He warned that the election was lost unless the Democrats in the big industrial states, "blue-collar, middle-minded and socially more conservative than our principal sources of support in the Democratic primaries," could be won back (White 1973, 217). This sage advice appears to have gone unheeded.

McGovern chose to emphasize immediate and total withdrawal from Vietnam in his appeal for votes. In selecting this issue in foreign relations, he chose to do battle on a field of policy in which voters reposed little confidence in the Democratic Party and even less in its candidate. The specific course he advocated, positioning him "to the left of them all," espoused a policy rejected by a clear majority of the public. And his rhetoric, characterizing the policy which the nation had pursued in Vietnam as dishonorable and on occasion besmirching the Americans who fought the war, offended the patriotic sentiments of many, even of those who thought the policy a grave mistake.

When McGovern addressed other issues during his campaign, he spoke the language of the New Politics and reinforced his position to the left of the majority of the public (Kirkpatrick 1976, 279; 1978, 90–93). That majority perceived him as an advocate of amnesty for war resisters, of emasculation of the military forces, of redistribution of wealth by confiscatory taxation and handouts to the idle, of seeking to reform rather than punish criminals, of toleration of the lifestyle of Haight-Asbury, Hollywood, and Greenwich Village.

No better example of an issue on which McGovern chose the unpopular side can be cited than school busing, which the Democratic platform declared "must continue to be available" to achieve desegregation and the Republican platform denounced as "unnecessary, counter-productive and wrong." The Center for Political Studies of the University of Michigan found 87 percent of the public closer to the Republican than the Democratic position on this subject. Wallace's strength in suburbia in the 1972 primaries was largely a response to his anti-busing stand. And in the November election Wattenberg's prediction that the Democratic platform's endorsement of busing would bring defeat in Michigan's Macomb County seems to have been borne out. Sixty-three percent of Macomb's vote was cast for Nixon in 1972, in contrast to the 30 percent which the county gave him in 1968. And whereas Humphrey was given 55 percent of the county's vote in the three-candidate race of 1968, McGovern's share four years later fell to 35 percent.

Especially damaging to the Democratic campaign was the aura of confusion and incompetence which surrounded it. Benjamin Page argued that the conduct of the campaign "conveyed an impression that McGovern was indecisive, weak, and incapable of making a tough decision and sticking to it" and that these "negative views of McGovern's personal characteristics . . . were probably the strongest factor pushing voters against him" (Page 1978, 142, 251–55). Introducing McGovern as the Democratic presidential candidate by an acceptance speech aired after the bedtime of a substantial part of the nation was an initial gaffe of a chaotic campaign. Probably the most harmful of the blunders were the grant and then the painful gradual withdrawal of "1000 percent support" of Senator Eagleton as vice presidential nominee, followed by the lengthy and embarrassing search for someone willing to be George McGovern's running mate. The weeks including and following the Democratic convention brought a series of self-inflicted wounds from which McGovern never recovered. Campaign themes that might have been persuasive with an electorate never completely trustful of Richard Nixon lost their edge in McGovern's clumsy hands. Skepticism about the president stopped short of accepting Democratic charges comparing him to Hitler and condemning his administration as the most corrupt in history.

The offenses related to the Watergate break-in and to the attempts to cover it up became clear to the public only after the election was over. Although Watergate was to have disastrous consequences for the Republican party later—in the off-year election of 1974 and to a lesser degree in the 1976 contests—in October 1972 a Harris poll found that 62 percent of the public dismissed Watergate as "mostly politics."

Finally, the desertion by organized labor was a decisive blow to the Democratic presidential ticket in many parts of the land. For the first time in its history the AFL-CIO failed to endorse the Democratic candidates and to provide the funds and the foot soldiers which it was capable of pouring into a campaign. The individual most responsible for labor's abstention from the presidential campaign was George Meany. His aversion to any candidate advocating "surrender" in Vietnam was reinforced as he witnessed the degradation of labor's role in the Democratic convention operating under its new rules. Although he did not cast his vote for Nixon in November (it appears that Mrs. Meany did), he joined the president for a conspicuous round of golf at the Burning Tree Country Club in a foursome that signaled to union members at least an attitude of benevolent neutrality in the presidential race.

In addition to depriving McGovern of the personnel and resources needed for his campaign to overcome the deficiencies of party organizations, the stance of labor leaders and mainline unions was of incalculable importance in other ways. It sent a message to union members that loyalty to the Democratic Party did not require a vote for the party's presidential candidate in 1972. The response is reflected in the finding of the University of Michigan Center for Political Studies that 57 percent of union members voted for Nixon and 43 percent for McGovern. The faithful Democrats responsible for this drastic departure from past voting patterns undoubtedly included a large number of Catholic unionists and their families.

Although the leaders and the national organization of labor avoided involvement in the presidential campaign, they participated vigorously in congressional contests. The unprecedented gap between the vote for McGovern and that for Democratic congressional candidates in major industrial states suggests how powerfully labor's involvement affected elections.

Postmortem Appraisals of the Election

Commonweal, the organ of a group of liberal lay Catholics, strongly supported McGovern. After the election it praised him as "a humane man, a man of courage, a man of wisdom and moral concern." His defeat it attributed to the blunders of his chaotic campaign in allowing himself to be perceived as "the candidate of the counterculture, a proponent of Abortion, Marijuana, and Amnesty" and in his handling of the dismissal and replacement of Senator Eagleton on the ticket. After the election *Commonweal* published a symposium under the title "Four More Years" in which several Catholics of Democratic inclination assessed the results. The participants agreed that "McGovern strategists decided to ignore the traditional ethnic base of the Democratic party." Eugene McCarthy, whose youthful antiwar constituency McGovern sought to inherit, observed that those who had been rejected in 1968 "with the help of new rules and procedures, controlled a convention and a campaign which effectively alienated one-third or more of the traditional Democratic voters" (*Commonweal* 1972, 204). Andrew Greeley explained that McGovern was rejected by Catholic voters "not so much because of campaign issues but apparently because of visceral dislike of the man" (Greeley 1992, 5).

McGovern blamed his defeat on "the forces of irrationalism and fear" which Nixon exploited to build a coalition of Republicans and "defecting Democrats—Wallaceites." It was "a southern strategy extended nationwide" tapping "the seeds of racism, the fear of change, the fear of the young, of the black" which explained the landslide victory of the Republicans (quoted by Novak 1972b, 262). The blind spot which afflicted McGovern during the campaign still affected his judgment after the election. The defecting Democrats were not all Wallaceites. Nixon's vote in 1972 exceeded by 6 million the combined vote which he and Wallace received in 1968, and 25 percent of the Wallace voters of 1968 chose McGovern.

There were many millions of Democrats and Independents who voted against McGovern simply because he seemed unresponsive to, even unaware of, their concerns and unappreciative of their values. Eugene McCarthy thought that much of McGovern's campaign focused on matters irrelevant to these voters. Michael Novak rendered a less charitable judgment that McGovern showed "contempt for the portion of the electorate that rejected him." Novak, then a liberal Democrat closely attuned to the Catholic ethnic population, who had served as a speechwriter for Sargent Shriver in the campaign, wrote that "thirty-five million registered Democrats" had been regarded by his party's presidential candidate as "irrational, racist, fear-ridden and," he concluded, "that's why they rejected McGovern" (Novak 1972b, 262).

The distribution of the presidential vote in 1972 seemed to some to signify a massive shift of party allegiance on the part of the electorate. That the South had ceased to be a Democratic stronghold had been apparent earlier. No Democratic presidential candidate had carried all eleven states of the Confederacy since 1944. McGovern, however, was the first to lose all eleven. The 1972 election confirmed the conclusion that a substantial realignment of southern voters had occurred. The confirming indicators were more than voting behavior in a series of presidential elections. Republicans could point also to steady gains in winning congressional seats as well as state and local offices in the South. And throughout the region Republican registrants had become a constantly increasing percentage of the total electorate (Black and Black 1992, ch. 11).

The behavior of Catholic voters was more difficult to interpret. It had shown no such consistent trend. That Catholics in 1972 had broken substantially from their voting pattern in the three presidential elections of the 1960s was clear enough. But whether this was a temporary negative reaction to the Democratic candidate rather than an abandonment of the Democratic Party was not clear. Nor, if a large body of Catholics was abandoning the Democrats, was it clear that they were ready to join the Republicans rather then to detach themselves from parties to become independents or even ally themselves with a third party.

Survey data do not reveal a great shift of party affiliation to the Republican side on the part of Catholics in 1972 despite a massive switch in voting behavior. Andrew Greeley argued after the 1972 election that the Catholic population remained overwhelmingly attached to the Democratic party and that the shift to Nixon was no greater than that registered by other groups of voters (Greeley 1977b, 202). In fact, the shift among Catholics between 1968 and 1972 was considerably greater than the change registered by the general voting population. Yet, withal, in their vote for president, Catholics remained less Republican than the electorate as a whole by a margin of eight percentage points. And Father Greeley was right in saying that the Catholic population held more Democrats than Republicans. Looking at long-range trends, however, one can discern in survey data a marked shrinkage in the Democratic advantage among this volatile group in the electorate.

The 1976 Election

The presidential contest in 1976 was extraordinary in many ways. The incumbent to whom the office had devolved by succession to a President who had resigned to escape removal by impeachment was pitted against a born-again Baptist peanut farmer and one-term governor of a southern state. Campaign discourse dwelt on subjects decidedly different from the staples of electioneering in the past. The new topics included the skulduggery connected with Watergate, the blanket pardon granted to Nixon to avert criminal prosecution, born-again Christianity, lust, and abortion.

This last subject drew the nation's Catholic bishops into the political arena in a more conspicuous and energetic role than ever before. In response to the Supreme Court's decision in *Roe v. Wade*, the National Council of

Catholic Bishops launched a campaign to amend the Constitution with the objective of revoking the holding in that case. In 1975 a plan to organize opponents of the decision in each of the 435 congressional districts was initiated. The plan was, in effect, superseded with the formation of the National Right to Life Committee, an organization open to all opponents of abortion and less formally related to a religious group. In the committee's membership, nevertheless, Catholics and evangelical Protestants seem to be especially numerous.

In 1974 and 1975 the Senate Judiciary Committee held hearings on two variants of a proposal called the Human Life Amendment to the Constitution designed to effect reversal of the Supreme Court's decision on abortion. Pro-life forces, the advocates of the Human Life Amendment, were unable to secure more than a committee hearing from the Senate and not even that from the House of Representatives. Undeterred, they turned their attention to the prospective presidential candidates as the 1976 campaign drew near.

Jimmy Carter, former governor of Georgia, shed the status of a dark horse regional candidate by virtue of his showing in the Iowa primary, in which he succeeded in identifying himself with the pro-life cause. Thereafter he had to exercise considerable ingenuity obscuring his position on the Human Life Amendment, a proposal he could not endorse without forfeiting the hope of nomination by a Democratic National Convention. In an editorial the Jesuit weekly *America* accused Carter of "indifference" to the issue of abortion manifested by a "response . . . [that] has shifted constantly from the Iowa primary through the platform hearings to the post-convention maneuverings" (*America* 1976, 42). Such criticism led Carter, complaining that he was "in trouble with the Catholics," to seek advice from the president of the University of Notre Dame, Theodore Hesburgh, who urged him to sidestep the question by pointing out that the Constitution gave the president no part in the process of amending the constitution (Hesburgh 1990, 271–72).

In their campaigns both Carter and Ford made more public overtures to the Catholic bishops than had been customary in previous contests. It was Carter who took the lead, inviting the National Conference of Catholic Bishops (NCCB) to send a representative to his home in Plains, Georgia to brief him on the prelates' concerns. The invitation brought from Washington not a bishop but a low-level staff representative whose presence was not newsworthy and who further refused to talk to the press after his meeting with the candidate. Eventually Carter had his session with a group of bishops, but the result was not what he sought. Questioned by the press after the meeting, which took place in the Mayflower Hotel in Washington, Archbishop Joseph Bernardin, president of the NCCB, responded that he and his colleagues were "disappointed" with Carter's position on abortion.

The Bishops' Conference then received an invitation to confer with President Ford. The delegation found Ford willing to support a constitutional amendment leaving the regulation of abortion to the states. Although this was less than the bishops sought through the Human Life Amendment, it was more of a concession than Carter offered, and Bernardin characterized Ford's position as "encouraging."

The effect of the contrasting comments about the candidates' views was, in the minds of many within and without the Church, to position the bishops on the Republican side in the presidential contest. Apparently in response to a wave of criticism, the administrative committee of the NCCB released a statement to dispel "public misperceptions concerning the nature and purpose of the meetings with the candidates." Rejecting the notion that the bishops were "indicating a preference for either candidate or party," the statement noted "elements of agreement and disagreement on many issues between our positions and those of the major parties, their platforms and their candidates." Further, the statement seemed to signal that the bishops were not single-issue voters by listing among their concerns not only protection of the unborn but also unemployment, education, food policy, housing, health care, human rights, arms limitation, and social justice (Reese 1992, 192–95; Byrnes 1991, ch. 5).

The platforms of the major parties took contrasting stands on proposals to amend the Constitution to reverse the decision in *Roe v. Wade*. The Democratic Party declared "undesirable" any attempt to enact an amendment of this sort. The Republican platform was less abrupt. It agonized over the "difficult and controversial" question of abortion, noted a lack of consensus within the party on the Supreme Court's decision, which it said permitted "abortion on demand," and urged continuation of "the public dialogue on abortion." It ended its contribution to the dialogue, however, with an expression of support for "those who seek . . . a constitutional amendment to restore protection of the right to life for unborn children."

Both parties advocated somewhat cautiously a measure of aid to families with children in nonpublic schools through some form of relief from taxation. The Republicans, however, promised such families more than the Democrats did by calling for granting a share of "education funds" to nonpublic schools on a constitutionally acceptable basis.

There were other provisions of the Republican platform that carried a message designed for some Catholics, though not exclusively for them. Among such were the planks favoring a constitutional amendment permitting prayer in public schools and bestowing lavish praise on ethnics, with special attention to Hispanics.

In 1976, as in 1968, the presidential candidate who started the campaign as the underdog closed the gap only to lose by a narrow margin on Election Day. This time it was President Gerald Ford who ran a catch-up race, beginning thirty-three percentage points behind his opponent in the polls in late July and losing by two points in the popular vote in November.

Ford regarded the blanket pardon he granted to Nixon as the decisive factor in his defeat (Ford 1979, 429). But other things were equally or more important. How tarnished the label Republican had become by events stemming from Watergate was forcibly demonstrated in the election returns of 1974 resulting in the loss of forty-eight Republican House seats and five Republican Senate seats. In an effort to shed the millstone of Republican issue, the president's advisers in the 1976 campaign urged him to shun identification with the party which Ford had served during all his political life. The president was cautioned specifically to refrain from attending Republican Party fundraising events and from endorsing Republican candidates for other offices.

A sluggish economy was another of Ford's handicaps in the 1976 campaign. Between 1973 and 1975 all significant economic indicators registered negative results—a decline of 6 percent in median family income, a 73 percent increase in the unemployment rate, and an inflation rate close to double digits. The incipient recovery reflected in the statistics for 1976 came too late to erase the perception that the economic policy of the Ford administration had been a failure. How important the public's view of the economy was in affecting votes in 1976 is indicated by the fact that 76 percent of the voters regarded the performance of the economy as the most important problem. Thirty-three percent were most concerned about recession and unemployment; 27 percent, about inflation. These findings of the University of Michigan Center for Political Studies marked a change from three prior presidential contests in which issues of foreign policy were dominant.

Neither of the major candidates conducted a campaign free from blunders. Carter's confession to *Playboy* that he had been guilty of lust in his heart and his defense of maintaining ethnic purity in the neighborhoods of big cities raised questions about qualities of character and intellect. Ford's limitations as an orator and campaigner were recognized by his advisers, who planned that the bulk of presidential activity designed to win votes would be conducted in the shelter of the White House. The wisdom of this plan became clear on several occasions, notably in the second debate, when the president declared, "There is no Soviet domination of Eastern Europe." Poland, he asserted, "is independent, autonomous; it has its own territorial integrity." The president had in mind a defensible proposition that the fierce national pride and the thirst for independence of the Polish people had not been extinguished by thirty years of Soviet occupation of their country, but he was not deft enough either in the debate or in several subsequent attempts to clarify his views to dispel the impression that he was woefully out of touch with reality.

The eagerness with which both Ford and Carter pursued meetings with the bishops representing the U.S. Catholic Conference was one indication of the importance both parties attached to the Catholic electorate in 1976. The plan drafted to guide the Ford campaign defined as a "target constituency" upwardly mobile blue-collar and white-collar workers in the suburbs, "many of whom are Catholics." It described "upwardly mobile Catholics" as a group becoming more independent and conservative . . . and the key to victory in the northern industrial states where they are from twenty-five to forty-eight percent of the voters" (Witcover 1977, 530, 536).

In recognition of the importance of this constituency, Ford's limited campaign schedule included fairly numerous appearances in a Catholic milieu. The president addressed an audience of 100,000 at a Eucharistic Congress with Philadelphia's Cardinal John Krol presiding and, on the Sunday before the election, he attended a mass in Buffalo at which the local Bishop Edward D. Head preached a sermon denouncing abortion.

The advice which Jimmy Carter received from his pollster, Pat Caddell, also reflected a concern about Catholic voters. In a memorandum dated 11 September 1976, Caddell warned that "the Catholic situation is serious. In most of the industrial states we barely carry the Catholic vote, and in Illinois, Michigan and California we are actually losing that segment." Caddell noted that the defection of Catholics was in part offset by Carter's "excellent showing (for a Democrat) with Protestants," but, he added, "If we expanded our margin to even a respectable Democratic showing in the urban Catholic centers, then all these key states would be held by wide margins." (Schram 1977, 283).

When the votes were counted, Ford trailed Carter among Catholics, but by historic standards the level of support which Catholic voters gave the Republican candidate was high. Gallup found 57 percent of Catholic ballots were cast for Carter, 42 percent for Ford. The CBS/*New York Times* poll reported the vote was split 54 to 44. Roughly double the share of their vote that Catholics had cast for Nixon in 1960 and for Goldwater in 1964 was registered for Ford. Ford's showing among Catholics was also substantially better than Dewey's in 1948 and Nixon's in 1968, and it was comparable to the Catholic vote cast for Eisenhower in 1952.

How well Ford did in attracting the vote of Catholics can be judged when one compares his 42 to 44 percent with the size of the group of Catholics who were then adherents of the Republican Party. According to the Gallup poll, in 1976 only 15 to 18 percent of the Catholic voting population regarded themselves as Republicans. This was the lowest level of Republican strength among Catholics in all the years of Gallup's polling.

Among the factors accounting for the Democratic resurgence in 1976 from the depths of 1972, the return of organized labor to the fray after sitting out the McGovern campaign had great importance. The AFL-CIO reported spending $4 million. Its more important contribution lay in fielding 100,000 "volunteers" in a get-out-the-vote drive and mailing out 70 million pieces of campaign literature from its Washington headquarters.

According to the CBS survey, Carter received 63 percent of the vote cast by union members, a massive gain in comparison with the 46 percent which McGovern garnered in 1972. "We were the margin," George Meany declared in a statement celebrating victory the day after the election, claiming credit particularly for the fifty-two electoral votes Carter gained from Pennsylvania and Ohio. Whether or not Meany's boast contained some element of hyperbole, undoubtedly the vigorous campaign which labor conducted on Carter's behalf had a significant impact on the voting behavior of union members and their families, including a high percentage of Catholics.

Another vote shift crucial to Carter's success was the return of the South to the Democratic fold. Of the eleven states of the Confederacy, the Democratic ticket carried all but Virginia. As a southerner Carter benefited from regional pride. As an active Baptist—indeed, a Sunday School teacher—he enjoyed the confidence of many who felt estranged by cultural influences represented by the Democratic Party leaders of 1972. As a graduate of Annapolis and a former naval officer, he could not be suspected of sharing that loathing of the military so widespread among McGovern's followers. On the contrary, he could be trusted to honor the uniform and keep America strong.

The South that Carter won back was not the South that had solidly supported Democratic presidential nominees down to the late 1940s. Elections in Dixie were no longer lily-white. The contest of 1976 was the first presidential election in which the power of black voters was demonstrated throughout the entire South. By 1976, 63 percent of southern blacks were registered to vote, contrasted with only 29 percent sixteen years earlier. Encouraged by Andrew Young and Martin Luther King Sr. to turn out on Election Day, they cast 90 percent of their vote for Carter, providing one-third of his vote in his home region. At least three states in Dixie—Texas, Louisiana, and Mississippi—were carried by the Democratic presidential ticket because of a black vote substantial and solid enough to overcome the pluralities Ford received from white voters.

After the election Pat Caddell pointed out that the Carter triumph rested on a coalition significantly different from that of the New Deal era. He singled out as decisive elements in the outcome certain "nontraditional groups" that provided a larger Democratic vote in 1976 than in past elections, thereby offsetting Carter's relatively weak performance in many traditionally Democratic strongholds. Prominent among these nontraditional groups were "white Protestants," "rural, small-town voters," and "better-educated white-collar people." Caddell chose not to highlight the fact that in the South a large share of the rural and small-town voters who supported Carter had voted for Wallace in 1968.

Jimmy Carter won the vote of 46 percent of the Protestant electorate. With the exception of the Johnson landslide of 1964, no Democratic presidential candidate in the half century since 1944 had fared as well with this religious group. On the other hand, although favored by a clear majority of the Catholic voters, Carter did not receive from them a margin comparable to Humphrey's in 1968. And in the coalition that elected Carter, Catholics played a smaller role than they had in electing Democratic presidents in earlier years.

One analyst, John R. Petrocik, called Catholic support for the Democratic ticket in 1976 "anemic," noting that "only a bare majority—53 percent—voted for Carter" (Petrocik 1981, 96). A Catholic journalist and loyal Democrat, Jim Castelli, drew a more upbeat conclusion from the returns, asserting that Carter got 85 percent of the "normal" vote a Democratic presidential candidate could expect from Catholics "under the best of conditions" (Castelli 1976, 780–81). If this was praise, it was faint indeed. For it would be hard to imagine more favorable conditions for a Democratic candidate than those of 1976. Jimmy Carter ran against an unelected incumbent who had served only a fraction of a term, who won renomination by the skin of his teeth, who bore the label of the party associated with Watergate, who had pardoned Nixon, and who had occupied the White House during a period of sluggish performance by the economy.

The 1976 election made the point that the days when two-thirds to three-fourths of Catholics voted for Democratic candidates were clearly past. The election of 1972 was more than a temporary aberration. A permanent change had taken place. Lost to the Democratic Party were millions of Catholics who would have enlisted under its banner in earlier times. Most had not become Republicans. They were adrift in a state of independence awaiting a candidate, a cause, a party more congenial to their values than the party of their fathers had become by the dawn of the decade of the seventies.

8

The Political Homogenization of American Catholics 1980–1998

In the two final decades of the twentieth century the political landscape changed significantly. A Republican was chosen to occupy the White House in three successive presidential elections during the 1980s, and for six years during the decade Republicans controlled the Senate. Although Bill Clinton, running as a New Democrat, was twice elected to the presidency in the nineties, his victories were achieved without winning a majority of the popular vote in either contest. In 1994 Republicans took control of Congress, returning divided government to Washington but with Democratic and Republican roles reversed from the arrangement familiar during the Nixon and Reagan and Bush years.

The loosening of the ties of voters to the major parties, evident in the 1970s, gathered momentum in the eighties and nineties. Manifestations of this trend included the significant vote for the presidency which Ross Perot received in two elections and in the victories of third-party candidates in gubernatorial contests in four states. In addition to growth in the ranks of Independent voters, the electorate evidenced some shifting of loyalties between the major parties. The change was in part geographic, in part economic, in part cultural, and in part racial. The Democrats gained adherents in the Northeastern region of the nation, among the most highly educated and affluent classes, among mainline Protestants, secularists, and the literary, artistic, and entertainment world, and won almost total support from the black community. Republican gains were registered among white southerners, Catholics, evangelical Protestants, blue- and white-collar workers, and middle-income suburbanites.

The 1980s brought a surge of political activism on the part of women that expanded in the following decade. The number of female candidates and officeholders increased dramatically at all levels of government and in all its branches. By 1997 sixty women were serving in Congress; twenty years earlier there had been only eighteen. The heightened feminine activism was not neutral in its effects on the fortunes of the two major parties. Democratic women in the Congress in 1997 outnumbered Republican women two to one. Further, a fissure appeared in the 1980s between men and women in voting behavior. In the five presidential elections between 1980 and 1996 the Republican candidate drew a larger share of the male than the female vote. In presidential balloting in the 1950s and 1960s, on the other hand, women voted more heavily Republican than men. In 1976 Carter drew 50 percent of the male and 50 percent of the female vote.

Ronald Reagan was the dominant political figure of the 1980s. He brought to the management of the nation's affairs a brand of conservatism which shifted the direction and emphasis of public policy, slowing the expansion of government's domestic agenda and building up the nation's military power.

The 1984 election demonstrated Reagan's popularity. Carrying forty-nine states, he received more votes than were cast for any other candidate down to the end of the twentieth century. And in 1988 the public's approval of the Reagan administration was probably the decisive factor in the triumph of George Bush.

By far the most important change in the world in the 1980s was the dramatic collapse of the Communist system in the Soviet Union and Eastern Europe, symbolized by the destruction of the Berlin Wall during the Bush administration. Some saw in these events the fruit of the policies of Ronald Reagan who had stood beside that wall and called on Khrushchev to tear it down.

The adoption of supply side economics (or Reaganomics), brought a reduction of income tax rates and curbed the growth of spending for domestic programs. Reagan staked out a position on the conservative side of the cultural divide on abortion, pornography, prayer in school, school choice, and punishment of criminals. Except for cutting off much public financing of abortion, however, the Reagan administration did not significantly effect change in policy in these fields.

During Reagan's two terms substantial economic progress was recorded, reflected in a healthy growth rate in the gross domestic product and in employment. Deficits mounted, however, and the goal of a balanced budget was further away in 1988 than in 1980.

Many social indicators told a story of continuing decay—increasing incidence of violent crime, overflowing prisons, slumping SAT scores, illegitimacy rates, single-parent families, and hordes of homeless who suddenly appeared on the streets of our cities.

Immigration, principally from Asia and Latin America, brought about changes in the demography of the nation, adding to its cultural, racial, and linguistic diversity. The problems of absorbing a large element of immigrants, many illegal, led to enactment of an important revision of the immigration laws and to significant frustration and resentment on the part of the native population, especially in the heavily impacted Southwest.

After defeat in 1988 the Democratic Party began to alter its message, avoiding the word "liberal" and softening aspects too directly challenging what middle America regarded as moral and economic virtues. The engine of change was a group within the party formed as the Democratic Leadership Council which succeeded in recasting the party's image, in moving it to the "vital center," and in winning the Democratic presidential nomination in 1992 for its former leader, Bill Clinton. As a result of the changes wrought in the party's stance in the administration of a New Democrat, issues defining the parties became somewhat blurred and political debate took on an increasingly conservative tone.

Catholics in the 1980s

Catholics continued to ascend the socioeconomic ladder. The Americanization of older European ethnics proceeded as their neighborhoods disappeared from the cities, churches in which their language was used were closed (often converted into houses of worship for black Protestants), and the residents moved to suburbia (Alba 1995, 3–18).

The Church became more Hispanic as a result of immigration. In contrast to the system of separate national parishes established to serve immigrant groups in earlier times, Hispanics were generally integrated into existing territorial congregations that were multiethnic in character.

In the 1980s a notable realignment of Catholic voters took place. The proportion of Catholics of Democratic affiliation and voting habits shrank; the ranks of Catholic Republicans and Independents increased; and the activist cadres in the Republican Party were diversified by an infusion of Catholics in party and public office.

Pollster Richard Wirthlin called these changes a "rolling realignment." The shift was not an earthquake on the political Richter scale, not sudden or dramatic. It whittled down, but did not eliminate, the margin by which Catholic Democrats outnumbered Catholic Republicans.

Surveys of the party preference of voters can yield results that vary one from another depending on such factors as their timing and the phrasing of the question put to interviewees. Despite some differences in results, several surveys confirm the trend toward a rolling realignment of Catholics. According to the University of Michigan Center for Political Studies, the margin by which Democratic Catholics exceeded their Republican coreligionists shrank from 43 percentage points in 1952 to 22 percentage points in 1986 (Miller and Traugott, 1989, 93).

Figures from other sources reflect a similar trend of Republican gain and Democratic loss during this period. An analysis by the Roper organization found that whereas 62 percent of the Catholic population reported Democratic affiliation in 1952, only 39 percent did so at the end of the eighties. During these years, it also reported, the percentage of Catholics of Republican affiliation rose from 17 to 28 (*American Enterprise* 1991, 93). These figures lead to the conclusion that, between the end of the Truman administration and the beginning of the Bush White House years, the Democratic party experienced a loss equal to almost 40 percent of its Catholic membership. The gain in Republican adherents, though significant, did not match the Democratic loss. The Democratic decline also brought growth in the ranks of Catholic Independents.

A third study, the Survey of Religious Identification conducted in 1990, reached the startling conclusion that, among white Catholics, Republicans outnumbered Democrats, 34 to 29 percent. In the total Catholic population, however, it found more Democrats than Republicans because of a lopsided Democratic margin among Hispanic and black Catholics (Kosmin and Lachman 1993, 199).

In the three presidential elections of the 1980s, Republican candidates fared well with Catholic voters. Ronald Reagan in his two races ran substantially ahead of his Democratic opponents. In 1984, Reagan (according to Gallup) received 61 percent of the vote cast by Catholics—a triumph unmatched by a Republican in any earlier presidential race. Four years later the vote cast by Catholics appears to have been divided evenly between Bush and Dukakis, with a majority of white Catholics however, voting for Bush.

In the years after the Second World War Catholics became more numerous in the ranks of Republican activists as holders of, and candidates for, public office as well as participants in party organization. The emergence of Catholics in such roles is reflected in the sizable increase in the number of Catholics on the Republican side of the aisle on Capitol Hill (table 8-1).

A similar trend reflecting increased Catholic representation among Republican activists is found in the changing religious composition of Republican national nominating conventions (table 8-2).

In the 1980s the Catholic hierarchy assumed a more visible role than had been its custom in addressing public policy issues. The bishops spoke out as a body on nuclear weapons in a statement *The Challenge of Peace* (1983) and on the economic system in *Economic Justice for All* (1986). Both statements were widely construed as critical of the direction of policy taken by the Reagan administration in these fields. On the matter of abortion, on the other hand, the bishops were on the side of Presidents Reagan and Bush. In both the 1984 and 1988 campaigns some prelates indicated a clear preference

TABLE 8–1. Number of Catholic Republican Members of Congress, 1948–1999

	Senate	*House*	*Percent of Republican Membership*
80th Congress (1947–48)	1	13	4.7
86th Congress (1959–60)	0	14	7.5
90th Congress (1967–68)	2	22	10.7
104th Congress (1995–96)	9	56	23.0
106th Congress (1999–2000)	11	49	21.5

for the Republican presidential ticket. Notable among them was Cardinal O'Connor of New York.

In 1983 the Congress cleared the way for resumption of formal diplomatic relations with the Vatican by repealing a legal obstacle dating back to 1867. Early in January 1984 President Reagan appointed William A. Wilson Ambassador to the Holy See. Up to that time Wilson had served as the president's personal representative to the pope. The change in title and status conferred on Wilson, though modest, involved some political risk. When Harry Truman had proposed a similar step in 1951, the storm of protest it provoked led the president to back away from his idea, the Congress to submerge it, and the prospective appointee, General Mark Clark, to decline the honor.

Concern that old passions might be reignited by the appointment of an ambassador to the Vatican led to cautious handling of the repeal of the 1867 ban. It was done almost by stealth in 1983 through an amendment added to the State Department authorization bill on the Senate floor and accepted in conference by the House without a hearing or a roll call vote in either chamber.

"Times and attitudes do change—and so do institutions" the *Christian Century* observed on 25 January 1984, explaining why it was not "frothing at the mouth in righteous rage over the . . . move to establish full and formal

TABLE 8–2. Religious Affiliation of Delegates to Four Republican National Conventions (As Percentage of Total Delegates)

	1948	*1972*	*1984*	*1988*
Protestant	87.1	79.0	66.4	66.7
Catholic	6.1	17.0	23.7	21.8
Jewish	0.7	2.0	2.8	2.5
Mormon			1.9	1.5
Other	2.6	1.0	4.4	5.5
No religious affiliation	3.5	2.0	—	2.0

Sources: 1948: David et al., *The Politics of National Party Conventions* (1960), 331; 1972: Jeane Kirkpatrick, *The New Presidential Elite* (New York: Russell Sage Foundation, 1976), 86; 1984 and 1988: analysis by staff of Republican National Committee (unpublished).

ties between the United States and the Vatican" after it had vigorously opposed the same initiative when proposed by President Truman thirty years earlier. "Thanks in large part to Pope John XXIII, the Second Vatican Council and the humanizing reforms they initiated" as well as the national experience during the Kennedy administration, the paper said fear that Catholicism threatened religious liberty had abated and distrust of the Papacy had declined.

Indeed, the relatively feeble protest against sending an ambassador to the Vatican demonstrated that anti-Catholicism had lost much of its political punch. And, correspondingly, the tepid response of the nation's Catholics suggested that this gesture brought little political gain to its sponsors.

The 1980 Election

Ronald Reagan's victory signaled a change in the Republican Party—a reordering of priorities more than a change of goals or policy. The social issue, perhaps more accurately described as a complex of cultural issues, was elevated to major status in the party platform and in campaign rhetoric.

Getting government off the backs of the taxpayers was a major theme of the Reagan campaign—government said to be bent on taxing too much, regulating too much, forcing busing on schoolchildren while forbidding them to pray, protecting pornographers, promoting abortion, giving handouts to welfare queens, subsidizing illegitimacy, and making minority status instead of individual merit a test for employment and promotion in the job market and for admission to college. Such issues were not new, but in earlier campaigns they had lesser status than economic programs, and candidates like Gerald Ford were somewhat uncomfortable with them. Now they were front and center, touted by a candidate who did not shrink from exploiting them.

In addition to giving stronger emphasis to these cultural issues, the platform on which Ronald Reagan ran also abandoned one old issue by omitting any statement of support for the Equal Rights Amendment. Although past Republican platforms had endorsed the ERA—indeed, had boasted that the Republican Party had supported it since 1940—qualms about the purposes of its most vocal advocates in the feminist movement and about the interpretation it might be given by a Supreme Court that had discovered a right to abortion in the Constitution led to silence about the ERA in the 1980 platform.

With regard to foreign policy, the change in the stance of the Republican Party under Reagan was more subtle. Anti-Communism had long been associated with the Republican Party, but Reagan seemed more aggressive in repeating old battle cries—so much so that the Democrats warned that electing him would risk plunging the nation into war with the Soviet Union. President Carter sought to exploit this concern that Reagan's recklessness would lead to conflict and to downplay any Communist issue by denouncing "inordinate fear of Communism."

The Democratic platform staked a claim to the votes of the feminists whose major demand had met with a rebuff from the Republican Party. The Democrats championed the cause of the Equal Rights Amendment as the Republicans abandoned it. The platform adopted by the Democratic convention went far beyond a call for the constitutional amendment. It also required that Democratic Party funds be withheld from candidates opposed to the ERA and that states which failed to ratify the proposed amendment be boycotted.

The homosexual constituency of the Democrats, which placed six openly gay people on the platform committee, secured its major objective with the adoption of a civil rights plank which added "sexual orientation" to the list of impermissible reasons for discrimination, along with the older well-established categories of race, religion, gender, and age.

On the ERA and on homosexual rights the opposing positions of the parties were conveyed by the contrast between Republican silence and an explicit Democratic statement. On the subject of abortion, on the other hand, the two platforms were in stark and explicit contrast to each other. The Republican platform staked out a strong antiabortion position including advocacy of an amendment to the Constitution to overturn *Roe v. Wade*, opposition to government financing of abortion, and support for the appointment of judges committed to the right to life. The Democratic platform opposed an amendment to alter the Supreme Court's decision on abortion and endorsed government financing of abortions for the poor. President Carter accepted the stand taken in the platform on the constitutional amendment but notified the convention of his personal opposition to federal funding of abortion. The stands taken by the candidates for president were not satisfactory to the National Organization for Women, which withheld its endorsement from both Carter and Reagan because of the abortion issue.

The Influence of Religion in 1980

The most visible group of religious participants in the 1980 campaign came from the ranks of Protestant evangelicals, particularly the Moral Majority under the leadership of the Reverend Jerry Falwell. A significant bloc of voters and campaign workers emerged from the pews of conservative churches. With the enthusiasm of amateurs committed to the cause of saving the nation, they registered new voters, operated telephones, mailed out literature, got their people to the polls, and performed all the chores that go with a political campaign. The effort that was mounted was substantial. It is not surprising that Reagan campaign strategists regarded evangelicals as the primary target group among religious bodies in 1980.

Although less emphasis was given to appealing to the nation's Catholic voters, this group was not neglected. Under the chairmanship of Bill Brock, the Republican National Committee had placed on its staff a priest educator, Donald Shea, as an adviser on the concerns of Catholics. When 1980 came around, Father Shea had held his position for three years. He had become a familiar figure to Republican officeholders and party officials, serving as a consultant to them as well as to candidates facing constituencies with significant numbers of Catholics.

Collectively the Catholic bishops maintained a low profile in the 1980 campaign. This time they held no meetings with the candidates and issued no declarations which could be construed as an expression of preference for either major party. They did issue a statement on "political responsibility," an exhortation that candidates campaign on issues and that voters make rational conscientious judgments on the range of policy choices at stake in the election. They warned against single-issue voting, appearing to some critics within the Church thereby to downplay the importance that Catholics should accord to abortion in forming their voting decision.

Individual bishops, however, did become involved in campaigns, usually stressing the issue of abortion. The most direct and clear episcopal intervention intended to influence Catholic voters involved congressional contests in Massachusetts and California. Humberto Cardinal Medeiros, in a statement read in the 410 churches of the archdiocese of Boston on the eve of the

Democratic primary, asserted that voters who "elect those lawmakers . . . who make abortions possible by law" share in the guilt for a "horrendous crime and deadly sin" (*New York Times*, 16 September, 18 September, 19 September 1980). Despite this strong admonition, the two candidates who were the Cardinal's apparent targets, Barney Frank and James C. Shannon, won nomination and were subsequently elected to the House of Representatives. According to the *New York Times*, Catholics made up 75 percent of the population of Congressman Shannon's district and 45 percent of Frank's constituency.

In California, a Ku Klux Klan leader running for Congress publicly opposed by Bishop Leo Maher of San Diego was defeated. As reported in the *New York Times* on 5 October 1980, the bishop declared that a vote for Democratic nominee Tom Metzger would be sinful. Since Metzger was repudiated generally by local opinion leaders, including most of his own party, the bishop's share of the credit for the outcome cannot be quantified, but presumably his intervention helped to bring about the result. It is significant that Bishop Maher did not suffer the kind of criticism heaped on Cardinal Medeiros for involvement in politics. The actions of the two ecclesiastics were similar, but the concerns which prompted their intervention were quite different.

Two other members of the hierarchy clearly signaled their preferences in the 1980 campaign. Archbishop John Whealon of Hartford strongly criticized the Democratic Party in a signed column in his archdiocesan newspaper, and he was joined by the other Connecticut bishops in urging Catholics to vote against candidates supporting abortion (Castelli 1980, 650–51). Cardinal John Krol of Philadelphia joined Reagan at a breakfast meeting and criticized Carter for his stand on abortion and on tax credits for nonpublic school students in a speech to 250 of his priests the following day (Castelli 1980, 650–51).

Religion and Voting Behavior in 1980

In 1980 the presidency was returned to the Republican party. In the election for the third time since World War II, voters were faced with a choice among three presidential candidates enjoying appreciable support. When the votes were tallied, the third-party candidate, John Anderson, received 7 percent of the total, with his main supporters found in the ranks of Jewish voters, college graduates, and the young. It seems reasonably clear that Anderson's candidacy helped to enlarge Reagan's margin of victory, siphoning off more votes from the president than from his Republican challenger. As a sort of born-again liberal and an articulate former member of the House Republican leadership, Anderson was an attractive alternative to Carter for Republicans who considered Reagan too far right and for Democrats who thought Carter too pious.

Carter's percentage of the total national vote fell off by nine percentage points from the 50 percent he had received in his first race. Reagan, who received almost 51 percent of the votes, improved on Ford's showing by three percentage points.

According to Gallup's figures, Carter's losses among Jews amounted to nineteen percentage points, among Catholics eleven, and among Protestants seven. Compared with the vote Ford had received, Reagan's gains among Catholics and Jews were equal—five percentage points among each group—whereas Protestants gave him only one percentage point more of their vote than they had cast for Gerry Ford.

The media were fascinated with the Moral Majority's part in Reagan's victory, but these figures suggest that although the movement may have had a local or regional impact, in the nation as a whole it failed to marshal a vote of abnormal size for its presidential candidate. The results tend to confirm the conclusion reached by two respected political scientists after surveying the evangelical vote that the "efforts to mobilize a religious constituency . . . had no measurable effect in the 1980 elections" (Lipset and Raab 1981, 31).

The changes in the voting behavior of both Catholics and Jews attracted little media attention, but they were more substantial than those of the Protestant population. Unlike Jewish voters who were more inclined to turn to Anderson, Catholic switchers voted predominantly for Reagan. Polls agree that Reagan captured more votes from Catholics than Carter but disagree about his margin. Gallup reported that Catholics split 47 percent for Reagan, 46 for Carter, and 6 for Anderson whereas the CBS pollsters found Reagan ahead of Carter 50 to 42 percent. Either way, the 1980 election can be regarded as another in which a plurality of Catholics voted for a Republican presidential candidate as they had in 1956 and 1972. This election has been called the election Watergate postponed, and there are grounds for the belief that, along with other elements of the population, many Catholics returned to a track toward Republicanism on which they had been traveling for at least a decade.

A particularly noteworthy aspect of the 1980 election was the emergence of a sharp gender gap. The reasons for this phenomenon are in dispute. Gallup reported that in part the Democrats strong advocacy of the Equal Rights Amendment was responsible for the divergence between male and female voting patterns. The ABC exit poll offered some confirmation of this judgment, finding that the candidates' position on the ERA influenced the vote of 16 percent of the electorate and that 69 percent of this group cast their votes for Carter. Clearly, however, this is not a sufficient explanation of the gender gap, which was to endure long after ERA ceased to be an issue.

The considerations that appear to have been most important in Reagan's victory lay in the fields of economic and foreign policy. Runaway inflation and unemployment levels were the economic concerns. The apparent impotence of the United States to secure the release of American diplomats held hostage in Tehran was the major foreign policy problem significantly affecting voting behavior.

These specific concerns contributed powerfully to a sense that the nation was in decline as the rest of the world, including our adversaries, forged ahead. President Carter complained that a vague malaise was affecting the country for which the administration appeared to have no cure. When Ronald Reagan put to the public the question, "Are you better off than you were four years ago," even his opponent seemed to be giving a negative response.

Catholics, like the rest of the nation, pronounced a negative verdict on the leadership of the Carter administration. The majority which the Democratic presidential ticket had eked out from this segment of the electorate in 1976 evaporated in a pronounced shift back toward the direction that Catholic voters had taken in 1972.

Surveys suggest that the reasons for the change in the voting pattern of Catholics in 1980 were not unlike those motivating the nation at large. Although the stand on abortion taken in the Republican platform may have helped to steer some Catholics toward Reagan, relatively few voters—6 percent nationwide—told ABC pollsters that their vote was influenced by the candidates' position on this question. And Reagan's support from them—52 percent of the group—was less than overwhelming. These findings probably reflect considerable confusion in public perception of the issue in the campaign abetted by President Carter's disagreement with the Democratic platform on public funding of abortion and by the failure of both candidates to win the seal of approval of the National Organization for Women.

In summary, the 1980 Republican presidential ticket appears to have won approximately half of the vote cast by Catholics. Contributing to this result was a band of voters, in great part blue-collar Catholics, that came to be known as "Reagan Democrats." They constituted a considerable segment of the large number of Democrats—25 percent of those who voted, according to the CBS/*New York Times* poll—who defected from Jimmy Carter.

E. J. Dionne Jr. concluded a searching analysis of Catholic voting behavior in 1980 by declaring, "Catholic ties to the Democrats are undoubtedly weaker, but there has yet to be a clear conversion of Catholics to the Republican cause" (1981, 316–18). The estrangement of Catholic voters from the Democrats he called "dealignment" rather than realignment.

Although the 1980 election did not produce a Republican majority of decisive dimensions among the nation's Catholics and indeed left doubt about the durability of the attachment to Republicanism of many Catholics who voted for Reagan, Republicans could claim to have secured a greater share of this historically Democratic vote than in any previous comparable presidential election. In 1968, the most recent contest among three serious candidates for the presidency, Nixon received only one-third of the Catholic vote. Beside this, the share cast for Reagan, roughly 50 percent, was an impressive gain.

The Election of 1984

In a year-end survey of religious news, the *Christian Century* expressed its conclusions for the year 1984 in the caption "Religion in Politics: 84's Top Story." Press coverage of the presidential campaign justified the headline. The media's attention was directed principally toward the activities of evangelical Christians in behalf of the Reagan candidacy and reaction to them, as it had been in 1980. But in addition, this time Catholic personalities, lay and clerical, were involved in the campaign in ways prominent enough to provide abundant fodder for the press.

Religion and Morality

The morning after his renomination, Reagan addressed more than ten thousand people at a prayer breakfast in Dallas's Reunion Arena. In language almost identical to that once used by George Washington, he told his audience, largely evangelical in composition, that "politics and morality are inseparable. And, as morality's foundation is religion, religion and politics are necessarily related." Such sentiments, as well as the highly visible role of clergymen like Jerry Falwell and Pat Robertson in the convention and the campaign, drew the complaint that the Republicans had violated "a liberal consensus of the past half century . . . that religion ought to . . . be kept out of the public order" (Plotkin 1985, 48). Vice President Mondale joined the complainants, expressing respect for religion but criticizing Reagan for political exploitation of religious sentiments and organizations.

Along with this criticism directed principally toward Protestant clergy, some Catholic politicians and journalists deplored the activities of their own churchmen in the election contest. Governor Mario Cuomo told the *New York Times* on 28 July 1984 that his church was more "aggressively involved" in politics than ever before and accused Republicans of "pandering" to Catholic voters. Another staunch Democrat, columnist Mary McGrory, writing in defense of Geraldine Ferraro, observed that "the hierarchy of her church is acting like an arm of the Reagan re-election committee."

Ferraro herself after the election expressed particular bitterness toward Cardinal John O'Connor, who, she noted, had been a registered Republican in Pennsylvania before coming to New York and registering as an Independent. "I did not anticipate," Ferraro wrote, "that the Archbishop of New York would step out of his spiritual pulpit into the partisan political ring" (Ferraro 1985, 213; Shannon 1985, 302).

Geraldine Ferraro was chosen by Mondale as his running mate in response to feminist pressure to place a woman on the ticket. But she had much to recommend her besides femininity. She had won elections to Congress several times and served in the leadership of the House of Representatives. She had capably chaired the platform committee of the convention which nominated her. And she brought geographical balance to the ticket.

But the "rationale for choosing Ferraro," as William V. Shannon, former political reporter for the *New York Times* and, under Kennedy, ambassador to Ireland, saw it, was something else. It was that "as a wife and mother, a Catholic and an Italian American, she was expected to appeal particularly to socially conservative Catholic Democrats who in recent presidential elections had begun to stray from the party of their parents" (Shannon 1985, 302).

If this was the rationale for the selection of Ferraro, the election returns proved that the ticket makers had miscalculated badly. Wirthlin's postelection poll for Reagan found that only 1 percent of the Catholics who voted for the Democratic presidential ticket cited the vice presidential nominee as a reason for doing so. And even in the Irish-Italian congressional district in Queens which Ferraro had always carried handily, the Democratic presidential ticket received only 43 percent of the vote in 1984.

The rationale began to come apart in September when Cardinal O'Connor criticized Ferraro for expressing the view that "the Catholic position on abortion is not monolithic." Such was the stand Ferraro had taken two years earlier in a letter inviting members of Congress to hear the opinions of a paper organization called Catholics for a Free Choice which disagreed with the pope and the bishops on abortion and many other matters. There is but one position on abortion defined by those authorized to formulate the "Catholic" position, O'Connor asserted. Among them opinion is "not divided." "There is no variance, there is no flexibility, there is no leeway" (Ferraro 1985, 232; 213–18). When Ferraro subsequently appeared at a campaign rally in Scranton, Pennsylvania, Bishop James Timlin, successor to O'Connor as head of that diocese, called a press conference to condemn her position on abortion as "absurd" and "dangerous."

The Ferraro campaign encountered conflict with yet another member of the hierarchy in connection with the annual Columbus Day parade in Philadelphia. According to Ferraro's account of the incident, Cardinal John Krol blocked her participation in this event by threatening to withdraw the marching bands and children from Catholic schools from the celebration if she were among the dignitaries in the parade (Ferraro 1985, 232).

Cardinal O'Connor became involved in controversy also with Governor Mario Cuomo. In a speech carefully drafted in consultation with certain academic Catholic theologians that was delivered at the University of Notre Dame and widely publicized, Cuomo laid out a justification for the position on abortion which he and many other Catholic politicians were taking. Although accepting his Church's position that abortion was immoral, he warned against efforts to impose this moral view on others. "The values derived from religious belief will not—and should not—be accepted as part of the public morality unless they are shared by the pluralistic community at large, by consensus" (*New York Times*, 14 September 1984; McElwaine 1988, 94–96).

This position was implicitly challenged by the Cardinal when he declared that he could not understand how any Catholic could vote for a candidate favoring abortion. Cuomo responded vigorously, questioning whether this observation would bar a Catholic from voting for him or for Ferraro. O'Connor replied somewhat unconvincingly that he had not intended to urge voters to choose or reject any specific candidate (*New York Times*, 3 August, 4 August 1984).

O'Connor's preference for the Republican presidential ticket perhaps explains Mondale's decision to decline the cardinal's invitation to attend the Al Smith Memorial banquet in mid-October, an event that had usually attracted the candidates of the major parties in previous presidential election years. In 1984 Reagan appeared without his opponent, giving the dinner something of the appearance of a campaign rally.

O'Connor was not alone among the bishops in signaling a preference in the 1984 election contest and in basing his choice on the issue of abortion. The eighteen bishops of the New England states added their voices to the campaign dialogue in September by declaring abortion to be "the critical issue of the moment." Without going so far as to endorse a candidate, bishops in Buffalo, Hartford, Scranton, and Philadelphia made their preference for the Republican presidential ticket as clear as did the archbishop of New York.

From members of the hierarchy, based particularly in midwestern states, came statements that sounded somewhat discordant to ears attuned to the nuances of ecclesiastical discourse. In August Bishop James W. Malone of Youngstown issued a declaration on behalf of the bishops' conference cautioning the clergy against expressing support for candidates although approving statements defining Church teaching on the moral aspects of political issues (*New York Times*, 10 August 1984).

Perhaps the most significant pronouncement was made by Cardinal Joseph Bernardin of Chicago in an address at Fordham University in December of 1983. Probably in anticipation of the 1984 campaign, Bernardin argued for "a consistent ethic of life." Several issues affecting life, he reasoned, should be viewed as a whole—as "a seamless garment," in his words. Among them were abortion, euthanasia, capital punishment, and modern warfare (*New York Times*, 7 December 1983). The speech was a call to broaden the attack on existing or proposed policies threatening life. To some it seemed to be an attempt not only to discourage single-issue voting, but also to downgrade abortion as an issue in the coming campaign, and even to dilute opposition to it.

Such an interpretation reads far too much into the Bernardin statement. The "seamless garment" analogy does, however, discourage single-issue voting. The campaign statements of Bernardin's brother bishops in the East suggest that he achieved only limited success in making his point in the 1984 campaign.

Reemergence of the Republican Coalition of 1972

There is little doubt that Reagan's smashing victory in 1984 expressed the nation's satisfaction with its situation and its approval of the president's stewardship. Richard Nixon, in a memorandum predicting the outcome of the election, expressed his opinion that it would demonstrate the political axiom that "you cannot beat an incumbent President in peacetime if the nation is prosperous."

A year before the election Lee Atwater outlined a strategy that looked to the South and the West to provide a Republican victory (Germond and Witcover 1985, 423). When the returns were in, Reagan had scored a victory far broader than the sectional triumph Atwater aimed at, losing only the District of Columbia and (by a hair) Mondale's home state of Minnesota.

Only a few Democratic diehards perceived a silver lining in the results of the presidential voting. The *New York Times* was one, contending on 8 November 1984 that "the old New Deal coalition . . . remains very much alive" since, it noted, Mondale had won a majority of the vote cast by racial minorities, Jews, union members, big city dwellers, and the unemployed. A strange myopia prevented the *Times* from observing that the coalition had lost two components essential to victory in a national election—the South and the nation's Catholics. And, in the case of one of the minorities, Hispanics, Mondale had edged out Reagan by only the narrow margin of 53 to 47 percent of their vote.

The victorious coalition apparent in the election returns was that of 1972, not of the 1930s and 1940s. Catholics were a significant part of it although considerably less united than they had been as participants in the New Deal coalition.

The numerous surveys of voting behavior seem to concur that Reagan received a higher share of the vote cast by Catholics than any Republican presidential candidate as far back as the polls ran. Most reported that Reagan got between 54 and 57 percent of the Catholic vote—a variation within the expected margin of error. The Gallup poll, however, arrived at a result hard to square with other surveys, finding that an astounding 61 percent of Catholics cast their votes for Reagan.

The findings reported by the president's pollster, Richard Wirthlin, reveal interesting shifts on the part of religious groups when their 1984 vote is compared with that of 1980. Catholics and members of most Protestant denominations registered a swing of about the same magnitude toward the Republican presidential candidate. Two groups, however, moved in considerably greater strength from one party to another—Baptists from Democrat to Republican and Jews from Republican to Democrat. One can hazard the guess that the larger swings among Baptists and Jews were heavily influenced (though in opposite directions) by the same phenomenon, the fact that the Democrats replaced a born-again Christian with one of less fundamentalist reputation as their presidential candidate.

Wirthlin's surveys for Reagan in the 1984 campaign also sought to determine the motivating factors behind the vote which Catholics cast for Reagan. The reason most frequently cited by respondents was the President's job performance. The nation's Catholics were, however, far more united in their approval of Reagan's performance in the field of foreign than domestic policy. They accorded the administration high marks for keeping the peace, reestablishing the leadership role of the United States in international affairs, and managing relations with the Soviet Union.

When the questioning turned to specifics in the field of domestic policy, on the other hand, Reagan received a substantially lower level of approval from the Catholic voting public. His highest score was registered in the appraisal of his general economic policy. Yet the approval rating for the administration's measures to deal with unemployment, inflation, the drug problem, education—even for cutting taxes—was at best modest. A verdict of emphatic disapproval was rendered by Catholic voters on control of government spending during Reagan's first administration.

Reagan's coattails provided little help to his party's candidates for Congress in 1984. After the election Republicans held one seat fewer in the Senate than they had before. They gained seventeen seats in the House leaving them, however, still ten seats short of the number they had held after Reagan's first election in 1980.

Postelection polls indicated what the election returns for the Congress suggested: that the Republican Party was regarded by the general public considerably less favorably than was the president. From Catholics, responses to questions asked by Wirthlin's polltakers comparing perceptions of the major parties showed a continuing preference for the Democrats. When asked which party was more concerned about people like them, 54 percent of the Catholic respondents chose the Democrats, 32 percent the Republicans. By smaller but still decisive margins, Catholics found the Democratic Party more inclined to be fair, to enlarge opportunity, and more receptive to new ideas and to change than the Republicans. Only in one respect did as many of the Catholics questioned have as favorable an opinion of the Republican Party as of the Democrats. Thirty-six percent associated high ethical standards with the Republicans, 37 percent with the Democrats, and 9 percent with both parties.

Wirthlin concluded that most Catholics remained Democrats in 1984 despite the fact that a majority voted for Reagan. At election time he informed party leaders that, although Republicans and Democrats were neck and neck in the total electorate, among Catholics 51 percent regarded themselves as Democrats, 39 percent as Republicans, and the remainder as Independents. Nevertheless, the preponderance of Democrats among the Catholic population was eroding. One indicator pointing to this conclusion was the fact that the percentage of Catholics with a more favorable view of the Democratic Party than the Republican fell short of a majority on almost all questions designed to compare attitudes toward the parties.

Catholic voters in 1984 gave Ronald Reagan a vote of confidence for a healthy economy and a nation at peace as well as for personal characteristics which met with their approval. The personal qualities that voters found attractive melded into the social issues. They inspired confidence that Reagan would repress criminal activity and drug use and sexual license and squandering of taxpayers' money; that he would stand firm against tax increases and abortion on demand as well as disorder on the streets and in the schools.

After this precedent-shattering election, a few conclusions were established beyond doubt. The coalition that had put Democrats in the White House in the days of the New Deal was in shambles, having lost the white South and an important segment of the nation's Catholics. The Republicans had attained majority status among white Southerners and among a partially overlapping group just gaining political consciousness and cohesion—evangelical and fundamentalist Protestants.

The 1984 election demonstrated the limitations of the influence of organized labor. Although important in securing the nomination for Mondale and in conducting his campaign, labor was able to win for its candidate only the barest majority of the votes cast by union families. And feminists, having secured their objective of nominating a woman for the nation's second highest office, were unable to convince as many as 45 percent of women voters (or even 40 percent of white women) to cast ballots for the Mondale-Ferraro ticket.

This second successive defeat of a Democratic presidential ticket—this time by a mammoth margin—prompted the Democratic National Committee to commission studies to determine why voters had lost confidence in the party's candidates. Based on a national survey of five thousand people and a series of focus group interviews, CRG Communications Corporation, the public relations and marketing firm which conducted the research, concluded that both change in economic status and the social issue accounted for an erosion of support for the Democratic Party. The erosion, which had occurred in the last two presidential elections, was most severe among middle-class whites both in the South and in northern cities and suburbs (particularly among ethnics). Those who had turned their backs on the party saw it as controlled by liberal extremists and special interest groups with values and an agenda foreign to middle-class America. Gays and feminists they viewed as a social underclass threatening their families. Along with "an economic underclass that absorbs their taxes and even locks them out of a job, in the case of affirmative action," such groups, the CRG report asserted, "signify the present image of the Democratic party."

This explosive report never saw the light of day. Fearful that it would offend many of the party's faithful supporters, authorities at the Democratic National Committee withheld it even from members of the committee. The original copy was destroyed along with all but a few bootleg copies, and the report was effectively suppressed (Brown 1991, 198–200).

The Election of 1988

As in 1976 and 1980, the Republican candidate for president in 1988 started out well behind his Democratic opponent but narrowed the gap in the course of the campaign. In 1976 the momentum brought Ford close to an even split of the popular vote with Jimmy Carter; in 1988 George Bush had forged ahead of his opponent by Election Day, following a course in successive polls very similar to Reagan's in 1980 and winning by a comparable vote margin over his Democratic opponent.

In May of 1988 a Gallup poll reported that Catholics, by 49 to 29 percent, were more inclined to vote for an unnamed generic Democratic nominee for president than for a generic Republican. In November, when voters chose between two specific candidates after a campaign which subjected their records and views and personalities to exposure by friend and foe, the Catholic electorate was reported to prefer Bush to Dukakis by the narrow margin of one percentage point.

In a sense the election of 1988 must be regarded as Reagan's third victory. In great part it was another referendum on the administration in which George Bush had served. Postelection surveys found that the element that correlated most strongly with voting for Bush was approval of his predecessor's policies and of the condition in which Reagan had left the nation after eight years in power. Ninety-five percent of those who wished "to continue Reagan's policies" voted for Bush, and five of every six votes cast for Bush came from Reagan voters of 1984.

Voter turnout in 1988 was the lowest in sixty-four years, barely 50 percent of the population of voting age. Richard Scammon after the election interpreted the low turnout as an indicator of satisfaction with the status quo. It may also have indicated that voters were unimpressed by either Bush or Dukakis. A poll conducted by the *New York Times* and CBS in late October reported that almost two-thirds of the respondents wished they had a choice other than the candidates offered by the two major parties. This opinion is perhaps not surprising in view of the media campaign to stigmatize Bush as a wimp and Dukakis as one of the Seven Dwarfs.

Voting of Religious Groups in 1988

As in 1984, the most Republican of religious groups was white fundamentalist/evangelical Christians (81 percent for Bush, according to the *New York Times*–CBS poll), followed by mainline white Christians (66 percent for Bush), then Catholics (52 percent), and finally Jewish voters (35 percent). From the polling data it is reasonable to conclude that the vote of Catholics was evenly split between Bush and Dukakis. This was the finding of the NBC pollsters, and this outcome was within the margin of error of the reports of other surveys. The *New York Times*–CBS poll reported that Bush received 52 percent of the vote cast by Catholics. At the other extreme was Gallup, crediting Bush with 48 percent of the Catholic vote. It also appears from survey data that a clear majority of "white" (i.e., neither Hispanic nor black) Catholics voted for the Republican candidate for president.

In three successive elections Catholic voters had now broken their historic habit of supporting the Democratic presidential ticket. And leading the Republican ticket this time was not an Irish name like Reagan but a Yankee with the patrician name of George Herbert Walker Bush.

The Democratic campaign made no perceptible effort to direct an appeal specifically to Catholics. Dukakis, unlike Mondale, attended Cardinal O'Connor's Alfred E. Smith Memorial dinner and humorously pointed out the similarities between himself and Smith, even as to stature. But he avoided appearances on Catholic college campuses, fearing that his position on abortion would provoke hostility in such a setting.

Revision of the Democratic Platform

A comparison of the platform adopted by the Democratic National Convention in 1988 with platforms of prior years reveals two significant differences in the treatment of matters bound to be of concern to many Catholics—education and abortion. In earlier presidential campaigns the Democratic platform had contained a salute to the Catholic school system. In fact, in 1972 it promised to "channel financial aid by a Constitutional formula to non-public schools." In 1976 the platform read, "The party also renews its commitment to the support of a constitutionally acceptable method of providing tax aid for the education of all pupils in non-segregated schools in order to insure parental freedom in choosing the best education for their children." The 1980 and 1984 platforms in identical language declared, "Private schools, particularly parochial schools, are also an important part of our diverse educational system." They went on to reaffirm support for a "constitutionally acceptable method of providing tax aid for the education of all pupils in schools which do not discriminate." By contrast, the platform that came from the Democratic convention of 1988 contained no expression of approval of private or parochial schools, no recognition of any type of parental right in relation to education, and no pledge of financial assistance to children attending non-public schools.

The abortion plank underwent a somewhat parallel, although less drastic and less inconsistent, evolution in successive platforms. In 1976, 1980, and 1984 the Democratic platform contained a word of sympathetic understanding of the pro-life position, saying, "We fully recognize the religious and ethical concerns which many Americans have about abortion." In 1976 the Democratic platform makers modestly offered the opinion that it would be "undesirable to attempt to amend the U. S. Constitution to overturn the Supreme Court decision" in *Roe v. Wade*.

By 1980 the word "abortion" had disappeared from the lexicon of Democratic platform drafters, giving way to "reproductive freedom," which was declared to be "a fundamental human right." *Roe v. Wade* was explicitly endorsed and any attempt to amend the Constitution to overturn the decision denounced. In a convoluted sentence that seemed designed to conceal its import, the platform went on record in favor of government funding of abortions by expressing opposition to "government interference in the reproductive decisions of Americans especially denying their right to privacy by funding or advocating one or a limited number of reproductive choices only." President Carter generated more fog about this matter by commenting that he "personally opposed Federal funding of abortion" but adding that he was nevertheless sworn to "uphold the laws . . . and the Constitution" (*New York Times*, 14 August 1980).

The Democratic platform of 1984 echoed the 1980 platform's stand on abortion. By 1988, however, the last vestiges of obfuscation were discarded in a platform which affirmed "reproductive choice" to be a "fundamental right" which "should be guaranteed regardless of ability to pay."

Clearly 1988 was a milestone in the history of the Democratic Party. Through changes in its platform and through the conduct of its campaign for the presidency, the party gave unambiguous signals that courting that substantial segment of Catholic voters strongly attached to Catholic schools and firmly opposed to abortion had slipped downward in its scale of priorities.

Two members of the Catholic hierarchy responded by publicly announcing their withdrawal from the Democratic Party. One of the two, Archbishop John F. Whealon of Hartford, dramatized his announcement by burning his membership card in the party (*New York Times*, 26 August 1988). One other prominent Catholic cleric, Andrew Greeley, deplored the attitude of the Democratic high command in 1988 but did not go so far as to renounce the party. "Catholic voters," he wrote, "continue to be ignored by the party leadership because they are not 'politically correct' and never will be" (1992, 7).

Religious Themes in the Republican Campaign

Perhaps no Republican platform in history had more religious references than that of 1988. And much of the religious content seemed crafted to strike notes that Catholics were hearing in their churches and schools. For example, the platform emphasized the place of the Judeo-Christian moral system in American society. It repeatedly affirmed the principle of subsidiarity, noting especially the service rendered by churches in education and social welfare. "The God-given rights of the family," it declared, "come before those of government. This separates us from liberal Democrats. We seek to strengthen the family. Democrats try to supplant it." Asserting that the "right and responsibility" for education belongs to parents and that "values are the core of good education," the platform called for "choice in education" and tax credits to assist students in nonpublic schools. It favored requiring daily recitation of the pledge of allegiance in schools, voluntary prayer, and the teaching of abstinence from premarital sex and from drug use.

In a passage emphasizing concern for Catholics in particular, the document condemned as "wrong, bigoted, and a massive violation of the First Amendment the current attempt by the American Civil Liberties Union to tax the Roman Catholic Church or any other religious institutions."

Like most platforms, this one drew many of its provisions from past declarations of the party, again endorsing a human life amendment to the Constitution, opposing government funding of abortion, denouncing quotas, and (in what was to be the last time) calling for freedom and self-determination for the captive nations.

The platform on which George Bush ran in 1988 set the stage for a campaign to capitalize on the good will toward Ronald Reagan as he left the White House, on the religious coalition which had supported him, and on strong negative themes painting Dukakis and his party as weak and inexperienced in foreign affairs and as far-left liberals in domestic policy. Bush won principally because he promised a continuation of the Reagan administration. Two savants analyzed the election as one in which the elements needed for Republican victory came together as they had in 1980 and 1984, overcoming the preponderance of Democrats in the electorate. The economy was performing well. In addition, attention "focused upon conservative issues (crime, traditional morals and values) and problems on which voters find the Republicans more competent than the Democrats (dealing with foreign adversaries, providing for a strong defense)." In these circumstances, they said, the "post-New Deal party system, although tilted in favor of the Democrats, will elect Republican presidents" as labor union families, Catholics, and white Southerners who are nominally Democrats or Independents cast Republican ballots (Petrocik and Steeper 1989, 7–9).

Several surveys suggest that abortion policy was more important in affecting voting behavior in 1988 than in any prior presidential campaign and that it worked to Bush's benefit. The poll conducted by ABC provided the most impressive evidence of these conclusions. Given an unlimited number of choices to name important issues, more respondents (33 percent of the total) cited abortion than any other single issue. In 1984, in response to a parallel question, somewhat differently phrased, 15 percent of those surveyed included abortion among the important issues. This poll reported that Bush received the vote of 57 percent of those who regarded abortion as important and Dukakis the vote of 42 percent. In 1984 Reagan was the choice of 63 percent of voters considering abortion important.

Some confirmation of the findings of the ABC poll were provided by another major survey. CNN/*Los Angeles Times* reported that abortion was more frequently cited as an important issue than any other except the deficit and defense. Sixty-three percent of those who cited it declared they had voted for Bush, 36 percent for Dukakis.

A CBS exit poll, limiting responses more strictly and therefore not completely comparable to the two surveys cited above, found that 11 percent of Michigan's voters and 4 percent of New Mexico's placed abortion among the most important matters influencing their choice of candidate with voters in the other forty-eight states in between these extremes.

Interest in the matter of abortion was undoubtedly heightened in 1988 in the states of Colorado, Michigan, and Arkansas where it appeared on the ballot as a referendum question. In all three states a majority of the electors endorsed a pro-life position. In Arkansas the state constitution was altered as the voters adopted by 52 to 48 percent the "Unborn Child Amendment" declaring life to begin at conception and banning the use of state funds for abortion. In Michigan, by a vote of 58 to 42 percent, publicly financed abortion was prohibited except to save the life of the mother. In Colorado an attempt to reverse a 1984 ban on the use of state funds for abortion was rejected by 60 percent of those voting on the issue.

It appears that Bush derived a significant advantage in 1988 from his stand on abortion. It would be inaccurate to consider this issue a decisive factor in the outcome of the election, but it influenced more votes than many matters that the media chose to highlight in analyzing the result. Commentators tended to assign great influence to questions relating to the Pledge of Allegiance in schools and to prison furlough policy. Both matters were introduced in the campaign by Republicans in attacks on the Democratic ticket. As governor of Massachusetts, Dukakis had vetoed a bill requiring school children to recite the pledge. And, the horrible crimes of kidnapping and rape committed by one Willie Horton, a black prisoner free on furlough while serving a life sentence in a Massachusetts penitentiary, were cited as the consequences of lax treatment of felons. Compared with the issue of abortion, these matters were of concern to a rather limited group of voters. The ABC poll, which found that 33 percent of the voters considered abortion an important issue, reported that a far smaller group—12 percent—thought the Pledge of Allegiance and prison furlough (read Willie Horton) to be important.

The Election of 1992

George Bush joined Taft, Hoover, Ford, and Carter to become the fifth president in the twentieth century to lose a bid to continue in office after serving one term or a fraction of a term in the White House. Two other presidents—Truman and Johnson—abandoned plans to seek election for a second time in the face of compelling evidence that they would lose the race. In all these instances the unity of the party holding the presidency was shattered. In 1912, 1968, and 1980 a major third-party candidate emerged who threatened to draw off a substantial number of votes from the party of the incumbent president. The threat materialized once more in 1992 in the person of Ross Perot. These seven instances in which the incumbent's departure from his office after one elective term or less was not completely voluntary demonstrate that incumbency, although conferring certain advantages, is far from a guarantee of reelection.

Invariably the campaign of a sitting president becomes a referendum on the state of the nation and on his performance in his first term. Following the success of Desert Storm, the brief and virtually bloodless military response to Iraq's invasion of Kuwait, Bush's approval rating in the polls soared. So strong did the prospects for his reelection appear that several potential Democratic candidates reached a decision to stay out of the 1992 presidential race. After mid-1991 the president's standing in the polls eroded steadily. By the spring of 1992 it became clear that the incumbent was no longer a prohibitive favorite in the approaching election.

At that time a consultant in the Bush campaign described the situation as "our worst political nightmare," citing twenty months of "recession," polls reporting that 78 percent of the public thought the country was "on the wrong track," and "a Southern conservative Democrat" as the probable opponent in the election (Goldman et al. 1994, 648). At the same time that riots in which fifty-two people were killed erupted in Los Angeles, the president's polls showed that his lead over his prospective foe—whether Bill Clinton or Paul Tsongas—had vanished.

James Carville's well-publicized campaign slogan "It's the economy, stupid" capsulized the dominant factor in Bush's defeat. The signs of recovery that began to appear in 1992 failed to overcome voter dissatisfaction with the performance of the economy and their uneasiness about the future as downsizing threatened the job security of middle-class America. Mammoth deficits and a broken pledge of "no new taxes" reinforced the impression that the administration had failed as a steward of government's responsibility to promote a healthy economy.

There were other factors than economic considerations which contributed to Bush's defeat. One was the end of the Cold War with the collapse of Communist regimes in Europe. Paradoxically, this development had mixed consequences for the Republican Party, on whose watch it had occurred. Its negative effect was to eliminate an issue which had long bolstered Republican fortunes. One insightful commentary called the 1992 contest "the first election 'at the end of history,' the first since 1932 when the survival of the cause of democracy did not appear to be at stake." Anti-Communism had been "the glue that helped hold the Republican coalition together." It had also been "a solvent corroding the Democratic coalition." The end of Communism "removed the security issue as a problem inside the Democratic coalition and paved the way for the exit of many 'Reagan Republicans' from the GOP" (Ceaser and Busch 1993, 15–18).

The on-and-off candidacy of Ross Perot, while a handicap to both major candidates, inflicted more serious damage on Bush, the principal object of Perot's attack, than on Clinton. During the campaign Bush had to fend off two opponents. Perot's attacks also made the case against the president credible to a segment of voters disinclined to heed Democratic critics.

The judgment voters passed on the Bush administration can be read in a few figures. The total vote cast in 1992 was 13 million more than in 1988; the vote cast for George Bush dropped by almost 10 million. Bill Clinton, although receiving 3 million more votes than Michael Dukakis had in 1992, was still the choice of only 43 percent of those who went to the polls. The Democratic share of the total vote fell by 6 percent from the 1988 level while Bush's share dropped by 30 percent. It is clear that the voter stampede away from Bush in 1992 headed not for Bill Clinton but mainly for Ross Perot, who amassed an impressive vote, just short of 20 million.

There were times in the 1980s when the dissolution of the New Deal coalition seemed so final that some pundits concluded that Republicans had a lock on the White House. The 1992 election put a stop to this talk, but in its place an equally fallacious interpretation of the Democratic victory gained some currency. The *New York Times* on 5 November 1992 found in the election returns evidence that Clinton's supporters "resembled the old New Deal coalition." Even so respected a political scientist as Seymour M. Lipset reached the surprising conclusion that "the social correlates of Clinton and Bush voters resembled those for Roosevelt and Landon in 1936" (Lipset 1993, 11–13).

Neither southerners nor Catholics, essential elements of the New Deal coalition, flocked back to the Democratic Party in numbers reminiscent of the years before World War II. Clinton, although a southern governor, was edged out by Bush in the aggregate vote of the eleven states of the Confederacy. The continuing strength of southern Republicanism was clear also in the fact that when states were ranked by the percentage of their vote cast for Bush in 1992, Mississippi won first place as the most Republican state in the nation; Alabama, second; South Carolina, third; and Virginia, fifth.

Catholics rejected the Republican presidential ticket impressively, but the beneficiary of their switch was Ross Perot. After giving Bush about half of their vote in 1988, they cast little more than a third of it for him this time. One indicator of the decline is found in the vote of 110 counties in which Catholics constituted a majority of the population in 1980. Reagan carried 75 of these counties in 1984; Bush carried 50 in 1988 and only 39 in 1992.

The voter apathy of 1988 evaporated in 1992. Catholics, like other Americans, increased their turnout by perhaps 10 percent above the level of the previous election. They appear to have given Clinton about the same number of votes as they had cast for Dukakis, but, because of the larger turnout, a smaller percentage of their vote. Among Catholic voters, Clinton's plurality over Bush exceeded 2 million, attributable largely to margins rolled up in eastern and far western states.

The Catholic voting pattern in 1992 reflects a marked departure from that of previous presidential elections. Whereas in the past Catholics consistently voted more heavily Democratic than the total electorate, this time the distribution of the vote of Catholics among the three leading contenders for the presidency was almost identical to the pattern for the nation as a whole.

Even in the Democratic rout of 1972, George McGovern's share of the Catholic vote was eight percentage points higher than the percentage he was given by the total electorate. In 1992, by contrast, the difference between the Democratic vote share from Catholics and that from the total voting population was only one percentage point. Clinton received 43 percent of the total vote and 44 percent of the Catholic vote.

This aspect of the 1992 election underlined the homogenization of Catholics into the electorate that occurred in the second half of the twentieth century. Yet, when compared with voters of other religious denominations or with secularists, Catholics retained a certain distinctiveness in their voting behavior. They were less Republican than white evangelical Protestants on the one hand and less Democratic than Jewish and secular voters on the other. They also evidenced a stronger propensity to behave as swing voters from one election to another.

The exit polls of 1992 revealed divisions in the voting pattern of Catholics when the total community was broken into subgroups (table 8-3). Race, economic status, ethnicity, region of residence, and age were the factors most clearly in play when Catholic voters made their choice among the candidates. The Catholic subgroups that gave Clinton greatest support were blacks, Hispanics, families below an income level of $15,000 (obviously overlapping groups), and those over sixty years of age. Catholic women gave Clinton a clear margin over Bush. Catholic men narrowly preferred Bush to Clinton. Bush was preferred by the more affluent and the college-educated (but not by holders of graduate degrees). In terms of geography Bush outpolled Clinton only among southern Catholics.

In the electorate as a whole the 1992 contest evidenced a split on the basis of what has come to be called religiosity. Fifty-five percent of those who voted for Bush attended church at least weekly, a habit shared by only 35 percent of Clinton's supporters and 33 percent of Perot's. Of the voters who professed no religious affiliation, 62 percent voted for Clinton, 20 percent for Perot, and 18 percent for Bush.

When the votes were in, it was clear that the nation had failed to give either major party or its candidates a vote of confidence. Millions of voters including a substantial bloc of Catholics seemed to be in search of a new political home.

The Republican Victory of 1994

In 1994, in an election which Walter Dean Burnham called "a seismic event" (Campbell and Rockman 1996, 363) voters replaced the regnant Democratic Party and its officeholders at all levels in all regions of the nation. To find a

TABLE 8–3. Catholic Voting Behavior in the 1992 Presidential Election

	Clinton	*Bush*	*Perot*
All voters	43	37	19
All Catholic voters	44	35	20
White Catholics	42	37	22
Gender			
Catholic men	37	39	24
Catholic women	44	36	20
Income			
Below $15,000	62	17	21
$30,000–$50,000	38	41	21
$75,000 and above	30	51	19
Region			
East	45	34	21
Midwest	44	35	21
South	41	42	17
Southern whites	34	48	18
West	47	31	22
Western whites	40	36	24
Age			
18–29	39	39	22
30–44	38	37	25
45–59	37	40	24
60+	53	32	16
Religious observance (white Catholics)			
Weekly churchgoers	39	41	20
Less than weekly churchgoers	44	33	24

Source: Exit Poll, Voter Research and Surveys.

shift of comparable cataclysmic proportions from Democratic to Republican preponderance, one must go back almost fifty years to 1946.

Democratic majorities in both houses of Congress were swept away. A decisive majority of the governorships ended up in Republican hands. And in state legislative bodies collectively, the Republican Party gained 486 seats, winning away from the Democrats control of eighteen chambers. Significantly, in the 1994 races no Republican incumbent candidate for governor or either house of Congress failed in a bid for reelection. A relatively heavy toll was taken of Democratic incumbents, on the other hand, including the speaker of the House, the chairmen of two of its most important committees, and the governors of Texas and New York.

So sweeping was the rejection of Democratic candidates that one scholarly group interpreting the outcome declared, "America is indeed in the midst of a historic period of party realignment" (Tuchfarber et al. 1995, 694; Ladd 1995, 23). Another rendered the verdict that "after years of gradual disintegration, the New Deal religious coalition is now in shambles, and with it the Democratic lock on congressional and state government" (Kellstedt et al. 1995, 21).

For Catholic voters, the major component of that New Deal religious coalition, the 1994 election was a historic milestone. For the first time since the advent of scientific polling, Democrats failed to win a majority from the nation's Catholics in the aggregate vote for the House of Representatives. Fifty-two percent of all Catholic voters cast ballots for Republican House candidates. Of white Catholic voters, 55 percent did so, and of male Catholics, 60 percent (Kellstedt et al. 1995, 18–21; Ladd 1995, 72–74).

The hefty Democratic margins of old are not found in the voting behavior of Catholics in the 1990s. The new pattern shows a Catholic vote which has lost much of its distinctiveness. In 1994, as in 1992, the distribution among the parties of the vote cast by Catholics closely paralleled the distribution of the total national vote.

Table 8-4, based on exit polling in the off-year election of 1994, reflects a striking correspondence between the voting pattern of Catholics and that of the entire electorate. This correspondence appears also when the vote is analyzed in terms of subgroups based on gender, income, party affiliation, and ideology. In some especially noteworthy respects, the Catholic subgroup appears to be more heavily Republican than the general voting public. One such instance is found in age groups under 45; another, in college graduates.

Catholics in lower educational and income subgroups, on the other hand, provide strong support for Democratic candidates. These subgroups include a relatively high representation of Hispanics.

Any analysis of Catholic voting behavior requires a separation of Hispanics from so-called "white" Catholics, for the pattern of the two diverges sharply. In the election for the House of Representatives in 1994, for example, Republican House candidates received the vote of only 32 percent of Hispanic Catholics while gaining 55 percent of the white Catholic vote.

In several respects the election of 1994 broke the mold of typical off-year contests of the past. It was successfully nationalized by Newt Gingrich's Contract with America, which gave common themes for Republican

TABLE 8–4. Catholic Vote for the House of Representatives in 1994: Homogenization Demonstrated (Percentage Voting Republican)

	All Voters	*Catholics*		*All Voters*	*Catholics*
Total	52.5	52			
Men	57	60	Women	46	44
White	58	55	Hispanic	40	32
Age 18–29	49	53	Age 30–44	53	59
Age 45–59	52	48	Age 60+	50	46
		Education			
Less than high school	40	28	High school grad	52	48
Some college	58	53	College grad	50	64
		Income			
Below $15,000	37	36	$15,000–$29,999	47	40
$30,000–$49,999	54	54	$50,000–$75,000	57	58
$75,000–$100,000	—	68	Over $100,000	—	65
		Political Orientation			
Liberal	18	21			
Moderate	42	44			
Conservative	80	79			
Democrat	11	11			
Independent	42	44			
Republican	92	90			

Source: Exit Poll, Voter News Service.

House candidates to run on. It was ideological, emphasizing specific poll-tested conservative measures that received strong popular support.

Analysts of voting behavior discerned two significant characteristics of the electorate that participated in choosing the members of the House of Representatives in 1994. First, as Fred Steeper pointed out, the Republican victory was based on cultural issues and on the strong support of voters who identified themselves as conservatives (Steeper 1995 4–6, 10–11). Whereas no marked change from past elections appeared in the behavior of liberals and moderate voters, conservatives voted Republican in unprecedented numbers casting 80 percent of their ballots for the GOP in House races.

Secondly, religiosity had much to do with the outcome of the 1994 election. As Lyman Kellstedt and his associates found, "new forms of ethno-religious politics are emerging, with the GOP drawing the more religiously observant voters, at least among whites, and the Democrats attracting the least observant in the major traditions, seculars, and various minority groups." Among Catholics, a clear-cut difference now appeared between the regular churchgoers (57 percent voting Republican) and less than regular churchgoers (49 percent casting Republican ballots) (Kellstedt et al. 1995, 20–21).

Surveying the election results of 1994 and the President's standing in the polls, the Times-Mirror Center opined in a press release of 11 January 1995, "Bill Clinton needs a miracle, not a comeback, to win in 1996. . . . Clinton's current ratings are comparable to those of landslide losers."

This appraisal was also the conventional wisdom among Republicans anticipating a victory in 1996 in which their presidential candidate would command strong support from Catholic voters (Gillespie 1996, 18–23). This confidence was bolstered by the history of mounting Republican strength in congressional elections capped by the success of 1994. In the off-year elections of 1958 and 1962 Republican House candidates received only 27 percent of the vote cast by Catholics. The figure rose to between 41 and 43 percent in the years 1984–1990. And in 1994 it reached 52 percent. Some analysts, arguing that off-year elections for the House of Representatives are the most accurate barometers of party strength, interpreted this trend as an indication of a Catholic realignment.

Yet the demonstrated volatility of the Catholic vote gave ground for doubt that the 1994 election results signified for many Catholics more than short-term enlistment in the Republican Party. The great erosion of Catholic voter support for George Bush in 1992, measured from the level he reached in 1988 or the heights Reagan attained in 1984, was evidence that this group was a swing vote. Many Catholics—about 35 percent, according to some polls—regarded themselves as Independents. This status had been emphatically asserted by one out of five Catholics who cast their ballots for Ross Perot in 1992.

The size of the Catholic swing vote was one reason for doubt that the support which Catholics gave Republican candidates in 1994 would prove to be secure and durable. Another was the untapped pool of potential Democratic voters in the Hispanic community.

The Campaign of 1996

The Democratic campaign began well in advance of the usual season. From mid-1995 on, President Clinton was in a campaign mode, advocating poll-tested initiatives with minor budgetary consequences, separating himself from Democratic liberals by speaking up for smaller government and a balanced budget and by signing bills reforming welfare and blocking gay marriages. Other Democrats launched a negative campaign demonizing Newt Gingrich (and other Republicans as his clones) charged with the intention of doing damage to Medicare, education, and the environment. To the tune of $35 million, organized labor joined the attack against selected Republican members of Congress whom it deemed vulnerable in election contests.

The president was an articulate and skilled campaigner. He carried on an unrelenting public relations effort, making unprecedented use of the White House (even the Lincoln bedroom) for fundraising and party-building purposes. Before 1995 ended, he had succeeded in rehabilitating himself in the eyes of a substantial part of the public which had repudiated him in the 1994 election. The rehabilitative process was helped by the shutdown of government brought about by an impasse over budgets for which the press and the public blamed congressional Republicans. It was also helped by a drumbeat of negative political advertising targeting Republicans that was carried on after mid-1995 without audible response.

At no time was there a serious threat that the President would be challenged for renomination by any prominent Democrat. Thus during the primary season Clinton was able to maintain a unified party, enjoy immunity from attack from within its ranks, and build his financial base for the post-convention period.

Senator Dole enjoyed no such tranquil respite. Embroiled in bitter primary contests against Pat Buchanan, Steve Forbes, Lamar Alexander, and several others, he was kept busy defending his record against vigorous attack from within his own party. Although Dole's nomination was assured in early spring with a series of victories beginning in South Carolina, the primary contests left him battered and financially exhausted.

For many reasons Dole was a weak candidate in a nationwide contest in the age of campaigning by television in the last years of the twentieth century. He was not articulate, tending to talk in ellipses and to use a form of Washington-speak intelligible to senators in their cloakroom but not to most other Americans in their home environment.

In his prior bids for the White House in 1980 and 1988, Dole's weaknesses as a candidate had been exposed. After his losing race for the presidential nomination against Bush in 1988, he had, according to one account, acquired a reputation for running mismanaged campaigns and generally for being "an evil-tempered loose cannon who, on top of that, couldn't organize a two-car funeral" (Germond and Witcover 1989, 147).

In the 1996 caucuses and primaries, in spite of the support of popular Republican governors and other state officials and a campaign treasury far exceeding that of any opponent, Dole ran behind Buchanan in New Hampshire, Alaska, Missouri, and Louisiana and behind Forbes in Arizona and

Delaware before his victories in Super Tuesday contests in March turned the tide in his favor.

Catholic Voting Behavior in 1996

Before receiving the Republican presidential nomination, Senator Dole addressed the annual convention of the Catholic Press Association, a group whose invitation Clinton spurned. His speech contained the proper buzzwords endorsing positions welcome to this audience on such matters as partial-birth abortion, school choice, a tax credit for charitable contributions, and the principle of subsidiarity. Restoring fundamental values "to their rightful place in our society," he declared, "is what my campaign for president is all about." In the following months, Dole largely ignored this message as he careened from one theme to another in search of what his campaign was really all about.

The exuberant expectation of Republican Party leaders that they would reclaim the White House in 1996 with impressive support from the Catholic voting population faded long before Election Day. As the expectation was discarded, campaigning for the Republican presidential ticket was curtailed and abandoned in one after another of the states rich with Catholic votes.

Exit polls indicated that, for the first time in twenty years, a majority of Catholic voters had favored a Democratic presidential candidate. Clinton, winner of 49 percent of the nation's vote, was the choice of 53 percent of the Catholics who went to the polls. Perhaps as much as one-half of the plurality of 8.2 million given to the President in the total vote was provided by Catholic voters.

Senator Dole received 40 percent of the total vote and 37 percent of that cast by Catholics. In only three elections in the preceding fifty years had a Republican presidential candidate gained as small a share of the Catholic vote. In Rhode Island and Massachusetts, the two states with the largest proportion of Catholics in their population, Dole's vote fell below 30 percent of the total recorded.

Voter Turnout in 1996

The 1996 election is noteworthy for registering the lowest voter turnout in seventy-two years. Somewhat fewer than 50 percent of the voting age population bothered to vote. Not since the dull contest of 1924 had a presidential election drawn to the polls so small a fraction of the potential national electorate.

In every state the percentage of eligible voters casting ballots declined from the 1992 level, dropping about six percentage points nationwide.

Despite population growth adding 7 million to the voting age population, relaxed registration systems like motor voter, and record campaign spending, the total vote cast fell approximately 8 million short of the total in 1992. A more valid measure of the fall-off in voter participation is 12 million; this is the number of additional ballots that would have been cast if the percentage of the potential electorate voting in 1996 had matched the percentage that voted in 1992.

According to the Committee for the Study of the American Electorate, in fourteen states new records for low turnout were set in 1996. Among them were Rhode Island, Massachusetts, New York, New Jersey, Illinois, Minnesota, and New Mexico—all with more than average Catholic representation in their population.

White, non-Hispanic Catholics were a conspicuous component of the stay-at-home population. The turnout of this majority element of the Catholic population appears to have fallen by 1.5 million from its 1992 level. The Hispanic electorate (largely Catholic), on the other hand, exceeded its 1992 turnout by about 1 million votes. As a result, the Catholic vote of 1996 was different in ethnic composition from that of 1992—or, indeed, from any previous election. Although only a rough estimate, the Hispanic component of the Catholic vote rose from perhaps 9 percent of the total in Bill Clinton's first race for the presidency to somewhere in the neighborhood of 14 percent when he sought reelection, a change that greatly benefited Democratic candidates across the board.

A Disappointed Conservative Constituency

The Republican campaign of 1996 was unfocused and devoid of passion. It did not pierce the armor of the administration it was seeking to replace, nor did it rebut persuasively the charges that it would cripple programs bringing health care to the elderly and education to children and protecting the environment against depredation. Small wonder that it won plaudits from Democratic commentators for adhering to the high road.

To the dismay of conservative supporters, the conduct of the campaign deemphasized the issues of their cultural agenda. When Dole addressed such issues, he was so obviously uncomfortable as to sound insincere. Columnist Don Feder in the *Boston Herald* on 6 November 1996 observed that Dole's message to cultural conservatives was, "You are an embarrassment and a hindrance. We will grudgingly accept your votes, but don't expect us to embrace your agenda." Professor James Hitchcock, a leading conservative, raised a question that troubled many in a column syndicated in the Catholic press captioned "How Pro-Life Is Bob Dole?" Noting that Dole had turned aside questions on the subject, once claiming to be unfamiliar with the platform language on the issue of abortion, again ignoring the topic in a speech at Jesuit-run St. Louis University, Hitchcock warned that in comparing Dole and Clinton "pro-lifers need to think very hard about how preferable Dole really is" (Hitchcock 1996). After the election Pat Robertson explained, as reported on 7 November 1996, in the *Richmond Times-Dispatch*, that religious conservatives had given Dole a much smaller vote than they had cast for Bush in 1992 because Dole "muted social issues in favor of money issues."

Why Clinton Won

Dole's awkward efforts to distance himself from religious and other cultural conservatives, especially obvious during the Republican convention, unquestionably weakened his appeal to an important Republican constituency. But in producing Dole's defeat and Clinton's victory, other factors were probably more important. The relatively vigorous economy and the threat-free international climate of 1996 were tremendous advantages for any incumbent president and a decided handicap for his challenger.

Among other factors contributing to Clinton's reelection and Dole's defeat were the following:

- Clinton was articulate; Dole was not.
- Dole was in his seventies, Clinton not yet fifty.
- Clinton sounded enough Republican themes to soften his liberal image; Dole failed to exonerate himself from the charge that he would weaken Democratic programs like Medicare.
- Clinton began to campaign early and never lacked funds; Dole was slowed by primary opposition and financial restraints.
- Clinton stuck to his campaign message; Dole shifted from tax reduction to liberalism to character as his issues, never moving a significant number of voters by use of any of the three.
- Ross Perot, though playing a weaker role than in 1992, assured Clinton's reelection against any candidate the Republicans might have offered.
- Media bias favored Clinton and disfavored Dole, operating as it would have to the detriment of any possible Republican candidate except Colin Powell.

Throughout the campaign polls showed that voters judged Dole superior to Clinton in moral stature, finding him more honest, truthful, and trustworthy than the president. It was only toward the end, however, that an issue of character appeared to influence voters strongly and then principally as a result of revelations of unsavory fundraising practices on the part of the Democratic Party. A contrast between the candidates seemed to sharpen in the public perception, and the lead which Clinton held in the polls contracted to single digits.

The Issue of Partial-Birth Abortion

For the Catholic hierarchy partial-birth abortion was unquestionably the dominant issue in 1996, and it was an issue on which their stand was diametrically opposed to the position of President Clinton. After Clinton vetoed a bill banning this practice, the bishops launched an unprecedented effort to persuade Congress to reverse the outcome. The nation's cardinals, having inspired a barrage of several million postcards to the Congress calling for overriding the veto, resorted to the unusual tactics of picketing the White House and conducting a press conference on the steps of the Capitol to draw attention to their message. Although successful in the House, the motion to override failed by nine votes to gain the support of the required two-thirds of the Senate.

The actions of the bishops in the struggle over partial-birth abortion were the clearest and most vigorous expressions of episcopal disapproval of a presidential candidate's position on an issue of public policy in recent history. They were accompanied by other signs of rejection of the president by Church officials. Clinton was the first presidential candidate of a major party to be denied an invitation to the Al Smith dinner of the archdiocese of New York.

A strong majority of the nation's Catholics were allied with their bishops and opposed to the president on the question of partial-birth abortion. A survey taken by a leading pollster found that 77 percent of Catholics disagreed with the veto and only 16 percent gave it their approval.

The retired archbishop of New Orleans, Philip M. Hannan, went so far as to declare bluntly, "No Catholic should vote for any officeholder who believes in abortion. No Catholic should vote for the President or Mary Landrieu" (the Democratic nominee for the United States Senate). Hannan's successor and other bishops in the state dissociated themselves from the advice on how to vote; indeed, Hannan later declared that he "spoke only for himself" (*Catholic Standard*, 7 November 1996).

Archbishop Hannan's statement seems to have had slight effect on those to whom it was addressed. Dole succeeded in finishing ahead of Clinton in only one of Louisiana's sixteen parishes in which Catholics constitute a majority of the residents. In the senatorial contest, a poll conducted by Professor Edward Renwick of Loyola University reported that only 11 percent of Catholic voters said they were more likely to vote against Landrieu because of Hannan's statement; 7 percent said they were more likely to vote for Landrieu because of it; and sixty-seven percent said it would not affect their vote. Mary McGrory, liberal Catholic columnist, noting that most Catholics in voting in 1996 had ignored the apparent preference of their bishops, wrote, "clerical clout . . . is a thing of the past" (quoted by Shaw 1996, 3).

It is clear that Catholic voters did not accord to the issue of abortion the same priority as did the hierarchy. Some argue that the bishops' message has always been muddied at election time by other actions they have taken. In 1996, as in previous election years, a Statement of Political Responsibility was released in the name of the bishops by the staff of the U.S. Catholic Conference defining policy positions in a number of fields, one of which was abortion. The statement, as Bishop James McHugh of Camden wrote, gave the impression that all matters in this laundry list were of equal importance, thereby denying any special emphasis to the issue which had provoked the strongest reaction from the hierarchy (McHugh 1997, 15).

Individual churchmen, too, sent conflicting signals. Father Robert Drinan, S.J., law professor at a prestigious Catholic institution and a former congressman, published an Op-Ed column in the *New York Times* on 4 June 1996 vigorously defending Clinton's veto of the partial-birth abortion bill. And Cardinal Bernardin, then near death, made a well-publicized visit to the White House to receive the Presidential Medal of Freedom from Clinton on the very day he joined fellow clergy at the opposite end of Pennsylvania Avenue to denounce the veto and call for Congress to override it. In the last analysis, however, the issue of partial birth abortion failed to generate a stronger protest vote from Catholics against the Clinton veto not because of ambiguous signals from clerics but because of the reluctance of Republican candidates to make it a major issue in their campaign.

The Hispanic Vote

From 40 to 50 percent of the 8.2 million plurality by which Clinton defeated Dole in the popular vote in 1996 can be attributed to Catholics. This margin was about double the plurality which Catholic voters gave the victor in 1992. The improvement in Clinton's fortunes was due principally to the vote of Catholic Hispanics and Catholic women.

In an election in which almost all other identifiable groups recorded a sharp drop in voter turnout, an upsurge occurred among Hispanics. Contributing about 14 percent of the Catholic vote—up from 9 percent in 1992—Hispanics provided about one-half of the 4 million margin by which Clinton's vote among Catholics exceeded Dole's.

Writing in the *New York Times* after the election, Linda Chavez argued that Hispanics were motivated to vote in unprecedented numbers in reaction to the immigration and welfare legislation enacted by the 104th Congress. (Chavez 1996). Along with the campaign in California to end affirmative action by referendum, these laws generated a backlash damaging to Republicans while largely sparing Democrats, even though the federal legislation was signed by the president. The turnout of Hispanic voters was abetted by a massive campaign launched by the Immigration and Naturalization Service which in the year ending in September 1996 reaped a harvest of more than 1 million new citizens and, undoubtedly, a substantial number of Democratic votes (*Washington Times*, 25 February 1997).

Ronald Reagan and George Bush had received a respectable share of the vote of the Hispanic community—between one-third and 40 percent—and, from Cuban-Americans, mainly in Florida, a strong majority. In fact, Bush's plurality of 100,000 in Florida in 1992 could be largely accounted for by Hispanic votes. In 1996, along with higher turnout than in the past, the Hispanic community registered in exit polls a stronger shift toward Clinton than any other significant category of voters, preferring him to Dole by 72 to 21 percent. Florida's Cuban-American electorate abandoned the Republicans in droves, dividing its vote equally between the two parties.

The Gender Gap Among Catholics

When the Catholic vote is analyzed by gender, a marked difference between male and female behavior emerges (table 8-5). The gender gap is not peculiar to Catholic voters. Exit polling in 1996 found that, of all subgroups sampled, in only one, Asian-Americans, did the vote of male members correspond closely to that of females.

In the 1996 presidential contest, if the vote had been restricted to men, it can be argued that Robert Dole would have been elected president by an electoral college vote of 277 to 261. According to the exit polls of Voter News Service, ten states casting 118 electoral votes ended up in Clinton's column because the plurality which women gave the president exceeded Dole's margin from male voters. This overriding of the male preference by female voters occurred in the populous midwestern states of Michigan, Missouri, Ohio, and Wisconsin as well as in Florida, Tennessee, Kentucky, New Mexico, Nevada, and New Hampshire (Dougherty et al. 1997, 108–11).

The cause of the gender gap is disputed. Pro-choice Republicans argue that the official party position on abortion drives women away. Their case has still to be made, for analysis of the vote in the senate race in Massachusetts in 1996 reveals that the popular pro-choice Republican candidate, Governor William Weld, ran afoul of the same gender gap as the party's pro-life candidates.

TABLE 8–5. The Gender Gap in Voting Behavior, 1996

				Change from 1992		
	Clinton	*Dole*	*Perot*	*Democrat*	*Republican*	*Independent*
All voters	49	41	8	+6.7	+3.7	-10.4
All Catholics	53	37	9	+9	+2	-11
All men	43	44	10	+2	+6	-11
Catholic men	47	41	10	+10	+3	-14
Protestant men	35	54	9	+1	+7	-10
All women	54	38	7	+9	+1	-10
Catholic women	59	34	7	+15	-2	-13
Protestant women	47	46	7	+8	+2	-10
White men	38	49	11	+1	+8	-11
Catholic white men	41	46	12	+4	+7	-12
White women	48	43	8	+7	+2	-11
Catholic white women	54	37	8	+10	+1	-12
Black men	78	15	5	+1	n.c.	-4
Black women	89	8	2	+3	-1	-3
Hispanic men	65	25	8	—	—	—
Hispanic women	78	17	4	—	—	—

Source: Exit Poll, Voter News Service.

A more plausible explanation has been offered by Jody Newman of the Roper Center for Public Opinion Research. Her analysis concludes that women vote Democratic more often than men because they desire government to exercise a greater role than do men—an important difference when issues such as education, Medicare, and help for the disadvantaged arise (Newman 1997, 102–6).

A complementary explanation of the reasons for the gender gap is suggested when the marital status of voters is introduced into an analysis. David Frum (1997, 24–25) of the Manhattan Institute found a clue to the gender gap in another gap in voting behavior—that separating the married from the unmarried. Unmarried women gave Clinton a margin of better than two to one over Dole. Married women, by contrast, preferred Clinton to Dole by the relatively narrow margin of 48 to 43 percent. Married men voted for Dole in preference to Clinton, 48 to 40 percent, and 10 percent were for Perot. Unmarried men gave Clinton about the same percentage of their vote as did married women, but they supported Perot in greater strength.

Why unmarried women are so strongly Democratic Frum explains by pointing out that 40 million women "form a new American proletariat"—10 million widows, 10 million divorced women, 5 million unmarried mothers, and 15 million single childless women. Disproportionate numbers of them are poor and dependent on government or on others (1997, 25).

The gender gap is most plausibly explained by the popular impression that Republicans, the party of wealth and privilege, has little compassion or concern for those struggling to stay afloat in the tempests that afflict their lives.

Traditional and Modernist Catholics: A Political Fault Line?

That sharp differences have developed in voting behavior, party affiliation, and policy views separating evangelicals and fundamentalists from adherents to mainline Protestant churches has been established in several studies. Whether a parallel split exists within Catholicism is less clear. Scholars such as David Leege of the University of Notre Dame (1993) and the prolific authors of *Religion and the Culture Wars* (Green et al. 1996, ch. 14), as well as the pollsters of the Times-Mirror Center for the People and the Press (*Diminishing Divide* 1996) seem to believe it does. Analysis of the 1996 election gives some support to this opinion.

A scholarly study of voting by religious groups in 1996 declared that "modernist Catholics" and "Hispanics and other non-white Catholics" were "the key to Clinton's success" in winning a decided majority of the vote cast by Catholics (Green et al. 1997, 38). As shown in table 8-6, among white modernist Catholics, Clinton's vote surpassed Dole's by twenty-six percent-

TABLE 8–6. Religious Attitudes and the 1996 Election

	Distribution of Vote (as percent of each group)		
Religious Orientation	*Clinton*	*Dole*	*Perot*
Catholic			
White			
Traditional	39	52	9
Modernist	57	31	12
Hispanic	75	19	6
Black/other	82	18	0
Protestant			
White evangelical			
Traditional	22	74	4
Modernist	42	48	10
White mainline			
Traditional	31	63	6
Modernist	54	42	4
Black	95	5	1
Hispanic/other	55	32	13
Secular			
Fully secular	53	27	20
Nominally religious	58	30	12
Jewish	81	19	0
Mormon	21	74	5
Other Christian	48	41	11

Source: 1996 National Survey of Religion and Politics, University of Akron. Published in John C. Green, James L. Guth, Corwin E. Smidt, and Lyman A. Kellstedt, "Who Elected Clinton? A Collision of Values," *First Things* no. 75 (August/September 1997): 37.

age points, whereas among white traditional Catholics Dole ran thirteen points ahead of the president. Among Hispanic Catholics Clinton's share of the vote exceeded Dole's by 56 percentage points; among black Catholics the margin was even greater.

This study found a gender gap among both categories of Catholics. Fifty-eight percent of male Catholic traditionalists supported Dole, but only 47 percent of female Catholic traditionalists. Among modernist Catholics Dole secured 43 percent of the vote cast by males and a low 20 percent of that cast by women.

Traditionalist groups, Catholic and Protestant, "strongly pro-life," according to the study, "gave high priority to social issues in 1996." Commenting on the Dole campaign strategy, the academicians involved in the study declared that the candidate's "lukewarm approach to late-term abortions and other social issues failed to mobilize the full potential of the traditionalist vote" (Green et al. 1997, 39).

The Election of 1998: A Stand-Off

Those in the media who judge and interpret elections were quick to pronounce the contest of 1998 a defeat for the Republican party. Strangely, in a break with the tradition of putting the best face on an electoral setback, even Republican spokesmen seemed to share this view. Dissatisfaction with the outcome among Republican members of Congress erupted in a campaign to replace the party's high command in the House of Representatives leading Speaker Gingrich to abdicate his position.

In fact, the election, registering the lowest turnout for an off-year contest since 1942 was a stand-off. The Republicans managed to cling to their majority status in both houses of Congress and in governorships. The party division in the Senate remained at 55 Republicans and 45 Democrats after each party surrendered three seats to its opponent. In the House a small ripple reduced Republican strength by four seats from the number won in the 1996 election. Republican governors were elected to replace Democrats in three states; Democrats took three governorships from Republicans; and in Minnesota, a former professional wrestler running as an Independent in a three-candidate race was chosen to replace a Republican governor.

In California, the most populous state, the Democratic party won a spectacular victory taking control of the governor's office and virtually all other agencies of state government.

In 31 states which are home to two-thirds of the nation's voters, however, Republicans held the office of governor in the wake of the 1998 election. This fact alone should be enough to puncture the pessimistic appraisal of the Republican showing in 1998 widely accepted as the conventional wisdom.

But other facts can be cited to challenge this appraisal. The 1998 election gave Republicans control of both houses in three consecutive Congresses—a victory streak which the Party had not been able to match in the preceding 70 years.

In only three elections since World War II—in 1946, 1994, and 1996—have Republican candidates held more seats in the House of Representatives than they won in the 1998 elections. More Republican members were to serve in the House in this 106th Congress than in any Congress during the presidency of Eisenhower, Nixon, Reagan, or Bush.

In the case of the Senate, only twice since the adoption of the Seventeenth Amendment requiring popular election of senators has a Congress assembled with more Republican senators than the 55 serving in the 106th Congress.

In its results the election of 1998 at the national level did not depart significantly from the pattern of 1994 and 1996. It did little to change the distribution of political power. As in 1996, voter turnout was low—the lowest for an off-year since 1942 when the war kept millions from the ballot box. Another continuing trend, related to low turnout, was an increase in the number of seats in the House of Representatives which one of the major parties conceded to its opposition by failing to nominate a candidate. In the 1998 House races 55 Republican candidates and 37 Democrats were elected without facing a major party opponent—twenty percent of the total membership of the lower chamber.

Catholic voters gave to Democratic candidates for the House of Representatives 53 percent of their vote, the same percentage as they had cast for Clinton in 1996. Their vote for Republican House candidates was not significantly different from the degree of support Catholics gave Republicans running for House seats in earlier elections in the 90s, except for 1994.

A reversal of the usual pattern of voting behavior in 1998 was revealed in exit polls in statewide races in New York and Illinois. In both states, contrary to all precedent, Catholic voters gave stronger support to the Republican candidates for governor and for the United States senator than did Protestant voters. This phenomenon can be explained only in part by the extraordinary effort made in both states by the Democratic party to mobilize black churches to turn out the electorate.

A strong increase in the black vote appeared also in other states, notably Alabama, California, Georgia, Maryland, and North Carolina, contributing powerfully to Democratic victories in those states.

On the other hand, there was evidence of a comeback for Republican candidates among Hispanic voters, particularly strong for the Bush brothers in their races for governor in Florida and Texas.

A noteworthy aspect of the 1998 senatorial elections lay in the religious affiliation of the successful Republican candidates. Of the four Republicans who became freshmen senators in 1999, three are Catholic. Representing Illinois, Kentucky, and Ohio, they were the only Republicans to win seats in the upper chamber held up to that time by Democrats.

Political Parties at the End of the Century

For only two of the 20 years between 1981 and 2001 did the nation vote to entrust control of the White House and of both chambers of Congress to the same party. With the election of Bill Clinton to a second term and the renewal of Republican control of Congress in 1996 and 1998, separating powers by putting executive and legislative branches in the hands of rival political parties had become the normal pattern.

Divided government reflected a competitive situation between the parties in the nation as a whole. In the 1990s, the major parties were evenly matched. Surveys reported that neither party could claim the adherence of a majority of the voters.

During this time, changes in the party system which had begun earlier continued to unfold leaving both major parties seriously weakened (Wattenberg, Martin 1994). Although retaining the capacity to raise gigantic amounts of money, Republicans and Democrats found their power to lure voters to the polls and to deliver votes on the basis of party loyalty diminished.

Catholic voters in the mid-nineties displayed their independence. In their party preference they were almost equally divided, but perhaps as many were unattached to either party as could be classified as Republican or Democrat. In their voting behavior in elections after 1968 they no longer behaved as reliable Democrats. On the other hand, after strongly backing Reagan in the election of 1984 and dividing evenly between Bush and Dukakis in 1988, they deserted Republican presidential candidates in the nineties.

As the twentieth century closes, Catholics have, beyond doubt, become the largest swing vote in American politics.

9

The Catholic Voter: Summarizing Conclusions

The most indisputable conclusion emerging from scrutiny of the pattern of Catholic voting behavior in national elections, particularly since World War II, is that the Democratic Party has suffered a substantial loss and the Republicans have realized a moderate gain. As the ranks of Catholics calling themselves Democrats have thinned, the ranks of Catholic Republicans have grown—but not in equal measure. There has been growth, too, in the Catholic component of Independent voters eschewing attachment to either major party, prone to split tickets, and to oscillate from one party to another in successive elections.

It was in the 1980s the nation experienced a major reshuffling of party attachments as is demonstrated in table 9-1. Its effects extended to all religious groups but were most marked in the Catholic electorate as the Republican share of this constituency rose by 80 percent, the Democratic share dropped by 40 percent, and those without partisan attachment increased by 13 percent.

TABLE 9–1. Changing Party Affiliation 1978–1996: The Nation and Major Religious Groups (As Percentage of Group Total)

	1978		*1989–91*		*1996*	
	R	*D*	*R*	*D*	*R*	*D*
The Nation	23	48	33	34	31	34
Catholic	16	56	29	32	29	33
Protestant	28	45	35	34	35	33
Jewish	10	64	—	—	15	56

Source: Gallup polls reported by Roper Center for Public Opinion Research (Dougherty 1997, 58).

Analysis of the behavior of Catholic voters in both presidential and congressional elections since World War II reveals a long-range trend toward the Republican party (tables 9-2 and 9-3).

Three times in the twentieth century, a perceptible drift of Catholic voters from the Democratic Party has been arrested and reversed. The first instance began in the late 1920s with the candidacy of Al Smith, which in combination with the depression, greatly enlarged the Catholic base of the Democratic Party in a protest against both anti-Catholicism and hard times.

Again, in 1960 the nomination and election of John F. Kennedy had similar results, benefiting the Democrats by winning back Catholics who had

TABLE 9–2. Presidential Vote Cast by Catholics, 1928–1996 (Percentage Voting Republican)

Year	*Republican Percentage*
1928	10–15
1932	10–15
1936	19
1940	27
1944	27
1948	34
1952	44
1956	49
1960	22
1964	24
1968*	33
1972	52
1976	45
1980*	50
1984	56
1988	53
1992*	35
1996*	38

* Election in which third party candidate drew substantial vote.

Sources: 1928–48, Estimates of George Gallup; 1952–72, Gallup Post-Election Surveys; 1976–88, CBS News Exit Polls; 1992, Exit Poll, Voter Research Service; and 1996, Exit Poll, Voter News Service.

strayed during the Eisenhower years and by making political activists of hitherto uninvolved Catholics, particularly youthful Catholics.

After the election of 1972, which brought the Republican Party the largest share of the Catholic vote it had gained in a presidential election up to that time, a third reversal of Republican fortunes occurred. The shorthand expression for the cause of the reversal was Watergate. Exposure of the complex of sordid and criminal campaign tactics and of mendacity in the attempt to cover them up led Catholics to join the stampede of voters to the Democratic Party in the off-year election of 1974. The reaction to Watergate, however, was relatively short-lived. By 1980, with a Republican presidential candidate unconnected with the party's disaster, Watergate had ceased to have a strong effect on voting decisions.

The question why a large segment of Catholic voters apparently has over the years moved out of the Democratic Party—much of it into the Republican Party—has no single simple answer. To put the question in this way may

TABLE 9–3. Aggregate Vote Cast by Catholics for House of Representatives, 1958–1998 (Percentage Voting Republican)

Year	*Republican Percentage*
1958	25
1962	27
1970	37
1976	35
1978	38
1980	41
1982	37
1984	43
1986	43
1988	43
1990	41
1992	42
1994	52
1996	46
1998	47

Sources: 1958–78, Gallup Post-Election Surveys; 1980–88, CBS/NY Times Exit Poll; 1990–92, Exit Poll, Voter Research Service; and 1994–98, Exit Poll, Voter News Service.

be misleading. The change with which we are concerned occurred over several years. It resulted less from the conversion of individuals from one party to another than from a process of generational replacement. Every survey of the party affiliation and voting behavior of Catholics in the last two decades of the twentieth century shows a substantially greater percentage of Republicans in younger age brackets than among the elderly.

As Democratic Catholics of a generation that had supported Al Smith and FDR passed from the scene, they were succeeded by more youthful Catholics without memories of the 1920s and 1930s, of the Ku Klux Klan and the depression. Successive new generations introduced a different mix to the Catholic electorate, including a higher percentage of Republicans. The Catholic age cohorts with the greatest percentage of Republicans are those that came to maturity in the 1980s during the presidency of Ronald Reagan.

How the Catholic People Changed

To explain why there are proportionately more Catholic Republicans or fewer Catholic Democrats in the latter half of the twentieth century than in an earlier period, a basic question to ask is how Catholics of today differ from their parents and grandparents. The most obvious answer is that they occupy a more elevated position in the socioeconomic order. They are better educated, richer, more secure. They hold better jobs, more power, and more influence.

It was the changed status of the Catholic population from underclass to middle class that the 1985 study, commissioned by Democratic party officials and later suppressed, fixed on to explain the party's losses among a constituency which the authors designated as "white ethnics." This study undertaken by the CRG Communications Corporation was prompted by the severe setback of the Democratic ticket in the election of 1984 (See Chapter 8).

The white ethnics had deserted, the study concluded, because of failure to adjust the Democratic program to respond to the interests of this upwardly mobile socio-economic group.

"The white ethnic voter is accurate," the draft report read, "when he says that the Democratic party left him . . . the Party stood by these voters when they were at the bottom, but did not move up with them. It maintained the same message and inherited the next classes at the bottom . . . The Republicans . . . inherited these Democrats. They have represented their hopes and fears, and they have cut their taxes."

To recapture the deserting white ethnics the report recommended that the Democratic party "reposition" itself to demonstrate interest in the concerns of the middle class and added, in the vernacular of the advertising world, ". . .

this requires a demarketing of the party to the social and economic underclasses."

Other changes in the Catholic population came hand in hand with middle class status for the descendants of European immigrants. Catholics were no longer foreigners. They no longer lived in ethnic enclaves. They no longer separated themselves from other Americans. They lost the minority mindset, brooding about discrimination and feeling out of place in the larger society. They no longer felt a need for government's support and protection. Tax cuts came to assume more importance to them than the level of the minimum wage.

All these generalizations have some validity in the case of the white Catholic of European extraction typically separated by two or more generations from immigrant ancestors. But among the most important changes in American Catholicism in the late twentieth century has been a modification of its ethnic composition resulting from Hispanic, and secondarily from, Asian immigration. The political effect of the growing importance of both groups—particularly Hispanics—has been to counteract the trend toward Republicanism in the white Catholic community.

How the Parties Changed

National elections since the 1970s have demonstrated the validity of the prophecies made by Scammon and Wattenberg. Cultural considerations have played an important part in bringing about a changed political alignment of Catholic voters. Particularly in the years when it was directed by the forces that George McGovern relied on in 1972, the Democratic Party seemed to reject a set of values held by most Catholics—indeed, as the election demonstrated, by most Americans.

In the estrangement of Catholics from the Democratic Party, two modifications of party policy made in the 1980s should not be overlooked, for they suggested an indifference to the Catholic constituency. One involved the question of abortion, on which an absolute and uncompromising pro-choice position was adopted—so uncompromising that Governor Robert Casey of Pennsylvania, who held a dissenting view, was not permitted to address the party convention in 1992. The second was the abandonment in the 1988 platform of a pledge of assistance to children in nonpublic schools.

As a result of its conduct in the 1960 presidential campaign, the Republican party effaced the last remnants of its anti-Catholic image, strong at its founding and throughout most of the nineteenth century, submerged in the early twentieth, but revived by its campaign against Al Smith in 1928.

In the 1970s and 80s the Republican party exploited "the social issue." On both abortion and aid to non-public schools, it took a stand opposed to that adopted by the Democrats.

How the Political Environment Changed

Issues of foreign and military policy tended in the period of the Cold War to incline many Catholics toward the Republican Party. They had an influence especially on voters whose bonds to other countries were still vigorous. As long as there was a Communist world, American Catholics were deeply conscious of a continuing struggle in eastern Europe and in Latin America. But by the 1990s the Communist issue was dead to most voters, surviving only among anti-Castro Cuban-Americans.

As issues of domestic policy tended to monopolize public attention, Republican candidates found themselves fighting on unfavorable terrain. Always regarded as representative of wealth and privilege, Republicans had an uphill fight to convince voters that they ever fully endorsed the New Deal, much less Medicare, Medicaid, and other popular programs of the Great Society. By centering their attack against George Bush on fears about the economy, the Democrats in 1992 defeated the President in whose administration Communist power disintegrated and an almost bloodless war against Iraqi aggression was won.

In a consideration of changes in the political environment in the late twentieth century, the rise of women and of blacks cannot go without recognition. The increased activism of both groups has had an important impact on the political agenda, highlighting issues that were ignored in earlier times and reshuffling the coalitions composing the parties. Feminists and blacks enlisted overwhelmingly in the Democratic party, offsetting its losses among groups such as Southern whites, evangelicals, and Catholics.

Some commentators like E. J. Dionne (1991, 108–109) have argued that "feminists cost Democrats and liberals votes" because of backlash against excesses of the movement. A larger group came to the conclusion that some part of the surging Republican fortunes from the 1960s on was attributable to racial motivation (Carmines and Stimson 1989; Dionne, 1991, 78–80).

The behavior of Catholic voters in some places and at some times was probably influenced by backlash against both movements. But the influence was never strong; it was localized, and it was for the most part temporary. Backlash does not provide the explanation of lasting changes in Catholic voting patterns.

The Catholic Voter in the Future

The presidential elections of the 1990s were severe setbacks for the Republican Party in the erosion of the beachhead in Catholic territory that it appeared to have established in the eighties. In both contests the support it received declined well below 40 percent of the Catholic vote.

On the other hand, Democrats did not receive strong support from the Catholic electorate. In 1992 only 44 percent of Catholics voted for Clinton. In 1996 the president fared much better, gaining 53 percent of the ballots of a Catholic electorate decidedly more Hispanic in composition. This vote is of respectable size, particularly in a three-candidate race, but it does not approach the share of the Catholic vote once common for Democratic candidates. And the fact that it was achieved in an election in which turnout hit historic low points gives ground for doubt about its significance.

Predicting future voting behavior is a risky enterprise. Nevertheless, it is clear that although the Democrats have ceased to be the party of a majority of the nation's Catholics. Republicans have yet to win the support of that majority. A careful analysis of Catholic voting behavior by two scholars based on elections of the seventies and eighties concluded, "Although Catholics are no longer the New Deal loyalists, blue collar, lower-income voters of past decades, they have not shifted into the Republican camp across the board" (Kenski and Lockwood 1990, 32). In the presidential contests of the 1990s the shift has been reversed. Issues that formerly attracted Catholics to the Republican Party have lost their importance to voters. Witness the exit poll finding that only 4 percent of the voters in 1996 were influenced by any foreign policy issue. The advantage Republicans once enjoyed as the more trustworthy custodians of the economy has evaporated as the economy has sustained a brisk pace under Democratic care and the attainment of balance in the federal budget is on the horizon. On cultural issues the emphasis placed by the Clinton administration on family concerns, particularly children, has cut into any Republican advantage. Finally, as Hispanics constitute an increasingly large proportion of the electorate, Republicans face an additional hurdle in winning a majority of the vote cast by Catholics.

The voting behavior of American Catholics, as the twentieth century draws to a close, suggests that independence and volatility will be its characteristics in the future. A large and crucial portion of Catholic voters will not be firmly tied to either major party—and probably not to a third party, should one develop. Catholics, no longer reliable Democrats, are likely to slip further from their historic fold to join the ranks of both Republicans and Independents. They will add particularly to the category of voters classified in surveys as "leaners," inclining toward one of the major parties but without a strong commitment to it, ready to switch their allegiance and split their tickets on Election Day. The melting pot will in all likelihood continue its work of making Catholics in their political attachments and sentiments less and less distinguishable from the rest of America.

References

Abbott, Walter M., ed. 1966. *The Documents of Vatican II*. New York: Guild Press.

Abramson, Harold J. 1973. *Ethnic Diversity in Catholic America*. New York: Wiley.

Alba, Richard D. 1985. *Italian Americans: Into the Twilight of Ethnicity*. Englewood Cliffs, N.J: Prentice-Hall.

———. 1995. "Assimilation's Quiet Tide." *The Public Interest* 119 (Spring): 3–18.

Allitt, Patrick. 1993. *Catholic Intellectuals and Conservative Politics in America, 1950–1985*. Ithaca: Cornell Univ. Press.

Allswang, John M. 1986. *Bosses, Machines, and Urban Voters*. Baltimore: Johns Hopkins Univ. Press.

Ambrose, Stephen A. 1987. *Nixon: The Education of a Politician, 1913–1962*. New York: Simon & Schuster.

———. 1989. *Nixon: The Triumph of a Politician, 1962–1972*. New York: Simon & Schuster.

American Enterprise. 1991. "Election Profile: Catholics' Political Inclinations." Sept/Oct. 2: 93–100.

Anbinder, Tyler. 1992. *Nativism and Slavery: The Northern Know Nothings and the Politics of the 1850's*. New York: Oxford Univ. Press.

Andersen, Kristi. 1979. *The Creation of a Democratic Majority, 1928–1936*. Chicago: Univ. of Chicago Press.

Balzano, Michael P. Jr. 1991. "The Silent versus the New Majority." *Richard Nixon: Politician, President, Administrator*, Leon Friedman and William P. Levantrosser. New York: Greenwood.

Banks, Nathaniel. 1856. *Banks Papers*. Washington, D.C.: Library of Congress.

Barker, Wharton. 1888. *Barker Papers*. Washington, D.C.: Library of Congress.

Basler, Roy P., ed. 1953. *The Collected Works of Abraham Lincoln*. New Brunswick, N.J.: Rutgers Univ. Press.

Bauer, K. Jack. 1985. *Zachary Taylor: Soldier, Planter, Statesman of the Old Southwest*. Baton Rouge: Louisiana State Univ. Press.

Bell, Daniel, ed. 1963. *The Radical Right*. Garden City, N.Y.: Doubleday.

Billington, Ray A. 1938. *The Protestant Crusade, 1800–1860: A Study of the Origins of American Nativism*. New York: Rinehart.

Black, Earl, and Merle Black. 1992. *The Vital South: How Presidents Are Elected*. Cambridge: Harvard Univ. Press.

Bobcock, John Paul. 1894. "The Irish Conquest of Our Cities." *Forum* 17 (April): 186–95.

Boldt, David R. 1990. "The Bishops Return to a Darker Era of U.S. Politics." *Philadelphia Inquirer* (1 July).

Brown, Peter. 1991. *Minority Party: Why Democrats Face Defeat in 1992 and Beyond.* Washington, D.C.: Regnery Gateway.

Brown, Thomas N. 1966. *Irish-American Nationalism 1870–1890.* Philadelphia: Lippincott.

Browne, Henry J. 1949. *The Catholic Church and the Knights of Labor.* Washington, D.C.: Catholic Univ. of America Press.

Brownlow, William G. 1974. *A Political Register Setting Forth the Principles of the Whig and LocoFoco Parties in the United States.* Jonesboro, Tenn., 1844 Reprint, Spartanburg, S.C.

Burner, David. 1968. *The Politics of Provincialism: The Democratic Party in Transition, 1918–1932.* New York: Knopf.

Byrnes, Timothy A. 1991. *Catholic Bishops in American Politics.* Princeton: Princeton Univ. Press.

Campbell, Angus, Philip E. Converse, Warren E. Miller, and Donald E. Stokes. 1960. *The American Voter.* New York: Wiley.

Campbell, Angus, et al. 1966. *Elections and the Political Order.* New York: Wiley.

Campbell, Colin, and Bert A. Rockman, eds. 1996. *The Clinton Presidency: First Appraisals.* Chatham, N.J.: Chatham House.

"Candidate Carter and Catholics." *America* 135 (1976): 42.

Cannon, James. 1928. "Causes of Governor Smith's Defeat." *Current History* 29 (December): 373–77.

Carroll, Anna Ella. 1856. *The Great American Battle or the Contest Between Christianity and Political Romanism.* New York: Miller, Orton & Mulligan.

Castelli, Jim. 1976. "How Catholics Voted." *Commonweal* 103 (3 December): 780–82.

———. 1980. "The Religious Vote." *Commonweal* 107 (21 November): 650–51.

———. 1987. "A Tale of Two Cultures." *Notre Dame Magazine* 15, no. 2 (summer): 33–34.

Castelli, Jim and Joseph Gremillion. 1987. *The Emerging Parish: The Notre Dame Study of Catholic Life Since Vatican II.* San Francisco: Harper & Row.

Ceaser, James W., and Andrew E. Busch. 1993. *Upside Down and Inside Out: The 1992 Elections and American Politics.* Lanham, Md.: Rowman & Littlefield.

Celio, Mary Beth. 1993. "Catholics: Who, How Many, and Where?" *America* 168 (9 January): 10–14.

Chavez, Linda. 1996. "The Hispanic Political Tide." *New York Times* (18 November): A17:3.

Church, Robert L., and Michael W. Sadlak. 1976. *Education in the United States: An Interpretive History.* New York: Free Press.

Clarkson, James S. 1884. *Clarkson Papers.* Washington, D.C.: Library of Congress.

Clubb, Jerome M., and Howard W. Allen, eds. 1977. *Electoral Change and Stability in American Political History.* New York: Free Press.

Coletta, Paolo E. 1964. *William Jennings Bryan: Political Evangelist.* Lincoln, Nebr.: Univ. of Nebraska Press.

Connaughton, Sister Mary S. 1943. *The Editorial Opinion of the Catholic Telegraph on Contemporary Affairs and Politics, 1871–1921.* Washington, D.C.: Catholic Univ. of America Press.

Connelly, James F. 1960. *The Visit of Archbishop Gaetano Bedini to the United States of America (June 1853–February 1854).* Rome: Pontificia Universitas Gregoriana.

Converse, Philip E. 1966. "Religion and Politics: The 1960 Election." In *Elections and the Political Order,* edited by Angus Campbell et al., 96–124. New York: Wiley.

Converse, Philip E., Angus Campbell, Warren E. Miller, and Donald E. Stokes. 1961. "Stability and Change in 1960: A Reinstating Election." *American Political Science Review* 55 (June): 269–80.

Cooper, Thomas V., and Hector T. Fenton. 1888. *American Politics Non-Partisan from the Beginning to Date: A Complete Tabulated History of American Politics.* Boston: B. A. Fowler.

Cox, James M. 1946. *Journey Through My Years.* New York: Simon & Schuster.

Crippen, Lee F. 1942. *Simon Cameron: Ante-Bellum Years.* Oxford, Ohio: Mississippi Valley.

Crosby, Donald F. 1978. *God, Church and Flag: Senator Joseph R. McCarthy and the Catholic Church, 1950–1957.* Chapel Hill: Univ. of North Carolina Press.

Curry, Earl R. 1973. "Pennsylvania and the Republican Convention of 1860." *Pennsylvania Magazine of History and Biography* 97, no. 2 (April): 183–98.

David, Paul T., and David H. Everson, eds. 1983. *The Presidential Election and Transition, 1980–1981.* Carbondale, Ill.: Southern Illinois Univ. Press.

David, Paul T., Ralph M. Goldman, Richard C. Bain. 1960. *The Politics of National Party Conventions.* Washington: Brookings Institution.

Davidson, James D. 1994. "Religion Among America's Elite: Persistence and Change in the Protestant Establishment." *Sociology of Religion* 55, no. 4: 419–40.

Davis, Cyprian. 1990. *The History of Black Catholics in the United States.* New York: Crossroad.

Degler, Carl N. 1964. "American Political Parties and the Rise of the City: An Interpretation." *Journal of American History* 51 (June): 41–59.

———. 1971. "American Political Parties." In *Electoral Change and Stability in American Political History,* edited by Jerome M. Clubb and Howard W. Allen. New York: Free Press.

DeSantis, Vincent P. 1960. "Catholicism and Presidential Elections, 1865–1900." *Mid-America* 42, no. 2 (April): 67–79.

———. 1965. "American Catholics and McCarthyism." *Catholic Historical Review* 51 (March): 1–30.

Desmond, Humphrey J. 1912. *The APA Movement: A Sketch.* Washington, D.C.: New Century.

The Diminishing Divide: . . . American Churches, American Politics. 1996. News Release (25 June). Washington, D.C.: Times-Mirror Center for the People and the Press.

Diner, Hasia R. 1983. *Erin's Daughters in America: Irish Immigrant Women in the Nineteenth Century.* Baltimore: Johns Hopkins Univ. Press.

Dionne, Jr., E. J. 1981. "Catholics and the Democrats." In *Party Coalitions in the 80's*, edited by Seymour M. Lipset. San Francisco: Institute for Contemporary Studies.

———. 1991. *Why Americans Hate Politics.* New York: Simon & Schuster.

Divine, Robert A. 1974. *Foreign Policy and U.S. Presidential Elections, 1952–1960.* New York: New Viewpoints.

Dolan, Jay P. 1985. *The American Catholic Experience: A History from Colonial Times to the Present.* Garden City, N.Y.: Image Books.

Dougherty, Regina, Everett C. Ladd, David Wilber, and Lynn Zayachkiwsky, eds. 1997. *America at the Polls 1996.* Storrs, Conn.: The Roper Center, Univ. of Connecticut Press.

Doyle, David Noel. 1976. *Irish Americans: Native Rights and National Empires: The Structure, Divisions and Attitudes of the Catholic Minority in the Decade of Expansion 1890–1901.* New York: Arno Press.

Ellis, John Tracy. 1952. *Gibbons.* Milwaukee: Bruce.

———. 1956. *American Catholicism.* Chicago: Univ. of Chicago Press.

———. 1967. *Documents of American Catholic History.* Chicago: Regnery.

Evans, John Whitney. 1960. "Catholics and the Blair Education Bill." *Catholic Historical Review* 46: 273–98.

Farley, James A. 1948. *Jim Farley's Story: The Roosevelt Years.* New York: Whittlesey House.

Farrelly, David G. 1955. "Rum, Romanism and Rebellion Resurrected." *Western Political Quarterly* 8, no. 2 (June): 262–70.

Felknor, Bruce. 1966. *Dirty Politics.* New York: Norton.

Fenton, John H. 1960. *The Catholic Vote.* New Orleans: Hauser.

Ferraro, Geraldine A. 1985. *Ferraro, My Story.* New York: Bantam Books.

Finke, Roger, and Rodney Stark. 1992. *The Churching of America, 1776–1990.* New Brunswick, N.J.: Rutgers Univ. Press.

Fite, Gilbert. 1951. "The Agricultural Issue in the Campaign of 1928." *Mississippi Valley Historical Review* 37 (March): 653–72.

Fladeland, Betty. 1955. *James Gillespie Birney: Slaveholder to Abolitionist.* Ithaca: Cornell Univ. Press.

Flynn, George Q. 1968. *American Catholics and the Roosevelt Presidency, 1932–1936.* Lexington, Ky.: Univ. of Kentucky Press.

Foik, Paul J. 1969. *Pioneer Catholic Journalism.* New York: Greenwood.

Foner, Eric. 1970. *Free Soil, Free Labor, Free Men: The Ideology of the Republican Party Before the Civil War.* New York: Oxford Univ. Press.

Ford, Gerald R. 1979. *A Time to Heal: The Autobiography of Gerald R. Ford.* New York: Harper & Row.

"Four More Years" (A Symposium). 1972. *Commonweal* (24 November): 195–204.

Friedman, Leon, and William F. Levantrosser, eds. 1991. *Richard M. Nixon: Politician, President, Administrator.* New York: Greenwood.

Frum, David. 1997. "On the Future of Conservatism." *Commentary* 103 (February), 24–25.

Fuchs, Lawrence H. 1967. *John F. Kennedy and American Catholicism.* New York: Meredith.

Gallup, George, and Jim Castelli. 1987. *The American Catholic People.* New York: Macmillan.

———. 1989. *The People's Religion: American Faith in the 90's.* New York: Macmillan.

Gannon, Robert I. 1962. *The Cardinal Spellman Story.* Garden City, N.Y.: Doubleday

Gelm, Richard J. 1990. "The United States Catholic Bishops: A Survey Research Perspective." Paper delivered at Annual Meeting of the American Political Science Association, San Francisco, Calif., August 30–September 2.

George, Carol R. V. 1993. *God's Salesman: Norman Vincent Peale and the Power of Positive Thinking.* New York: Oxford Univ. Press.

Germond, Jack W., and Jules Witcover. 1985. *Wake Us When It's Over: Presidential Politics of 1984.* New York: Macmillan.

———. 1989. *Whose Broad Stripes and Bright Stars? The Trivial Pursuit of the Presidency 1988.* New York: Warner Books.

Gerner, George W. 1995. "Catholics and the Religious Right." *Commonweal* 122, no. 9 (5 May): 15–20.

Gibson, Florence E. 1951. *The Attitudes of the New York Irish Toward State and National Affairs, 1848–1892.* New York: Columbia Univ. Press.

Gienapp, William E. 1985. "Nativism and the Creation of a Republican Majority." *Journal of American History* 72 (December): 529–59.

———. 1987. *The Origins of the Republican Party, 1852–1856.* New York: Oxford Univ. Press.

Gillespie, Edward. 1996. "The Catholic Vote." *Rising Tide* (May/June): 18–23 (a publication of the Republican National Committee).

Glenn, Charles L. 1988. *The Myth of the Common School.* Amherst, Ma.: University of Massachusetts Press.

Glenn, Norval D., and Ruth Hyland. 1967. "Religious Preference and Worldly Success: Some Evidence from National Surveys." *American Sociological Review* 32 (February): 73–85.

Goldman, Peter, Thomas M. DeFrank, Mark Miller, Andrew Murr, and Tom Matthews. 1994. *Quest for the Presidency 1992.* College Station, Tex.: Texas A & M Univ. Press.

Gonzalez, Roberto, and Michael LaVelle. 1985. *The Hispanic Catholic in the United States: A Socio-Cultural and Religious Profile.* New York: Northeast Catholic Pastoral Center for Hispanics.

Grant, Philip A. 1990. "The Priest in Politics: Father Charles E. Coughlin and the Presidential Election of 1936." *Records of the American Catholic Historical Society of Philadelphia.* 101 (Spring): 35–47.

Greeley, Andrew M. 1971. *Why Can't They Be Like Us? America's White Ethnic Groups.* New York: E. P. Dutton.

———. 1977a. *The American Catholic: A Social Portrait.* New York: Basic Books.

———. 1977b. "How Conservative are American Catholics?" *Political Science Quarterly* 92 (Summer): 199–218.

———. 1981. *The Irish Americans: The Rise to Money and Power.* New York: Harper & Row.

———. 1990. *The Catholic Myth: The Behavior and Beliefs of American Catholics.* New York: Scribner's.

———. 1992. "A Catholic Vote?" *Church* 8 (Fall): 5–7.

Green, John C., James L. Guth, Corwin E. Smidt, and Lyman A. Kellstedt. 1996. *Religion and the Culture Wars: Dispatches from the Front.* Lanham, Md.: Rowman & Littlefield.

———. 1997. "Who Elected Clinton? A Collision of Values." *First Things*, no. 75 (August–September): 35–40.

Harris, Joseph Claude. 1993. "Pennies from Heaven." *Commonweal* 120 (9 April): 8–9.

———. 1994. "U.S. Catholic Contributions—Up or Down?" *America* 170 (May 21): 14–16.

Harris, Louis. 1954. *Is There a Republican Majority? Political Trends 1952–1956.* New York: Harper.

Hertzke, Alan D. 1988. *Representing God in Washington: The Role of Religious Lobbies in the American Polity.* Knoxville: Univ. of Tennessee Press.

Hesburgh, Theodore M. 1990. *God, Country, Notre Dame: The Autobiography of Theodore M. Hesburgh.* New York: Doubleday.

Hesseltine, William B., and Rex G. Fisher, eds. 1961. *Trimmers, Trucklers, and Temporizers: Notes of Murat Halstead from the Political Conventions of 1856.* Madison: Univ. of Wisconsin Press.

Higgins, George G. 1993. *Organized Labor and the Church: Reflections of A "Labor Priest.* Mahwah, N.J.: Paulist Press.

Higham, John. 1955. *Strangers in the Land: Patterns of American Nativism, 1860–1925.* New Brunswick, N.J.: Rutgers Univ. Press.

Hitchcock, James. 1996. "How Pro-Life Is Bob Dole?" *Catholic Herald* (Arlington, Va.) (24 October).

Hofstadter, Richard. 1963. "Pseudo-Conservative Revolt." In *The Radical Right*, edited by Daniel Bell. Garden City, N.Y.: Doubleday.

Hollingsworth, J. Rogers. 1963. *The Whirligig of Politics: The Democracy of Cleveland and Bryan.* Chicago: Univ. of Chicago Press.

Holt, Michael F. 1973a. "The Antimasonic and Know Nothing Parties." In *History of U.S. Political Parties, 1789–1968*, edited by Arthur M. Schlesinger, Jr. New York: Chelsea House.

———. 1973b. "The Politics of Impatience: The Origins of Know Nothingism." *Journal of American History* 60 (September): 309–31.

———. 1978. *The Political Crisis of the 1850s.* New York: Wiley.

Hoover, Herbert. 1951–52. *The Memoirs of Herbert Hoover.* New York: Macmillan.

Hornig, Edgar Albert. 1961. "The Religious Issue in the Taft-Bryan Duel." *Proceedings of the American Philosophical Society* 105, no. 6: 53–537.

Huthmacher, J. Joseph. 1959. *Massachusetts People and Politics, 1919–1933*. Cambridge: Harvard Univ. Press.

Iseley, Jeter A. 1947. *Horace Greeley and the Republican Party, 1853–1861*. Princeton: Princeton Univ. Press.

"Is Protestant Support a Political Liability?" 1952. *Christian Century* 69 (26 November).

Johnson, Lyndon B. 1971. *The Vantage Point: Perspectives of the Presidency 1963–1968*. New York: Holt, Rinehart & Winston.

Johnson, Walter, ed. 1972–79. *The Papers of Adlai E. Stevenson*. Boston: Little, Brown.

Jones, Stanley L. 1964. *The Presidential Election of 1896*. Madison: Univ. of Wisconsin Press.

Julian, George W. 1899. "The First Republican National Convention." *American Historical Review* 4, no. 2 (January): 313–22.

Kantowicz, Edward R. 1983. *Corporation Sole: Cardinal Mundelein and Chicago Catholicism*. Notre Dame, Ind.: Univ. of Notre Dame Press.

Keefe, Thomas M. 1957. "The Catholic Issue in the Chicago Tribune Before the Civil War." *Mid-America* 57 (October): 227–45.

Kehl, James A. 1981. *Boss Rule in the Gilded Age: Matt Quay of Pennsylvania*. Pittsburgh: Univ. of Pittsburgh Press.

Kellstedt, Lyman A., John C. Green, James L. Guth, and Corwin E. Smidt. 1995. "Has Godot Finally Arrived? Religion and Realignment." *The Public Perspective* (June/July): 18–22.

Kenski, Henry C., and William Lockwood. 1990. "Catholic Voting: The Shift from New Deal Loyalist to Critical Swing Vote." Paper delivered at the Annual Meeting of the American Political Science Association, San Francisco.

———. 1991. "Catholic Voting Behavior in 1988." In *The Bible and the Ballot Box: Religion and Politics in the 1988 Election*, edited by James L. Guth and John C. Green. Boulder, Colo.: Westview.

King, James M. 1899. *Facing the Twentieth Century: Our Country, Its Power and Peril*. New York: Eaton.

Kinzer, Donald L. 1964. *An Episode in Anti-Catholicism: The American Protective Association*. Seattle: Univ. of Washington Press.

Kirkpatrick, Jeane J. 1973. "Revolt of the Masses." *Commentary* 55 (February), 58–62.

———. 1976. *The New Presidential Elite: Men and Women in National Politics*. New York: Russell Sage Foundation.

Kleppner, Paul. 1966. "Lincoln and the Immigrant Vote: A Case of Religious Polarization." *Mid-America* 48 (July): 178–95.

———. 1970. *The Cross of Culture: A Social Analysis of Mid-Western Politics, 1850–1900*. New York: Free Press.

———. 1982. *Who Voted? The Dynamics of Electoral Turnout, 1870–1980*. New York: Praeger.

Klinkhamer, Sister Marie Carolyn. 1956. "The Blaine Amendment of 1875." *Catholic Historical Review* 42: 15–49.

Knebel, Fletcher. 1959. "Democratic Forecast: A Catholic in 1960." *Look* (3 March), 13–17.

Knobel, Dale T. 1986. *Paddy and the Republic: Ethnicity and Nationality in Antebellum America.* Middletown, Conn.: Wesleyan Univ. Press.

———. 1996. *America for the Americans: The Nativist Movement in the United States.* New York: Twayne Publishers.

Kosmin, Barry A., and Seymour P. Lachman. 1993. *One Nation under God: Religion in Contemporary American Society.* New York: Crown.

Kremm, Thomas W. 1977. "Cleveland and the First Lincoln Election: The Ethnic Response to Nativism." *Journal of Interdisciplinary History* 7, no. 1 (Summer): 69–86.

Kwitchen, Sister Mary Augustine. 1949. *James Alphonsus McMaster: A Study in American Thought.* Washington, D.C.: Catholic Univ. of America Press.

Ladd, Everett C., ed. 1995a. *America at the Polls 1994.* Storrs, Conn.: Roper Center.

———. 1995b. "The 1994 Congressional Elections: The Postindustrial Realignment Continues." *Political Science Quarterly* 110: 1–23.

Ladd, Everett C., and Charles D. Hadley. 1978. *Transformations of the American Party System: Political Coalitions from the New Deal to the 1970s.* New York: Norton.

Lally, Francis. 1962. *The Catholic Church in a Changing America.* Boston: Little, Brown.

Lash, Joseph P. 1973. *Eleanor: The Years Alone.* New York: New American Library.

Leege, David C. 1993. *The Decomposition of the Religious Vote: A Comparison of White, Non-Hispanic Catholics with Other Ethnoreligious Groups, 1960–1992.* Paper delivered at American Political Science Association Convention, Washington, D.C., September.

Lichtman, Allan J. 1979. *Prejudice and the Old Politics: The Presidential Election of 1928.* Chapel Hill: Univ. of North Carolina Press.

Lipset, Seymour M., ed. 1981. *Party Coalitions in the 1980s.* San Francisco: Institute for Contemporary Studies.

———. 1993. "The Significance of the 1992 Election." *P.S. Political Science & Politics.* (March): 7–16.

Lipset, Seymour M., and Earl Raab. 1981. "Election and the Evangelicals." *Commentary* 71 (March): 25–31.

Liptak, Dolores. 1989. *Immigrants and Their Church.* New York: Macmillan.

Lubell, Samuel. 1956. *The Future of American Politics.* New York: Harper.

———. 1957. "Can the GOP Win Without Ike?" *Saturday Evening Post* 229 (January 26): 30+.

McAvoy, Thomas T. 1969. *A History of the Catholic Church in the United States.* Notre Dame, Ind.: Univ. of Notre Dame Press.

McCadden, James J. 1964. "Bishop Hughes Versus the Public School Society of New York." *Catholic Historical Review* 50, no. 2 (July): 188–207.

McElwaine, Robert S. 1988. *Mario Cuomo: A Biography.* New York: Scribner's.

McGreevy, John T. 1996. *Parish Boundaries: The Catholic Encounter with Race in the Twentieth Century Urban North*. Chicago: Univ. of Chicago Press.

McGurrin, James. 1948. *Bourke Cochran: A Free Lance in American Politics*. New York: Scribner's.

McHugh, James T. 1997. "Catholics and the 1996 Election." *First Things*, no. 70 (February): 15–17.

McKay, Ernest A. 1964. "Henry Wilson: Unprincipled Know Nothing." *Mid-America* 46: 29–37.

McLaughlin, J. Fairfax. 1885. *The Life and Times of John Kelly, Tribune of the People*. New York: American News Company.

McSeveney, Samuel T. 1972. *The Politics of Depression: Political Behavior in the Northeast 1893–1896*. New York: Oxford Univ. Press.

Marshall, Charles C. 1927. "An Open Letter to Governor Alfred E. Smith." *Atlantic Monthly* 139 (April): 540–49.

Martin, John Bartlow. 1976. *Adlai Stevenson of Illinois: The Life of Adlai E. Stevenson*. Garden City, N.Y.: Doubleday.

———. 1977. *Adlai Stevenson and the World: The Life of Adlai E. Stevenson*. Garden City, N.Y.: Doubleday.

Miller, Randall M., and Jon L. Wakelyn. 1983. *Catholics in the Old South: Essays on Church and Culture*. Macon, Ga.: Mercer Univ. Press.

Miller, Robert Moats. 1956. "A Footnote on the Role of the Protestant Churches in the Election of 1928." *Church History* 25 (June): 145–59.

Miller, Warren E., and Santa A. Traugott. 1989. *American National Election Studies Data Source Book 1952–1986*. Cambridge: Harvard Univ. Press.

Moore, Edmund A. 1956. *A Catholic Runs for President: The Campaign of 1928*. New York: Ronald.

Morison, Elting E., and John Blum, eds. 1951–54. *Letters of Theodore Roosevelt*. Cambridge: Harvard Univ. Press.

Mueller, Sam A., and Angela V. Lane. 1972. "Tabulations from the 1957 Survey on Religion." *Journal for the Scientific Study of Religion* 2, no. 1 (March): 76–98.

Murnion, Philip J., and Anne Wenzel. n.d. *The Crisis of the Church in the Inner City*. New York: National Pastoral Life Center.

Newman, Jody. 1997. "The Gender Story: Women as Voters and Candidates in the 1996 Elections." *America at the Polls 1996*. Roper Center: Storrs, Conn.

Nichols, Roy. 1923. "Some Problems of the First Republican Presidential Campaign." *American Historical Review* 28 (April): 492–96.

Nichols, Roy, and Jeanette Nichols. 1971. "Election of 1852." In *History of American Presidential Elections 1789–1968*, edited by Arthur M. Schlesinger Jr., 921–1006. New York: Chelsea House.

Nixon, Richard M. 1962. *Six Crises*. Garden City, N.Y.: Doubleday.

———. 1978. *RN: The Memoirs of Richard Nixon*. New York: Grosset & Dunlap.

Novak, Michael. 1972a. *The Rise of the Unmeltable Ethnics: Politics and Culture in the Seventies*. New York: Macmillan.

———. 1972b. "The Party in Question." *Commonweal* 97, no. 11 (15 December): 245, 261–63.

O'Brien, David J. 1968. *American Catholics and Social Reform: The New Deal Years*. New York: Oxford Univ. Press.
O'Connell, Marvin R. 1988. *John Ireland and the American Catholic Church*. St. Paul: Minnesota Historical Society.
O'Connor, Thomas H. 1984. *Fitzpatrick's Boston, 1846–1866: John Bernard Fitzpatrick, Third Bishop of Boston*. Boston: Northeastern Univ. Press.
O'Driscoll, Sister M. Felicity. 1937. "Political Nativism in Buffalo: 1830–1860." *Records of the American Catholic Historical Society* 48: 279–319.
O'Hare, William P., ed. 1989. *Redistricting in the 1990's: A Guide for Minority Groups*. Washington, D.C.: Population Reference Bureau.
Page, Benjamin I. 1978. *Choices and Echoes in Presidential Elections: Rational Man and Electoral Democracy*. Chicago: Univ. of Chicago Press.
Petrocik, John R. 1981. *Party Coalitions: Realignments and the Decline of the New Deal Party System*. Chicago: Univ. of Chicago Press.
Petrocik, John R., and Fred Steeper. 1989. "Wedges and Magnets." Unpublished paper, Detroit: Market Opinion Research.
Pew Research Center. 1996. *The Diminishing Divide . . . American Churches, American Politics*. Washington, D.C.: Pew Research Center for the People and the Press.
Phillips, Kevin P. 1969. *The Emerging Republican Majority*. New Rochelle, N.Y.: Arlington House.
Plotkin, Henry A. 1985. "Issues in the Campaign." *The Election of 1984: Reports and Interpretations*, edited by Gerald Pomper et al. Chatham, N.J.: Chatham House.
Pool, Ithiel de Sola, Robert P. Abelson, and Stewart L. Popkin. 1965. *Candidates, Issues, and Strategies: A Computer Simulation of the 1960 and 1964 Presidential Elections*. Cambridge: Massachusetts Institute of Technology Press.
Potter, David M. 1976. *The Impending Crisis 1848–1861*. New York: Harper & Row.
Potter, George M. 1960. *To the Golden Door: The Story of the Irish in Ireland and America*. Boston: Little, Brown.
Prendergast, William B. 1950. "State Legislatures and Communism: The Current Scene." *American Political Science Review* 44, no. 3 (September): 556–74.
"President's Surrender to the Pope." 1951. *Christian Century* 68 (31 October).
Princeton Religion Research Center. 1991. "Trends in Religious Preference Continue to Evolve Slowly." *Emerging Trends* 13, no. 7 (September): 1.
Rainwater, Lee, and William I. Yancey. 1967. *The Moynihan Report and the Politics of Controversy*. Cambridge: Massachusetts Institute of Technology Press.
Ravitch, Diana. 1974. *The Great School Wars New York City 1805–1973: A History of Public Schools as a Battlefield of Social Change*. New York: Basic Books.
Rawley, James A. 1955. *Edwin D. Morgan 1811–1883: Merchant in Politics*. New York: AMS.
Reese, Thomas J. 1992. *A Flock of Shepherds: The National Conference of Catholic Bishops*. Kansas City, Mo.: Sheed & Ward.
Reeves, Thomas C. 1982. *The Life and Times of Joe McCarthy: A Biography*. New York: Stein & Day.

Republican National Committee. 1961. *The Elections of 1960: Report of the Research Division*. Washington, D.C.

———. 1969. *The 1968 Elections: Report of the Research Division*. Washington, D.C.

Republican National Convention. 1893. *Proceedings of the First Three Republican National Conventions of 1856, 1860, and 1864 Including Proceedings of the Antecedent National Convention Held at Pittsburgh in February 1856 as Reported by Horace Greeley*. Minneapolis: C. W. Johnson.

Rice, Madeleine H. 1944. *American Catholic Opinion in the Slavery Controversy*. New York: Columbia Univ. Press.

Rieder, Jonathan 1985. *Canarsie: The Jews and Italians of Brooklyn Against Liberalism*. Cambridge: Harvard Univ. Press.

Robinson, Archie. 1981. *George Meany and His Times: A Biography*. New York: Simon & Schuster.

Rosenberg, Milton, Sidney Verba, and Philip Converse. 1970. *Vietnam and the Silent Majority: The Dove's Guide*. New York: Harper & Row.

Ruskowski, Leo. 1940. *French Émigré Priests in the United States, 1791–1815*. Washington, D.C.: Catholic Univ. of America Press.

Russell, Charles Edward. 1931. *Blaine of Maine: His Life and Time*. New York: Cosmopolitan Book Corp.

Ryan, John A. 1928. "A Catholic View of the Election." *Current History* 29 (December): 377–81.

Scammon, Richard J., and Ben Wattenberg. 1970. *The Real Majority*. New York: Coward-McCann.

Schlesinger, Arthur M. Jr., ed. 1971. *History of American Presidential Elections 1789–1968*. New York: Chelsea House.

Schram, Martin. 1977. *Running for President 1976: The Carter Campaign*. New York: Stein & Day.

Sellers, Charles. 1971. "The Election of 1844." In *History of American Presidential Elections 1789–1968*, edited by Arthur M. Schlesinger Jr., 747–861. New York: Chelsea House.

Shannon, William V. 1985. "The Election of 1984." In *History of American Presidential Elections 1789–1984*, edited by Arthur M. Schlesinger Jr. New York: Chelsea House.

Shaughnessy, Gerald. 1925. *Has the Immigrant Kept the Faith? A Study of Immigration and Catholic Growth in the United States*. New York: Macmillan.

Shaw, Russell. 1996. "Why Most Catholics Voted for Clinton." *Our Sunday Visitor* (24 November).

Sievers, Harry J. 1952. "The Catholic Indian School Issue and the Presidential Election of 1892." *Catholic Historical Review* 38: 129–55.

Silbey, Joel H. 1977. *The Partisan Imperative: The Dynamics of American Politics Before the Civil War*. New York: Oxford Univ. Press.

Silva, Ruth C. 1962. *Rum, Religion, and Votes: 1928 Re-Examined*. University Park, Pa.: Pennsylvania State Univ. Press.

Simpson, Craig M. 1985. *A Good Southerner: The Life of Henry A. Wise of Virginia.* Chapel Hill: Univ. of North Carolina Press.

Slawson, Douglas J. 1992. *The Foundation and First Decade of the National Catholic Welfare Council.* Washington, D.C.: Catholic Univ. of America Press.

Smith, Alfred E. 1927. "Alfred E. Smith, Catholic and Patriot, Replies." *Atlantic Monthly* 139 (May): 721–28.

———. 1929. *Up to Now: An Autobiography.* New York: Viking.

Smith, William E. 1933. *The Francis Preston Blair Family in Politics.* New York: Macmillan.

Sorensen, Theodore. 1960. "Catholic Vote—A Kennedy Staff Analysis." *U.S. News and World Report* 49 (1 August): 68–72.

———. 1965. *Kennedy.* New York: Harper & Row.

———. 1971. "The Election of 1960." In *History of American Presidential Elections 1789–1968*, edited by Arthur M. Schlesinger Jr., 3449–564. New York: Chelsea House.

Spalding, Martin J. 1855. "A Catholic Response to the Know-Nothings." In *Miscellanea, Comprising Reviews, Lectures, and Essays on Historical, Theological, and Miscellaneous Subjects.* Louisville: Webb, Gill & Levering.

Steeper, Fred. 1995. "This Swing Is Different: Analysis of 1994 Exit Polls." Unpublished paper, Steeper Market Strategies, Southfield, Mich.

Steinfels, Peter. 1994. "Future of Faith Worries Catholic Leaders." *New York Times* (1 June): 1.

Tansill, Charles C. 1940. *The Foreign Policy of Thomas F. Bayard 1885–1897.* New York: Fordham Univ. Press.

Theoharis, Athan G. 1970. *The Yalta Myths: An Issue in U.S. Politics 1945–1955.* Columbia, Mo.: Univ. of Missouri Press.

Trefousse, Hans Louis. 1989. *Andrew Johnson: A Biography.* New York: Norton.

Tuchfarber, Alfred J., Stephen E. Bennett, Andrew E. Smith, Eric W. Rademacher. 1995. "The Republican Tidal Wave of 1994: Testing Hypotheses about Realignment, Restructuring, and Rebellion." *P.S. Political Science and Politics* (December): 689–95.

Tyler, Samuel. 1872. *Memoir of Roger Brooke Taney, LL.D.* Baltimore: J. Murphy & Co.

U.S. Bureau of the Census. 1957. *Religion Reported by Civilian Population* (March). Current Population Survey, Series P20, no. 79.

U.S. Department of Labor. 1965. Office of Policy Planning and Research. *The Negro Family: The Case for National Action.* Washington, D.C.

"The Vatican Connection." 1984. *Christian Century* 101 (25 January).

Van Dusen, Glyndon G. 1967. *William Henry Seward.* New York: Oxford Univ. Press.

Verba, Sidney, and Norman H. Nie. 1972. *Participation in America: Political Democracy and Social Equality.* New York: Harper & Row.

Warner, William W. 1994. *At Peace with All Their Neighbors: Catholics and Catholicism in the National Capital.* Washington, D.C.: Georgetown Univ. Press.

Wattenberg, Ben J. 1995. *Values Matter Most: How Republicans or Democrats or a Third Party Can Win and Renew the American Way of Life*. New York: Free Press.

Wattenberg, Martin P. 1994. *The Decline of American Political Parties, 1952–1992*. Cambridge: Harvard Univ. Press.

Weed, Harriet A., ed. 1884. *The Life of Thurlow Weed Including His Autobiography and a Memoir.* New York: Houghton-Mifflin.

Weigel, George. 1992. "The New Anti-Catholicism." *Commentary* 93 (June): 25–31.

White, Theodore H. 1973. *The Election of the President, 1972*. New York: Atheneum.

———. 1978. *In Search of History.* New York: Harper & Row.

White, William Allen. 1926. "Al Smith: City Feller." *Colliers* 78 (21 August): 8–9.

Williams, Michael. 1932. *The Shadow of the Pope*. New York: McCann-Hill.

Witcover, Jules. 1977. *Marathon: The Pursuit of the Presidency, 1972–1976*. New York: Viking.

Additional Reading

Abbott, Richard H. 1972. *Cobbler in Congress: The Life of Henry Wilson, 1812–1875*. Lexington, Ky.: Univ. of Kentucky Press.

Abramowitz, Alan I. 1995. "It's Abortion, Stupid: Policy Voting in the 1992 Presidential Election" *Journal of Politics* 57: 176–86.

Abramson, Paul R., John H. Aldrich, and David W. Rhode. 1982. *Change and Continuity in the 1980 Elections*. Washington, D.C.: Congressional Quarterly Press.

———. 1986. *Change and Continuity in the 1984 Elections*. Washington, D.C.: Congressional Quarterly Press.

———. 1990. *Change and Continuity in the 1988 Elections*. Washington, D.C.: Congressional Quarterly Press.

———. 1994. *Change and Continuity in the 1992 Elections*. Washington, D.C.: Congressional Quarterly Press.

Barry, Colman J. 1953. *The Catholic Church and German Americans*. Washington, D.C.: Catholic Univ. of America Press.

Bartlett, Ruhl J. 1930. *John C. Frémont and the Republican Party*. Columbus: Ohio State Univ. Press.

Baum, Dale. 1984. *The Civil War Party System; The Case of Massachusetts, 1848–1876*. Chapel Hill: Univ. of North Carolina Press.

Blue, Frederick J. 1987. *Salmon P. Chase: A Life in Politics*. Kent, Ohio: Kent State Univ. Press.

Bradley, Martin B. 1992. *Churches and Church Membership in the United States, 1990*. Atlanta: Glenmary Research Center.

Broderick, Francis L. 1963. *Right Reverend New Dealer John A. Ryan*. New York: Macmillan.

Bukowczyk, John J. 1996. *Polish Americans and Their History, Community Culture and Politics*. Pittsburgh: Univ. of Pittsburgh Press.

Byrnes, Timothy A., and Mary C. Segers, eds. 1992. *The Catholic Church and the Politics of Abortion*. Boulder, Colo.: Westview.

Carlin, Sister Mary Angela. 1948. "The Attitude of the Republican Party Toward Religious Schools, 1875–1880." Master's thesis, Catholic Univ. of America.

Carmines, Edward G., and James A. Stimson. 1989. *Issue Evolution: Race and the Transformation of American Politics*. Princeton: Princeton Univ. Press.

Ceaser, James W., and Andrew E. Busch. 1997. *Losing to Win: The 1996 Election and American Politics*. Lanham, Md.: Rowman & Littlefield.

Clark, Dennis. 1973. *The Irish in Philadelphia: Ten Generations of Urban Experience*. Philadelphia: Temple Univ. Press.

Connor, Charles P. 1983. "Archbishop Hughes and Mid-Century Politics," *U.S. Catholic Historian* 3: 167–77.

Crandall, Andrew W. 1930. *The Early History of the Republican Party, 1854–1856*. Boston: Badger.

Cromartie, Michael, ed. 1994. *Disciples and Democracy: Religious Conservatives and the Future of American Politics*. Washington, D.C.: Ethics and Public Policy Center.

Cross, Robert D. 1958. *The Emergence of Catholic Liberalism in America*. Cambridge: Harvard Univ. Press.

Daniels, Roger. 1990. *Coming to America: A History of Immigration and Ethnicity in American Life*. New York: Harper-Collins.

D'Antonio, William V., James D. Davidson, Dean R. Hoge, and Ruth A. Wallace. 1996. *Laity, American and Catholic: Transforming the Church*. Kansas City, Mo.: Sheed & Ward.

Dolan, Jay P. 1975. *The Immigrant Church: New York's Irish and German Catholics 1815–65*. Baltimore: Johns Hopkins Univ. Press.

Edsall, Thomas Byrne, and Mary D. Edsall. 1991. *Chain Reaction: The Impact of Race, Rights, and Taxes on American Politics*. New York: Norton.

"Election '96: The Parties' Bases." 1996. *The Public Perspective* (October/November): 26–29. Roper Center for Public Opinion Research.

Elliott, Charles Winslow. 1937. *Winfield Scott, The Soldier and the Man*. New York: Macmillan.

Erickson, Robert S., and Kent L. Tedin. 1981. "The 1928–36 Partisan Realignment: The Case for the Conversion Hypothesis." *American Political Science Review* 95: 951–62.

Erie, Steven P. 1988. *Rainbow's End: Irish-Americans and the Dilemmas of Urban Machine Politics, 1840–1985*. Berkeley: Univ. of California Press.

Feldberg, Michael. 1975. *The Philadelphia Riots of 1844: A Study of Ethnic Conflict*. Westport, Conn.: Greenwood.

Flanigan, William H., and Nancy H. Zingale. 1992. *Political Bahavior of the American Electorate*. 6th ed. Boston: Allyn & Bacon.

Foner, Eric. 1983. *Politics and Ideology in the Age of the Civil War*. New York: Oxford Univ. Press.

Frawley, Sister Mary A. 1946. *Patrick Donohue*. Washington, D.C.: Catholic Univ. of America Press.

Fuchs, Lawrence H. 1957. "Presidential Politics in Boston: The Irish Response to Stevenson." *New England Quarterly* 30 (December): 435–47.

———. 1990. *The American Kaleidoscope: Race, Ethnicity, and the Civic Culture*. Hanover, N.H.: Wesleyan Univ. Press.

Galston, William, and Elaine C. Kamarck. 1989. *The Politics of Evasion: Democrats and the Presidency*. Washington, D.C.: Progressive Policy Institute.

Gamm, Gerald H. 1989. *The Making of New Deal Democrats: Voting Behavior and Realignment in Boston. 1920–1940*. Chicago: Univ. of Chicago Press.

Garfinkle, Adam. 1995. *Telltale Hearts: The Origins and Impact of the Vietnam Antiwar Movement*. New York: St. Martin's.

Glazer, Nathan, and Daniel P. Moynihan. 1970. *Beyond the Melting Pot*. Cambridge: Harvard Univ. Press.

Gleason, Philip. 1970. *Catholicism in America*. New York: Harper & Row.

Grasso, Kenneth L., Gerard V. Bradley, and Robert L. Hunt, eds. 1995. *Catholicism, Liberalism and Communitarianism: The Catholic Intellectual Tradition and the Moral Foundations of Democracy*. Lanham, Md.: Rowman & Littlefield.

Green, John C., James L. Guth, Corwin E. Smidt, and Lyman A. Kellstedt. 1994. "Murphy Brown Revisited: The Social Issues in the 1992 Campaign." In *Disciples and Democracy*, edited by Michael Cromartie. Washington, D.C.: Ethics and Public Policy Center.

Greer, Scott. 1961. "Catholic Voters and the Democratic Party." *Public Opinion Quarterly* 25, no. 4: 611–25.

Guth, James L., and John C. Green, eds. 1991. *The Bible and the Ballot Box: Religion and Politics in the 1988 Election*. Boulder, Colo.: Westview.

Hale, Jon F. 1995. "The Making of the New Democrats." *Political Science Quarterly* 110, no. 2 (Summer): 207–32.

Hale, William H. 1950. *Horace Greeley, Voice of the People*. New York: Harper.

Halsey, William M. 1980. *The Survival of American Innocence: Catholicism in an Era of Disillusionment, 1920–1940*. Notre Dame, Ind.: Univ. of Notre Dame Press.

Handlin, Oscar. 1941. *Boston's Immigrants, 1790–1865: A Study in Acculturation*. Cambridge: Harvard Univ. Press.

———. 1958. *Al Smith and His America*. Boston: Little, Brown.

Hanna, Mary T. 1979. *Catholics and American Politics*. Cambridge: Harvard Univ. Press.

Harrington, Fred H. 1948. *Fighting Politician: Major General N. P. Banks*. Philadelphia: Univ. of Pennsylvania Press.

Hattery, John W. 1967. "The Presidential Campaigns of 1928 and 1960: A Comparison of the Christian Century and America." *Journal of Church and State* 9 (Winter): 36–50.

Hennesey, James. 1981. *American Catholics: A History of the Roman Catholic Community in the United States*. New York: Oxford Univ. Press.

Herberg, Will. 1960. *Protestant, Catholic, Jew*. Garden City, N.Y.: Doubleday.

Hesseltine, William B. 1960. *Three Against Lincoln: Murat Halstead Reports the Caucuses of 1860*. Baton Rouge: Louisiana State Univ. Press.

Hohenberg, John. 1994. *The Bill Clinton Story: Winning the Presidency*. Syracuse: Syracuse Univ. Press.

———. 1998. *Reelecting Bill Clinton: Why America Chose a New Democrat*. Syracuse: Syracuse Univ. Press.

Hollander, Paul. 1992. *Anti-Americanism*. New York: Oxford Univ. Press.

Jelen, Ted, ed. 1989. *Religion and Political Behavior in the United States*. New York: Praeger.

Jelen, Ted. 1993. "The Political Consequences of Religious Group Attitudes." *Journal of Politics* 55: 178–90.

Kessel, John H. 1968. *The Goldwater Coalition: Republican Strategies in 1964*. Indianapolis: Bobbs-Merrill.

Ladd, Everett C. 1982. *Where Have All the Voters Gone? The Fracturing of America's Political Parties*. 2nd ed. New York: Norton.

———. 1985. "On Mandates, Realignments, and the 1984 Presidential Election." *Political Science Quarterly* 100: 1–25.

———. 1989. "The 1988 Elections: Continuation of the Post-New Deal System." *Political Science Quarterly* 104: 1–18.

———. 1993. "The 1992 Vote for President: Another Brittle Mandate?" *Political Science Quarterly* 108: 1–28.

Lawrence, David G. 1996. *The Collapse of the Democratic Presidential Majority*. Boulder, Colo.: Westview.

Layman, Geoffrey C. 1997. "Religion and Political Behavior in the United States." *Public Opinion Quarterly* 61, no. 2 (Summer): 288–316.

Leege, David C. 1996. "The Catholic Vote in '96," *Commonweal* 123, no. 16 (September 27): 11–18.

Leege, David C., Lyman A. Kellstedt, and John Green. 1993. *Rediscovering the Religious Factor in American Politics*. Armonk, N.Y.: M. E. Sharpe.

Lemert, James B., ed. 1996. *The Politics of Disenchantment: Bush, Clinton, Perot and the Press*. Cresskill, N.J.: Hampton Press.

Leonard, Ira M., and Robert D. Parmet. 1971. *American Nativism 1830–1860*. New York: Garland.

Levine, Edward M. 1966. *The Irish and Irish Politicians: A Study of Cultural and Social Alienation*. Notre Dame, Ind.: Univ. of Notre Dame Press.

Lichtman, Allan. 1983. "Political Reality and Ethnocultural Voting in the Nineteenth Century." *Journal of Social History* 16: 55–82.

Lopatto, Paul. 1985. *Religion and the Presidential Election*. New York: Praeger.

McAndrews, Lawrence J. 1991. *Broken Ground: John F. Kennedy and the Politics of Education*. New York: Garland Publishers.

McAvoy, Thomas T. 1960. *Catholicism and the American Way of Life*. Notre Dame, Ind.: Univ. of Notre Dame Press.

McCaffery, Peter. 1993. *When Bosses Ruled Philadelphia: The Emergence of the Republican Machine*. University Park, Pa.: Pennsylvania State Univ. Press.

McCaffrey, Lawrence J. 1984. *The Irish Diaspora in America*. Washington, D.C.: Catholic Univ. of America Press.

———. 1992. "Irish Textures in American Catholicism." *Catholic Historical Review* 78, no. 1 (January): 1–18.

McConville, Sister Mary S. 1928. *Political Nativism in the State of Maryland*. Washington, D.C.: Catholic Univ. of America Press.

McCormick, Richard L. 1979. *From Realignment to Reform: Political Change in New York State, 1893–1910*. Ithaca: Cornell Univ. Press.

Marshall, Charles C. 1928. *The Roman Catholic Church in the Modern State*. New York: Dodd, Mead.

Mayer, William G. 1996. *The Divided Democrats: Ideological Unity, Party Reform, and Presidential Elections*. Boulder, Colo.: Westview.

Meagher, Timothy J., ed. 1986. *From Paddy to Studs: Irish American Communities in the Turn of the Century Era, 1880–1920*. New York: Greenwood.

Menendez, Albert J. 1977. *Religion at the Polls*. Philadelphia: Westminster.

———. 1978. *John F. Kennedy: Catholic and Humanist*. Buffalo: Prometheus Books.

Michener, James A. 1961. *Report of the County Chairman*. New York: Random House.

Miller, Arthur H., and Martin P. Wattenberg. 1984. "Politics from the Pulpit: Religiosity and the 1980 Elections." *Public Opinion Quarterly* 48: 301–17.

Miller, Randall M., and Thomas D. Marzik, eds. 1977. *Immigrants and Religion in Urban America*. Philadelphia: Temple Univ. Press.

Miller, Warren E., and J. Merrill Shanks. 1996. *The New American Voter*. Cambridge: Harvard Univ. Press.

Morison, Elting. 1971. "Election of 1860." In *History of American Presidential Elections 1789–1968*, edited by Arthur M. Schlesinger Jr., 1097–1154. New York: Chelsea House.

Morris, Charles R. 1997. *American Catholic: The Story of the People, Passion, Politics Behind America's Largest and Most Influential Church*. New York: Random House.

Moynihan, James H. 1953. *The Life of Archbishop John Ireland*. New York: Harper.

Mulkern, John R. 1990. *The Know Nothing Party in Massachusetts: The Rise and Fall of a People's Movement*. Boston: Northeastern Univ. Press.

Muravchik, Joshua. 1997. "Why the Republicans Lost, and Won." *Commentary* 103 (January): 31–36.

Murphy, Robert J. 1928. "The Catholic Church in the United States During the Civil War Period, 1852–1866." *Records of the American Catholic Historical Society of Philadelphia* 39: 272–344.

Nevins, Allen. 1950. *The Emergence of Lincoln: Douglas, Buchanan, and Party Chaos 1857–1859*. New York: Scribner's.

Nichols, Roy F., and Philip S. Klein. 1971. "Election of 1856." In *History of American Presidential Elections 1789–1968*, edited by Arthur M. Schlesinger Jr., 1007–96. New York: Chelsea House.

Nie, Norman H., Sidney Verba, and John R. Petrocik. 1979. *The Changing American Voter*. Cambridge: Harvard Univ. Press.

Noonan, Carroll J. 1938. *Nativism in Connecticut*. Washington, D.C.: Catholic Univ. of America Press.

Nuesse, Celestine J. 1945. *The Social Thought of American Catholics, 1634–1829*. Washington, D.C.: Catholic Univ. of America Press.

O'Brien, David J. 1988. *Public Catholicism*. New York: Macmillan.

O'Connor, Thomas H. 1995. *The Boston Irish: A Political History*. Boston: Northeastern Univ. Press.

Olson, James S. 1987. *Catholic Immigrants in America*. Chicago: Nelson-Hall.

O'Toole, James M. 1992. *Militant and Triumphant: William Henry O'Connell and the Catholic Church in Boston 1859–1944.* Notre Dame, Ind.: Univ. of Notre Dame Press.

Paluszak, Sister Mary C. 1940. *The Opinion of the Catholic Telegraph on Contemporary Affairs and Politics 1831–1871.* Washington, D.C.: Catholic Univ. of America Press.

Peel, Roy V., and Thomas C. Donnelly. 1931. *The 1928 Campaign: An Analysis.* New York: New York Univ. Press.

Perko, F. Michael. 1989. *Catholic and American: A Popular History.* Huntington, Ind.: Our Sunday Visitor Press.

Phillips, Kevin P. 1982. *Post-Conservative America: People, Politics, and Ideology in a Time of Crisis.* New York: Random House.

Podhoretz, Norman. 1981. "The New American Majority." *Commentary* 71 (January): 19–28.

Pomper, Gerald, ed. 1977. *The Election of 1976: Reports and Interpretations.* New York: D. McKay.

———. 1981. *The Election of 1980: Reports and Interpretations.* Chatham, N.J.: Chatham House.

———. 1985. *The Election of 1984: Reports and Interpretations.* Chatham, N.J.: Chatham House.

———. 1989. *The Election of 1988: Reports and Interpretations.* Chatham, N.J.: Chatham House.

———. 1993. *The Election of 1992: Reports and Interpretations.* Chatham, N.J.: Chatham House.

———. 1997. *The Election of 1996: Reports and Interpretations.* Chatham, N.J.: Chatham House.

Powell, James M. 1996. "Catholics and American Politics." *America* 175, no. 3 (August 3–10): 8–11.

Radosh, Ronald. 1996. *Divided They Fell: The Demise of the Democratic Party 1964–1996.* New York: Free Press.

Ranney, Austin, ed. 1981. *The American Elections of 1980.* Washington, D.C.: American Enterprise Institute.

———. 1985. *The American Elections of 1984.* Washington, D.C.: American Enterprise Institute.

Ray, Sister Mary Augustina. 1936. *American Opinion of Roman Catholicism in the Eighteenth Century.* New York: Columbia Univ. Press.

Reedy, George E. 1991. *From the Ward to the White House: The Irish in American Politics.* New York: Macmillan.

Reichley, A. James. 1981. *Conservatives in an Age of Change: The Nixon and Ford Administrations.* Washington: Brookings Institution.

———. 1985. *Religion in American Public Life.* Washington: Brookings Institution.

———. 1992. *The Life of the Parties: A History of American Political Parties.* New York: Free Press.

Remini, Robert V. 1991. *Henry Clay: Statesman for the Union.* New York: Norton.

Rice, Arnold S. 1972. *The Ku Klux Klan in American Politics*. New York: Haskell House.

Riddleberger, Patrick W. 1966. *George Washington Julian: Radical Republican*. Indianapolis: Indiana Historical Bureau.

Rothan, Emmet H. 1946. *The German Catholic Immigrant in the United States 1830–1860*. Washington, D.C.: Catholic Univ. of America Press.

Segers, Mary C., ed. 1990. *Church Polity and American Politics: Issues in Contemporary American Catholicism* New York: Garland.

Shafer, Byron, and William J. M. Claggett. 1995. *The Two Majorities: The Issue Content of Modern American Politics*. Baltimore: Johns Hopkins Univ. Press.

Shannon, William V. 1963. *The American Irish*. New York: Macmillan.

Skerry, Peter. 1993. *Mexican-Americans: The Ambivalent Minority*. New York: Free Press.

Sousa, David J. 1993. "Organized Labor in the Electorate, 1960–1988." *Political Research Quarterly* 46: 741–58.

Spalding, Thomas W. 1973. *Martin John Spalding: American Churchman*. Washington, D.C.: Catholic Univ. of America Press.

Sundquist, James L. 1983. *Dynamics of the Party System: Alignment and Realignment of Political Parties in the United States*. Washington, D.C.: Brookings Institution.

Taft, Charles P., and Bruce L. Felknor. 1960. *Prejudice and Politics*. New York: Anti-Defamation League.

Thernstrom, Stephan, and Abigail Thernstrom. 1997. *America in Black and White*. New York: Simon & Schuster.

Thomas, Sister M. Evangeline. 1936. *Nativism in the Old Northwest, 1850–1860*. Washington, D.C.: Catholic Univ. of America Press.

Tomasi, Silvano M., and Madeline H. Engel. 1970. *The Italian Experience in the United States*. Staten Island, N.Y.: Center for Migration Studies.

Van Dusen, Glyndon G. 1953. *Horace Greeley, Nineteenth Century Crusader*. Philadelphia: Univ. of Pennsylvania Press.

Walch, Timothy, ed. 1988. *The Heritage of American Catholicism*. 28 vols. New York: Garland Publishing.

———. 1994. *Immigrant America: European Ethnicity in the United States*. New York: Garland.

Wattenberg, Martin P. 1991. *The Rise of Candidate-Centered Politics: Presidential Elections of the 1980s*. Cambridge: Harvard Univ. Press.

White, John Kenneth. 1988. *The New Politics of Old Values*. Hanover, N.H.: Univ. Press of New England.

White, Theodore H. 1961. *The Election of the President, 1960*. New York: Atheneum.

Wittke, Carl. 1956. *The Irish in America*. Baton Rouge: Louisiana State Univ. Press.

Zwierlein, Frederick J. 1956. *Theodore Roosevelt and Catholics, 1892–1919*. St. Louis: Victor T. Suren.

Index